Writing and Producing Television Drama in Denmark

Palgrave Studies in Screenwriting

Series Editors: **Ian W. Macdonald**, University of Leeds, UK; **Steven Maras**, University of Sydney, Australia; **Kathryn Millard**, Macquarie University, Australia; **J. J. Murphy**, University of Wisconsin-Madison, USA.

Advisory Board: **John Adams**, University of Bristol, UK; **Jill Nelmes**, East London University, UK; **Steven Price**, Bangor University, UK; **Eva Novrup Redvall**, University of Copenhagen, Denmark; **Kristin Thompson**, University of Wisconsin-Madison, USA; **Paul Wells**, Loughborough University, UK.

Palgrave Studies in Screenwriting is the first book series to focus on the academic study of screenwriting, exploring key topics and debates in this burgeoning area of research. It seeks to promote an informed and critical account of screenwriting, looking at the connections between what is produced and how it is produced, with a view to understanding more about the rich diversity of screenwriting practice. The scope of the series encompasses a range of study from the creation of texts (scripts, blueprints, screen objects), to the processes of production and composition behind those texts, to the structures that form those processes, and to the agents responsible for the texts themselves.

Titles include:

Ian W. Macdonald
SCREENWRITING POETICS AND THE SCREEN IDEA

Eva Novrup Redvall
WRITING AND PRODUCING TELEVISION DRAMA IN DENMARK
From *The Kingdom* to *The Killing*

Writing and Producing Television Drama in Denmark

From *The Kingdom* to *The Killing*

Eva Novrup Redvall

Department of Media, Cognition and Communication,
University of Copenhagen, Denmark

First published 2013 by
PALGRAVE MACMILLAN

Palgrave Macmillan in the UK is an imprint of Macmillan Publishers Limited, registered in England, company number 785998, of Houndmills, Basingstoke, Hampshire RG21 6XS.

Palgrave Macmillan in the US is a division of St Martin's Press LLC, 175 Fifth Avenue, New York, NY 10010.

Palgrave Macmillan is the global academic imprint of the above companies and has companies and representatives throughout the world.

Palgrave® and Macmillan® are registered trademarks in the United States, the United Kingdom, Europe and other countries.

ISBN 978-1-349-44991-0   ISBN 978-1-137-28841-7 (eBook)
DOI 10.1057/9781137288417

This book is printed on paper suitable for recycling and made from fully managed and sustained forest sources. Logging, pulping and manufacturing processes are expected to conform to the environmental regulations of the country of origin.

A catalogue record for this book is available from the British Library.

A catalog record for this book is available from the Library of Congress.

Contents

Figures

Acknowledgements

This book could not have been made without the help and guidance of numerous people within the world of academia as well as the world of screenwriting and television production. To begin with, I am thankful to the Danish Research Council for funding my research proposal on the writing and production of the Sunday night drama series from the Danish Broadcasting Corporation (DR). Studying writing and production processes is a time-consuming endeavour as is getting appointments with busy industry practitioners. The funding allowed me to spend substantial time following the emergence of new series, from the ideas stage in writers' rooms and all the way to the screen.

This research could not have been conducted without the openness and trust from a range of people at the DR in-house drama production unit DR Fiction. When the project was still a mere mission statement on paper, former Head of Drama Ingolf Gabold saw an opportunity to learn more about the mode of production of DR Fiction. This was before the international success of *The Killing* and *Borgen* made journalists take an interest in what British newspaper *The Guardian* branded as the Danish 'hit factory', and I am thankful to Gabold for supporting the project from the very beginning and opening many doors.

From the outset, the degree of access I was granted to many different kinds of rooms, meetings and processes has been remarkable. I have had the opportunity to follow the fragile, initial stages of development of a new high-profile series by head writer Maya Ilsøe and producer Christian Rank, with a number of writers and script consultants (Per Daumiller, Lolita Belstar and Vinca Wiedemann), directors (Jesper W. Nielsen, Heidi Maria Faisst, Jesper Christensen and Pernilla August) and the cast of the series accepting my presence during the storylining in the writers' room through feedback and pitch meetings until readings on set and script meetings with the actors. In a similar vein, the *Borgen* team has been incredibly welcoming, with creator Adam Price and writers Jeppe Gjervig Gram and Maja Jul Larsen allowing me to observe their writers' room and the development of episode 25 for the third season, followed by the work on the script through different feedback meetings until the reading for the cast and crew. Producer Camilla Hammerich, line producer Pernille Skov Sutherland and researcher Rikke Tørholm Kofoed found the time to talk to me in the midst of production. I am particularly thankful to Kofoed for helping out in numerous ways and continuously keeping me informed about new developments or changes in schedules.

It has been a great inspiration to experience how people at DR Fiction took an interest in the project based on a belief that they might learn something from having an outsider observe and analyse the work methods and practices of their everyday routines. This has also been the case among the many other producers, writers and executives at DR who agreed to meet me and discuss their work. Screenwriters Søren Sveistrup and Michael W. Horsten (*Forbrydelsen/The Killing*), Peter Thorsboe and Mai Brostrøm (*Rejseholdet/Unit One*, *Ørnen/The Eagle* and *Livvagterne/The Protectors*), and Stig Thorsboe and Hanna Lundblad (*Taxa/Taxi*, *Krøniken/Better Times* and *Lykke/Happy Life*) provided valuable information on the nature of their work and their perception of the DR Fiction mode of production, while producer Sven Clausen and former Head of Drama Rumle Hammerich contributed important insights into the developments of DR Fiction since the 1990s. Current Head of DR Fiction Nadia Kløvedal Reich found the time to discuss the present structures and strategies for production.

It was also insightful to follow the feedback of Reich and Head of Drama Piv Bernth at the National Film School of Denmark when students of the so-called TV term in January 2013 presented their ideas for potential new series. The TV term is a now institutionalized collaboration on television writing and production between DR, the Film School and the School of Design, and it was of great interest to observe the final pitch as well as teaching sessions during the term. Hanna Lundblad invited me to observe her class on television writing, and the students of the 2012–2013 term were all very welcoming. Head of the Screenwriting Department Lars Detlefsen, Head of the Producers' Department Ib Tardini and Jakob Ion Wille from the School of Design were all helpful, providing information on the structure of the term and sharing documents like the 'dummy paper' in the Appendix.

The extensive empirical data in this book is based on the help and support of all these people in the Danish film and television industry. I have also benefited from participating in industry events such as the first edition of the European TV Drama Series Lab in Berlin 2012, based on the generous invitation from the organizers Katrina Wood (MediaXchange), Nadja Radojevic, Maria Grau Stenzel and Lothar Mikos (Erich Pommer Institut). The Lab consisted of several presentations and panels on conceptions of best practice in the industry as well as writers' room simulations headed by US showrunners, which were informative in terms of tracing similarities and differences between different modes of production. Other industry events such as the Scandinavian Think Tank Symposium organized in 2010 by the Think Tank on European Film and Film Policy headed by Henning Camre, and the Nordic TV Drama Days at the Göteborg International Film Festival 2010–2013, organized by Cia Edström, have also been excellent opportunities to listen in on industry debates and presentations by both practitioners and scholars.

Within the world of academia, I am thankful to the many colleagues who have been helpful in a variety of ways. Ib Bondebjerg and Anne Jerslev at the University of Copenhagen have offered interesting perspectives on the research in this book over the years. Mette Hjort from Lingnan University, Hong Kong, has been a source of inspiration and a marvellous mentor for many years, and I also owe thanks to a number of other international colleagues with whom I have had enriching discussions during the making of this book. Patrick Vonderau and Petr Szczepanik have provided stimulating conversations on European production studies at seminars and conferences over the years, and a number of other colleagues have contributed with inputs, particularly at the annual conferences of the Society of Cinema and Media Studies, among them Miranda Banks, John Thornton Caldwell, Alisa Perren and Patricia Phalen.

Moreover, the research priority area Creative Media Industries, which I established together with professor Ib Bondebjerg at the University of Copenhagen in 2011, has proven to be a great setting for attracting international scholars. We are grateful to experts in their fields, such as David Hesmondhalgh, Jennifer Holt, Amanda Lotz, Horace Newcomb and Jeanette Steemers, for making the trip to Denmark and engaging in exciting conversations about topics related to current media industries. The research area has also opened up fruitful collaborations with scholars from a number of other Danish universities who have an interest in media production, television drama and creative processes, such as Heidi Philipsen, Gunhild Agger and Sara Malou Strandvad.

In terms of this book, I am thankful to the series editors Ian Macdonald, Steven Maras, Kathryn Millard and J. J. Murphy for taking an interest in the topic and to Palgrave editor Felicity Plester for launching this new series on screenwriting research. Above all, I want to thank Steven Maras for his always constructive criticism and precise feedback, making for a great writing process. This close collaboration with an admired colleague on the other side of the world has been an inspiring experience.

Since its establishment and the first conference on screenwriting research in Leeds in 2008, the Screenwriting Research Network has been important to my work as also the encouragements, writings and tireless efforts to further screenwriting studies and transnational collaborations by Ian Macdonald. The network has grown at an incredible speed. The annual conference, which I organized together with Mette Mortensen in Copenhagen in 2010, was one small step on the way to what has now become a global network of both practitioners and academics with an interest in screenplays and screenwriting. This book draws on the work and input of numerous screenwriting research colleagues. Parts of chapters build on material for conference papers and journal articles, which are referred to in the text, but all material in this book is written specifically with this context in mind.

On a more practical level, several people have offered their assistance. Gry Bak Jensen has helped with interview transcriptions, Professor Karin Wahl-Jørgensen from University of Cardiff was an apt reader in a time of need and Danish screenwriter Line Langebek has continuously been an online, London-based lifeline on textual matters and translations. At the daily newspaper *Information*, where I have been writing on film and television for many years, my editor Christian Monggaard has also been a source of informative points and tweets, with a more journalistic take on the latest developments in the wondrous world of old and new media. In the editorial process, I am thankful for the positive response and useful suggestions from the anonymous referees of the proposal and the manuscript and for the assistance of Chris Penfold at Palgrave Macmillan.

I am indebted to all these people as well as my friends and family who have taken part in the making of this book and have made the some-times exhausting process interesting and worthwhile. It is my sincere hope that the book will provide food for thought for new conversations and foster collaborations in the years to come.

Introduction

With large domestic audiences and four Emmy awards for best international drama since 2002, the high-profile drama series produced by the Danish Broadcasting Corporation (DR) have had a remarkable success in the past ten years. In the 2010s, US and UK audiences as well as critics discovered *Forbrydelsen/The Killing* (2007–2012) and *Borgen* (2010–2013), despite the traditional fear of subtitled content and the local nature of the stories and settings. *The Killing* won the international BAFTA award in 2011, beating US productions like *Mad Men* (AMC 2007–) and *Boardwalk Empire* (HBO 2010–). This kind of audience appreciation and acclaim has led to an interest in whether there is a certain approach to making one-hour quality drama series at DR, suddenly being labelled by some journalists as 'the Danish TV hit factory' (Gilbert 2012).

This book explores the approach to writing and producing television drama series of the DR in-house production unit DR Fiction. Based on an understanding of the development, writing and production of television series as a highly complex and collaborative endeavour, the book argues that while the quality and success of series like *The Killing* and *Borgen* stems from the work of gifted writers, directors, actors and producers with unique visions, there is much more to creating a successful series than a good idea and talented people to make it come alive. The series are also the result of several years of working with a certain mode of production within DR Fiction, and there are many more factors to take into account than the vision of a specific head writer or showrunner.

Drawing on a number of case studies of the production practice since the late 1990s until today and interviews with writers and producers at DR, this book intends to create a nuanced understanding of these varied elements informing the recent rise of Danish television series, as well as

1

considering key issues related to writing and producing television more generally. The book combines scholarly work on film and television with models and concepts from studies of creativity and collaborative work processes with the aim of providing insights into different modes of writing and production in particular production cultures. The book targets students and teachers with an interest in issues of writing and producing scripted fiction. Readers with a broader interest in screenwriting, drama series or the television industry will find that the book also addresses several industry debates based on an ambition to provide new perspectives about ongoing discussions, such as how to understand the role of the showrunner in a European production context or how to think of writers' rooms in production cultures with limited traditions for this way of working for high-profile drama series.

In the past few years, several series from DR have moved from the national realm to the international scene. Accordingly, the study of this specific, small-nation production culture not only offers analysis of the work of a particular public service broadcaster with domestic success but also provides knowledge about the structures and strategies, choices and collaborations behind series which have recently proven to attract interest beyond the neigbouring Nordic countries. Since the late 1990s, the one-hour, character-driven family and crime series from DR have continuously had large, national audiences when shown in the prime-time television drama slot on Sunday evenings at 8 pm. Several series have also found international acclaim since the first of now four Emmy awards for best international drama in 2002. However, it is the growing UK and US audience and critical interest in the Danish series in the 2010s which have created a more widespread desire to learn more about not only the creators of the series but also the nature of their mode of production.

The 2011 airing of *The Killing* on BBC4 found impressive audiences in spite of being foreign fare and attracted substantial press coverage. There were articles about how the portrayal of a modern welfare society mirrored the state of affairs in the UK, and coverage of gender issues related to the portrayal of the series' detective Sarah Lund. On a less serious scale, there were attempts at doing semiotic analysis of Lund's iconic sweater, and encouragements to readers to send pictures of their similar knitting designs. Following the success of *The Killing*, the political drama series *Borgen* about a female politician becoming the first prime minister of Denmark also appealed to UK audiences. Meanwhile, American audiences watched a remake of *The Killing* on US cable channel AMC, and a remake of *Borgen* is currently being planned. The Danish version of *Borgen* also made it onto American screens, but on a channel so difficult to find that the enthusiastic review in *The New York Times* was accompanied by a guide on how to locate the programme. As the reviewer concluded, '*Borgen* may be the hardest show to find on American television, but at the moment it's also one of the best' (Stanley 2012).

The review of *Borgen* in *The New York Times* point to the value of exploring different modes of production to better understand their specificity and to complicate discussions of institutional authorship and individual agency. As noted by reviewer Alessandra Stanley, '[T]he same team behind the original version of *The Killing* created *Borgen*, and it too focuses on a strong woman, only this time she leads not a homicide investigation, but an entire country' (2012). It is true that both series are from DR Fiction and that they share similarities by having strong female leads and an interest in larger societal issues besides aiming for an entertaining plot. However, the series were created and made by very different writers, producers and crews working within the same production framework. It is worthwhile investigating the extent to which this particular framework can be said to create certain kinds of productions and what might be said to characterize the mode of production at DR (Figure I.1).

Figure I.1 The cast of *Forbrydelsen/The Killing* (2007–2012) with Sarah Lund (Sofie Gråbøl) and the iconic sweater in front. Photo by Tine Harden. Courtesy of DR

For a small national production industry, the degree of international interest is quite unique and has given rise to discussion of a characteristic Danish approach to television production in the Nordic and European television industry (Bondebjerg and Redvall 2011; Redvall and Gubbins 2011; Redvall 2013). Many broadcasters and production companies are currently debating fiercely how to approach the future production of television drama in a media landscape marked by still more competition and media convergence. Audiences are now watching fiction on many other platforms than the television screen and new players like Netflix are moving into producing original content of their own. A pressing question for many European broadcasters is whether this is a great moment of opportunity for subtitled, scripted series on the international scene or whether this will lead to a decline in the popularity of the domestic series in the national realm with audiences now being able to (legally!) watch the latest episode of *Game of Thrones* (HBO 2011–) the day after its US airing on HBO Nordic or all 13 episodes of *House of Cards* (Netflix 2013–) in a row as part of a global, web-based release.

In 2012, a so-called European TV Drama Series Lab was organized to address some of the current challenges in the industry, particularly to try to understand what the European industry might learn from the American production framework with showrunners and writers' rooms. Several US executives and showrunners argued that the US mode of television production was 'broken', referring particularly to the vast amounts of money spent on developing projects in vain and the production of expensive pilots that never move into series (Redvall 2013, 5). A recurring point in several discussions at the lab was how DR has successfully implemented certain work methods from the American industry, but managed to integrate them into a public service mindset and the local production culture. Among the methods inspired by the US mode of production is the establishment of a head writer/episode writer structure of production since the late 1990s. Another method is the shooting of series as a 'relay', usually with blocks of two episodes, with different directors for each block and moving into production with only a few final scripts on hand, based on the intention of allowing for aspects of production to feed back into the writing process.[1]

Executives from DR Fiction like former Head of Drama Ingolf Gabold and producer Sven Clausen have been successful at creating a shared language around production and presenting an official story of the 'DR way of doing things' at both industry events and in the press. One can, thus, find discussions of a certain kind of 'Danish recipe' for television drama in the Nordic trade press and in, newspaper stories on the increased interest in television series from DR. Many of the concepts presented and debated, such as the concepts of 'one vision', 'double storytelling', 'producer's choice' and 'crossover', are naturally an important part of this book. However, the book does not attempt to offer any such thing as a recipe for how to write and produce television drama, based on the conviction that it is impossible to boil the complex processes down into a simple checklist, which can easily be digested and copied. As *Borgen* screenwriter Jeppe Gjervig Gram commented in an interview for this book, nothing upsets him more than when people think that there is a definitive recipe of how to write good television series, let alone an episode of *Borgen*; 'there is no final recipe, and the work is never easy' (Gram 2012). As the case studies in this book demonstrate, there can be many different approaches within the same production system. Some structural aspects do create a certain framework and a specific work environment, which can be highlighted as significant for the creative practitioners, but all writers and producers find their own way within the system.

Rather than trying to pinpoint one final recipe, the intention of this book is to analyse the complexity of the processes and collaborations and to insist on the value of using detailed case studies as a basis for understanding their particularity. Some elements like the idea of having a writer with 'one vision' at the centre of production will be discussed as influential across time and cases, but a concept like one vision is also equivocal and can mean a variety of things, both in its implementation and in the interpretation of its essence among people working in what is regarded as a 'one vision' production framework within DR.

Screenwriting and the Screen Idea System

Taking a particular interest in the writing of new television series, this book builds on the recent rise of screenwriting research within film and media studies. This new body of work has revolved around the Screenwriting Research Network and through new books focusing on the history, theory and practice of screenwriting and the nature of the screenplay (e.g. Murphy 2007; Maras 2009; Nelmes 2010; Price 2010). Whereas many classical studies of screenwriting practices have been particularly interested in the emergence of the continuity script or the structures of the US studio system (e.g. Bordwell, Staiger and Thompson 1985), research in the past few years has shown the value of a variety of approaches ranging from theoretical analysis of the ontology of the screenplay to practice-based analyses of screenplay development

Figure I.2 Birgitte Nyborg (Sidse Babett Knudsen) and her husband (Mikael Birkkjær) at the stairs of the seat of the Danish parliament Christiansborg (known as 'Borgen') at the end of the first season of *Borgen* (2010–2013). Photo by Mike Kollöffel. Courtesy of DR

and dealing with many different kinds of film and media cultures (Figure I.2).

The work growing out of this new field of screenwriting studies is often focused on the very process of how films or television series come into being. The research is not only on the development of the text and its properties but also on the complicated 'work groups' and production processes around the texts. Drawing on Helen Blair's concept of 'flexible work groups' (Blair 2001, 2003), Ian Macdonald has thus formulated the useful concept of the 'Screen Idea Work Group', which is to be understood as a grouping of the professional workers involved in conceptualizing and developing new works of fiction (2010). Bridget Conor has fruitfully investigated the labour conditions of British screenwriters (2010), and Steven Maras has proposed thinking about screenwriting as a process of 'scripting' where the stages of conception and execution are increasingly blurred with the coming of new tools and technologies (2009).

This book combines aspects of what Maras has described as the historical and the industrial/institutional trajectories in screenwriting research (2011, 278) with its interest in not only the development and nature of specific writing processes but also in 'the rules of the game' (Maras 2009, 154). Drawing on the work of the French sociologist Pierre Bourdieu, Ian Macdonald has insisted that the practice of screenwriting cannot be separated from the particular way of thinking about film and television drama at a certain point in time (2004). We need to include the beliefs and understandings behind judgements and distinctions of practitioners as well as gatekeepers guiding the decisions around the script. The research in this book similarly builds on a highly contextual approach to screenwriting, expanding Macdonald's concept of the Screen Idea Work Group to a Screen Idea System, based on thoughts and models from the field of creativity research.

Within the field of creativity research, Mihaly Csikszentmihalyi has outlined what he calls 'a systems view of creativity', arguing that talented people are of course crucial to the creation of original work, but that the work of individuals must always be considered in relation to the existing knowledge in the domain as well as to the experts of the field who decide what work to select for development and financing, production and distribution (1988, 1999). Based on the systems view of Csikszentmihalyi, this book proposes a Screen Idea System framework for understanding the writing and production of new television series as an interplay between the three main shaping elements of the individuals, the domain and the field. Creators of new series build on what is already produced within the domain of television drama and they are dependent on experts in the field to acknowledge the originality of their variation. The judgements of the experts are based on conceptions of quality or best practice in the current domain, and their decisions lead to the inclusion of new variations.

As analysed in later chapters, there are several aspects to consider in relation to the individuals, the domain and the field, such as the training and track record of the talent proposing new variations and the mandate, management and money of the experts making decisions on what to greenlight or not. As Csikszentmihalyi has remarked, creativity never exists in a vacuum (1999, 315). In creativity research, some scholars talk of 'the four P's of creativity', referring to the Person, the Process, the Product and the Press surrounding the three previous P's (Rhodes 1961). This book suggests similarly always considering what one can call 'the many P's of production'. Traditionally, film and television studies have tended to focus on the Person (as the artist) or the Product (the work of art). The intention in this book is to focus on the actual Process of how people develop new products in a specific, highly collaborative work context marked by many different types of constraints.

As I have previously demonstrated when studying collaborations between feature film directors and screenwriters (2009, 2010a, 2012b), screenwriters have become ever more influential in Danish filmmaking since the 1990s, but the director is still expected to be the driving force of new projects and to possess a vision of what is to be produced. The director is regarded as the artist or the auteur in the process, while the screenwriter is regarded as more of a craftsperson, helping to make the director's vision come alive. This focus on the director as an auteur has led to a marginalization of the screenwriter in many European film cultures (Finney 1996). However, the writer enjoys a much more respected position in the world of television, and a specific interest in the research presented in this book has been to explore the role of the writer in the production framework of DR Fiction and questions around who can be said to have the vision behind a series or be regarded as its creator or author. The collaborative nature of television production raises a number of important questions about individual, collective and institutional authorship, which this book attempts to shed more light on through the study of specific writing and production processes.

Television studies and media industries

While there is a long tradition of 'how to' books on writing for television and books about individual series and their reception from both an American and a European perspective, remarkably less has been written about the practice of making television from a scholarly perspective. Some of the classic studies have focused on the role of the producer, drawing on the understanding of television as a producer's medium (Cantor 1971; Newcomb and Alley 1983; Newcomb 1991). Studies of individual production stories exist (e.g. Elliott 1972; Levine 2001; Lotz 2004), but they are scarce, as are studies of the production culture of individual broadcasters such as Georgina Born's ethnographic study of the BBC, dealing with the work of the BBC drama unit as one part of an extensive book (2005). One of the values of several studies focusing on television production is their explicit focus on the collaborative nature of the processes, when discussing what has been called 'the polyauthorial' nature of work for television (Thompson and Burns 1990) and interpreted as the results of collective action (Sandeen and Compesi 1990).

In the 2000s, several scholars have analysed what is now discussed as 'quality television' (e.g. Jancovich 2003; Hammond and Mazdon 2005; McCabe and Akass 2007) or 'high-end' TV drama (Nelson 2007), sometimes linking the analysis of the emergence, nature and impact of much-admired cable series like *The Sopranos* (HBO 1999–2007) or *The Wire* (HBO 2002–2008) to more detailed discussions of how they are marked by the targeting of niche audiences rather than the mainstream mass audiences of network television. Recent books and chapters on television drama cultures have enriched the understanding of approaches to production in individual countries (e.g. Dunleavy 2010; Buonanno 2012) as well as of the intricate interplay between the television industries of the UK and the US (Hilmes 2011; Weissmann 2012). While recent years have thus seen a wide variety of valuable research on remarkable developments in the worldwide television drama industries, there are still few studies with a main focus on the actual on-going processes of creating a new series, moving through the stages from pitch to product. This book contributes new knowledge in this regard.

The lack of production research is often explained by film and media studies focusing more on content and aesthetic analysis or reception studies than on production analysis. However, there seems to be still more interest in studying different aspects of production in the film and media industries, not the least because of notable contributions from the field of media industry studies. Several books within this cross-disciplinary field of study have recently outlined the value of a range of possible approaches to studying media industries from local, regional and transnational perspectives (Holt and Perren 2009; Mayer, Banks and Caldwell 2009; Havens and Lotz 2012). Concurrently, books on specific production cultures have emphasized the importance of studying the self-understandings, 'deep texts' and rituals of not only the people thought of as 'above the line' in production but also of 'below the line' work processes (Caldwell 2008; Mayer 2011; Dawson and Holmes 2012).

Whereas there have previously been several studies on the wider implications of how to think of production and working conditions in the cultural or creative industries (Hartley 2005; Hesmondhalgh 2007), this new focus on media industry studies seems to further not only important issues from the perspective of critical political economy, such as questions of ownership or the larger economic or regulatory frameworks for production but also issues of the specific nature of creative work within various cultural industries (Deuze 2007; Hesmondhalgh and Baker 2010; Elefante and Deuze 2012). These studies often take a rather critical stance in relation to the labour issues and the precariousness of working in the creative media industries, and while these discussions are highly relevant in the world of screenwriting and television production, this book takes a greater interest in the nature of collaboration and the possibility that certain media industries might create enabling as well as constraining conditions for creative work.

Institutional authorship and individual agency

There can be many disadvantages in studying a small, national production culture, such as the somewhat limited number of players and productions in a country with only 5.6 million inhabitants and the fact that the national output is often of little interest outside the language barriers and borders. One advantage of studying the Danish context has been the relatively easy access to key people and work processes. This book is based on data obtained from having had access to in-house production documents, to people and to observing work processes like the development process of the forthcoming series *Arvingerne/The Legacy* (forthcoming 2014) and the writers' room of the third season of *Borgen* as well as pitches, note meetings, readings and other events around the writing and production. Observational studies of work spaces like writers' rooms provide the opportunity to deal with basic, but nonetheless important, questions like: Who is in the room? How are things discussed? What seems to be the notions of quality? How are disagreements dealt with? Who seems to have the final call?

As will be discussed later in this book, studies like Patricia Phalen and Julia Osselame's *Writing Hollywood: Rooms with a Point of View* (2012) outline some of the challenges of working in American writers' rooms for comedy and drama series, and it has continuously been fruitful to compare the workings of a smaller, national production culture with studies from the US television industry. In the US context, the showrunner is gaining still more ground as the professional role often defined as 'the creative force' behind a series (e.g. Del Valle 2008, 403). Showrunners such as Matthew Weiner (*Mad Men*) or Vince Gilligan (*Breaking Bad*, AMC 2008–2013) are singled out as the creators and creative voices of series, but according to Denise Mann's analysis, it seems still harder to allocate authorship in what she terms 'today's blockbuster-style television production circumstances' (2009, 100). She argues that the showrunner is no longer only in charge of running the writers' room, but is also in charge of managing the show as a multi-platform transmedia franchise and mentions one insider talking about a shift away from the single showrunner to 'a six-pack of executive producers' (2009, 100). Her discussion of what can be perceived as the many different 'authors' involved in a show like *Lost* (ABC 2004–2010) contains interesting perspectives on how to think of creativity, constraints and collaboration on major series. Focusing on the showrunner in relation to previous studies of the television producer, Alisa Perren has similarly provided enlightening examples of the work experiences of US showrunners through conversations on creativity in the contemporary cable industry (2011) and suggested how to think of showrunners as 'intermediaries' in the complex production processes (2013). Although there are, of course, major differences in the size, scope and speed of writing and producing television series in the US and Denmark, many of the fundamental questions about the nature of creative agency and issues of authorship remain the same.

A particular interest of the case studies in this book has been to analyse what the managerial concept of 'one vision' implies in a collective work process, and the extent to which one can say that the head writer of a new series in the DR model can carry his or her vision through during the many stages of production, since this concept of one vision is often highlighted as a major reason for the recent success of the DR series. However, it is one thing to put a concept down on paper in the official in-house mission statement of a public service drama unit and present it as crucial in the corporate storytelling of the department to the world; quite another is how this concept is at play during production and the extent to which it is regarded as implemented by the creative practitioners (Figure I.3).

Figure I.3   The writers Adam Price (on the right), Jeppe Gjervig Gram (in the middle) and Jannik Tai Mosholt (on the left) storylining in the writers' room of *Borgen* in November 2011. Photo by Peter Mydske. Courtesy of Polfoto

This book approaches the writing and production of Danish television drama from a scholarly perspective, but also with a clear ambition to offer constructive input and ideas for practitioners in the field. Much can be learned from bringing theory and practice closer together and from trying to bridge what is, at least in Europe, often a wide gap between academic film and television studies and the industry. This book is an attempt to bring the two worlds closer together and to provide food for thought to inspire future screenwriting, television and production studies as well as future productions.

Methodology and data

As John Thornton Caldwell has stated in relation to his seminal work on industrial reflexivity and critical practice in film and television, production cultures are 'far too messy, vast and contested to provide a unified code' (2008, 36). However, one can, as an 'interpretative bricoleur' (Denzin and Lincoln 2005, xv), try to offer a theoretically and methodologically transparent analysis of specific issues, grounding explanations and interpretations of the 'bricolage' in the material. There might not be a recipe or a unified code, but there can be meaningful interpretations of what is going on.

Besides the challenging messiness and vastness of production cultures, Caldwell has also emphasized how the fieldwork of production is complicated 'by the fact that film and television today reflect obsessively back upon themselves and invest considerable energy in overproducing and distributing this industrial self-analysis to the public' (2008, 1). There is a substantial amount of what he describes as 'corporate scripts' (2008, 3). As already mentioned, the public corporate script around DR exerts a significant force with executives from DR Fiction having told and retold their perception of the reasons behind the recent national and international success on several occasions to both the industry and the press. As demonstrated in the work of Caldwell, much can be learned from analysing this kind of corporate storytelling by a specific media institution and an 'industry's own self-representation, self-critique, and self-reflexion' (2008, 5), but it is also important to try to move beyond the official version of what is being done, to study what is actually going on in production. The intention to do this calls for not only asking practitioners how they describe and interpret their practice but also the opportunity to study the actual work processes.

Georgina Born has described the process of negotiating access for her fieldwork at the BBC like waging a military campaign (2005, 16). As mentioned in the acknowledgements, this has not been the case for this book. Whereas Born was investigating the BBC at what she described as a time of crisis, it has no doubt been easier to get access to DR at a time of perceived success. Besides the general sense of a time of successful best practice within DR Fiction, this is probably also due to the fact that the research was conducted at a time when one era could be seen as ending and a number of things were changing. There seems to have been a sense of value in having a researcher analyse the historical development and current practice in a drama department undergoing major generational and organizational changes, while the surrounding landscape for production and distribution was rapidly evolving.

One of the inherent risks of getting this kind of access and of conducting observational studies is to 'go native' and get smitten by the success story that most people and organizations would like to tell of themselves. This is not least the case when navigating among so-called elite respondents used to telling their story and presenting themselves in public. As argued by Caldwell, much can be learned from theorizing from the ground up and investigating the interpretative nature of practices (2008, 5). 'Looking over the shoulder' of practitioners can often offer more complex insights than direct talk, and what he has called 'embedded theoretical "discussion" ' among practitioners often contains important knowledge (2008, 26–7). It has been central to this study to do observational studies that would allow for investigation of the everyday practices, language and thoughts of production. Born has argued that one strength of fieldwork is to discern not only unifying features but also possible divisions, boundaries and conflicts (2005, 15). Fieldwork creates the opportunity to explore potential gaps between principles and practice, but it is also a fundamental way of gaining detailed knowledge about the routines and spaces for production as well as of the more tacit knowledge in a specific work environment. Much can be learned from interviewing, but there is great value in being able to study the actual work if one is constantly wary of one's own position as a researcher in the process.

The fieldwork conducted, primarily the case study of *Borgen*, has been marked by a sense of observing constructive work processes, which have later been interpreted as examples of best practice by the people involved. It seems important to note that observing the work of other series might have raised more critical points. During the writing of this book, there has sometimes been a sense of almost having to apologize for the lack of tension and conflict observed so as not to appear to be taking a cheerleading stance. As will be discussed later, observing the work processes at the competing public service broadcaster TV 2 would probably have painted a rather different picture of Danish television writing and production, and several of the *Borgen* practitioners have emphasized that their experience on this series has been rather unique in terms of the well-functioning writing collaborations and routines. As recently argued by television scholar Matt Hills when addressing the current state of television studies, there are good arguments in favour of doing 'failure studies' instead of always writing about acclaimed series and successful showrunners (Hills 2013). However, access to information on series considered to be failures is much harder to come by, and even if the degree of openness has been remarkable in the DR Fiction framework, it has proven hard to get detailed information on what was perceived as series which had been marked by substantial conflicts during their making.

This book thus primarily offers insights on what is considered to be best practice at a time of national and international success, building on extensive interviews as well as on the observations at DR. To gain a broader view of the production context, observational studies have also been conducted during the teaching of the so-called 'TV term' at the National Film School of Denmark in 2012–2013, while industry events like The European TV Drama Series Lab in Berlin 2012, the Nordic TV Drama Days at the Göteborg International Film Festival 2010–2013 and the Scandinavian Think Tank Symposium organized in 2010 by the Think Tank on European Film and Film Policy (Redvall and Gubbins 2011) have provided useful knowledge of current issues on the industry agenda and perceptions of best practice.[2] Combining the interview material and the observational studies with written sources like the in-house production principles (referred to as 'dogmas'), industry reports or statements from the press, the aim has been to provide a both informative and inspiring new perspective on writing and producing television drama.

Content of the book

Chapter 1 introduces the theoretical approach for studying television writing and production in this book. Referring to 'the four P's' in creativity research, the lack of production studies within the film and media studies' tradition of focusing on People and Products is discussed in relation to other fields of scholarship with a stronger interest in Processes and the Press surrounding them. The chapter suggests approaching film and media production as processes of problem finding and problem solving, focusing on the many choices of individuals in social situations with specific demands. These choices are always made in a particular context, and – drawing on Ian Macdonald's work on Screen Ideas (2004, 2010, 2012) and Mihaly Csikszentmihalyi's systems model for creativity (1988, 1999) – the chapter proposes the Screen Idea System framework for analysing the writing and production of new series based on a dynamic interplay between individuals, a domain and a field. The chapter also introduces other concepts for the analysis of creative work and practitioners' choices in the case studies to be discussed later in the book. Among them are different notions of individual versus collective authorship and of collaborations as different types of thought communities (John-Steiner 2000).

Chapter 2 provides 'a crash course' on Danish television drama, addressing major lines of development over the years. Part of the Screen Idea System is to always consider the trends, tastes and traditions in a particular domain as well as the specific mandate, management and money of the experts in the field when studying the emergence of new screen ideas. The chapter analyses major traditions in Danish television drama and some of the central discussions and concepts related to understanding TV series from a small nation public service broadcaster like DR. While there are obvious similarities related to, for instance, technological innovations or transnational trends in the development of television between countries, there are also a number of more nationally specific issues and challenges that are important for understanding the writing and production of television drama in a certain context. The chapter sets the stage for understanding the development from *Riget/The Kingdom* (1994) to *The Killing* (III 2012) and the case studies of current practice by establishing issues related to DR having a public service mandate and being in a monopoly position until the coming of TV 2 in 1988. The chapter defines the strong realist tradition in Danish television drama and outlines the development of more genre-oriented productions when moving away from an elitist TV theatre tradition towards serialized content with a more mainstream appeal. The chapter stresses how the current output by DR Fiction is almost exclusively one-hour family or crime series based on original ideas of writers and targeted at large audiences. Finally, the chapter addresses issues related to competing genres and channels as well as to international collaboration.

Building on the historical and institutional context of Chapter 2, Chapter 3 analyses the major aspects of the extensive reorganization of the production framework for television drama since the mid 1990s and the current structure and mandate of DR Fiction. The chapter tracks important concepts in the current framework back to changes in production when two film directors, consecutively taking on the job as Head of Drama, challenged the established mode of production. The concept of branding has emerged as still more important in a highly competitive television landscape (Johnson 2012), and one of the changes at DR was to focus on long-running drama series as branding flagships. This led to a new strategy of producing more mainstream 'quality within genre'-fare, combined with an ambition to copy work methods from the American television industry. The chapter traces how the spaces of production changed through the building of new studios and the establishment of so-called 'production hotels' envisioned to facilitate communication and collaboration in a similar way to what Mette Hjort has termed 'sites of synergy' in relation to new Danish cinema (2005, 20). Following successful series like *Taxa/Taxi* (1997–1999) and the first Emmy for best international drama with *Rejseholdet/Unit One* (2000–2004) in 2002, 15 'dogmas' for production were formulated to capture the tacit knowledge of what seemed to be the new recipe for producing successful series. The dogmas establish the concepts of 'one vision', 'double storytelling', 'producer's choice' and 'crossover', which are still a crucial part of the in-house understanding of how to produce good television drama. The chapter discusses the value of creating a shared language about processes and production and aspects of how to understand the recent developments in the mode of production as examples of 'peer-to-peer training' or 'family collaborations' before examining the structure of DR Fiction in the 2010s.

In the Screen Idea System framework for writing and production, important questions relate not only to the structures and mandate of the specific institution where the creative work is taking place but also to the background and training of the individuals working within this structure. Almost all writers and younger producers at DR are alumni of The National Film School of Denmark. As two examples, all writers of *The Killing* and all the episode writers of *Borgen* have an educational background in the Screenwriting Department of the School. The vast majority of the talent behind recent series thus have a background in the same educational institution with which DR has had an ongoing collaboration since the late 1990s. Chapter 4 analyses the ideas of best practice being taught to the new talent at the Film School and traces how teaching screenwriting for television gradually became an established part of the curriculum during the 2000s. This partly happened due to new developments in the domain of television drama, where US quality television series convinced people at the Film School that it was worthwhile to also take television seriously in an art school environment after years of focusing exclusively on film. However, central experts in the field from DR also played a major part in this development by encouraging collaboration, sharing their knowledge and taking an interest in the students to help ensure the emergence of strong television writers. Current Head of Drama Piv Bernth has called the collaboration between the two institutions one of the secrets behind the recent success of series from DR (Bernth in Pham 2012). Based on interviews with writers and producers from the School and a case study of the 2012–2013 edition of the so-called 'TV term', the chapter investigates the nature of this collaboration, where DR Fiction has actively engaged in training talent for future series. This has provided the opportunity to teach students a certain approach to television drama – based on a public service mandate and concepts like 'one vision' and 'double storytelling' from the production dogmas – as well as the opportunity to scout for new writers in a film school framework.

Chapter 5 explores the production framework at DR Fiction, focusing on the concept of 'one vision'. Based on interviews with writers, producers and executives at DR, the chapter traces the place of one vision in the DR mode of production since the 1990s. The analysis points to initial problems with establishing a head writer/episode writers structure, since neither head writers nor episode writers were used to this kind of division of labour in terms of the writing process. The chapter then outlines the gradual development of the one vision concept from the work of Stig Thorsboe and Hanna Lundblad (*Taxa, Krøniken/Better Times* and *Lykke/Happy Life*), Peter Thorsboe and Mai Brostrøm (*Unit One, Ørnen/The Eagle, Livvagterne/The Protectors*), Søren Sveistrup (*Nikolaj og Julie/Nikolaj and Julie* and *The Killing*) and Adam Price (*Borgen*) to the upcoming head writers Maya Ilsøe (*Arvingerne/The Legacy*) and Jeppe Gjervig Gram (*Follow the Money*, planned for 2015). The analysis points to how the idea of working with one vision comes in the shape of many types of collaborations depending on the head writer, and with producers, directors, production designers, actors and others involved to different extents. The chapter ends with a discussion on how to understand the concept of one vision in relation to the role of the 'showrunner'.

Whereas there can be many people in the writers' rooms for drama series in the US television industry, there are often only three writers in the rooms at DR, where writers and producers find three to be 'the magic number' for having the right energy in the room. Chapter 6 is based on a case study of the writing of episode 25 for the third season of *Borgen*, from the two week storyline in the writers' room over the different drafts and note meetings until the reading of the final draft the week before its shooting. The chapter offers a detailed analysis of the casting, the structure and the work process of the writers' room and of the nature of the collaboration between head writer Adam Price and episode writers Jeppe Gjervig Gram and Maja Jul Larsen. The chapter analyses what can be regarded as the different roles in the room, and seeks to understand the process as collaborative writing with one vision before proposing an idea of writers' rooms as different forms of thought communities.

Chapter 7 investigates the production story of Søren Sveistrup's crime thriller *The Killing*, illustrating how the emergence of new quality series is a result of an intricate interplay between individual talents, the domain and the field. After discussing the series as part of the new focus on 'Scandi-Crime' or 'Nordic Noir' and addressing how changes in the scheduling strategies of a broadcaster like BBC4 have been influential for the international success of the series, the chapter analyses the development of the series, focusing on the choices of content, structure and style as reflections of the ideas of quality hailed in the DR production dogmas. *The Killing* can be regarded as an example of allowing the creator Søren Sveistrup to develop a series based on his vision in spite of the original scepticism of whether it would be possible to have an extended murder mystery as the structure for 20 episodes. The three-layer structure of all three seasons – dealing with the police investigation, the political intrigues and the private lives of the victims of the different crimes – mirrors the idea of double storytelling with larger ethical and social connotations as an important part of the overall thriller set-up. Moreover, the idea of crossover between the film and television industry is present, not only in the choices of the people making the series come alive on screen but also in the initial ambitions of making cinematic drama for the small screen. The production story is interpreted as an example of a series where a practitioner with the outside recognition and the in-house track record to have earned the trust of the broadcaster is given the opportunity to propose a new kind of product. This product is based on the deliberate intention to reinvent the traditional approaches, and the process of making it draws on what is considered to be state of the art in the international domain. The DR dogmas should not be interpreted as principles that are necessarily discussed by all practitioners in the process, but as analytical categories, which reflect a certain approach by the experts in a production culture. The dogmas are thus an important part of assessing what might be the next series, which is – as most definitions of creativity stress – of high quality, original and appropriate to the task at hand.

The final chapter of the book synthesizes central points from the previous chapters and moves on to analyse the current conditions and cliffhangers for writing and producing television drama in an age of technological, economic and cultural convergence (as discussed in Lotz 2007 or Kackman et al. 2011). The current mode of production seems to be undergoing a number of changes. Within DR Fiction, the 2010s have been marked by major generational changes among executives and producers as well as writers. The domain is changing with DR experiencing more competition from other national broadcasters. Moreover, DR has to face the fact that a wealth of international product is now constantly available to national audiences on a variety of platforms.

This international competition is not only changing the game in terms of distribution. International players are also moving into the Nordic landscape of television production with Netflix producing the second season of the Norwegian series *Lilyhammer* (NRK 2012–) and HBO approaching DR about possible co-productions. Furthermore, national writing talent is suddenly being offered the opportunity to work abroad. As an example, Adam Price is set to collaborate with *House of Cards* writer Michael Dobbs on a new series for the BBC (Wind-Friis 2013). Despite the recent international interest in series from DR, DR Fiction insists on having the mandate to produce series for national audiences. It will be interesting to follow how the recent success might have unforeseen impacts on future productions by DR possibly having to engage with large-scale international collaboration or competition in the national production landscape for the first time, and potentially not being the first choice of talent with the whole world as their storytelling stage.

Summing up, a number of elements in the Screen Idea System framework are presently undergoing major changes with new experts in the field, new individuals writing series and new points of reference in the domain creating new demands for the nature of national quality TV series. The implications of these substantial changes for the process of writing and producing new television series remain yet to be seen. This book's attempt to create a detailed understanding of the Screen Idea System framework for writing and producing television drama in Denmark since the 1990s until now aims to be of use in a time of change.

1
Television Writing and the Screen Idea System

Introduction

Where do ideas for television series come from? How do writers, producers and broadcasters settle on the ideas to pursue and what are the stages and challenges in developing ideas into series for the screen? One would think that questions like these about the choices of practitioners and the nature of production were central to film and media studies, yet limited attention has been given to the creative process of developing and producing new works of fiction, let alone to the study of these in television.

One method that can prove useful for addressing such questions is, I argue, a Screen Idea System framework. This chapter introduces the Screen Idea System framework for the book, which builds on an understanding of the writing and production of television as a complex interplay between individuals, a domain and a field. The book links theories from film and media studies, approaches from the emerging area of screenwriting research, with concepts and models from the field of creativity research, insisting that one always needs to take what could be called 'the many P's in production' into account when analysing the emergence of new scripted series. Creativity scholars argue that when trying to understand the nature of creative work one has to include the Process, the Product and the Press and the understanding of the Person, with 'Press' referring to the environment in which the creative work takes place. This is the so-called 'four Ps' of creativity (see, e.g. Rhodes 1961; Mooney 1963).

Approaching the writing and production of television drama from this perspective, the chapter addresses how to understand this interplay as a system where individuals with a specific talent, training and track record

20

propose new screen ideas as variations on the existing trends, tastes and traditions in a domain, which then have to be regarded as being of high quality and appropriate in order to be accepted by gatekeepers with a specific mandate for production. A special focus of this chapter is the collaborative processes of television writing, analysed as the work of 'thought communities' who go through different stages in a problem-finding and problem-solving effort when moving from an original idea to a final product.

Studying television writing and production

While film and media studies do not have a tradition of extensive case studies of the nature of creative work, other fields of scholarship have taken a greater interest in the nature of artistic and cultural production. Sociologists Pierre Bourdieu and Howard Becker have written extensively on the field of cultural production and on art as collective action or 'art worlds' (e.g. Bourdieu 1993, 1996; Becker 1974, 1982). Sociologist Leo Rosten and anthropologist Hortense Powdermaker were among the first to conduct production-oriented studies of the American film industry (Rosten 1941; Powdermaker 1950).

More recently, studies coming from a 'production of culture' perspective have focused on how creative work in the cultural industries is the result of complex patterns and collaborations rather than a clear result of one person's vision (e.g. Peterson and Anand 2004), and this collective perception of cultural production also marks other cross-disciplinary publications and current studies of the nature of work life in the creative or cultural industries (e.g. Negus and Pickering 2004; Deuze 2007, 2010; Hesmondhalgh 2007; Hesmondhalgh and Baker 2010). These scholars are not alone. Coming from organizational studies, researchers like Paul DiMaggio and Paul M. Hirsch (e.g. DiMaggio and Hirsch 1976; DiMaggio 1977) have been investigating the structures in the cultural industries for quite some time, while others have been looking more specifically at film and media production, for instance, Helen Blair analysing work conditions in the film industry (Blair 2001, 2003).

Whereas the collective nature of most cultural production and the work processes in different cultural industries have interested researchers for a number of years, few studies combine this interest with the development of a specific product or the nature of the product itself. As noted in a sociological study of different processes of art making 'from start to finish' there has, for instance, always been 'a blind spot in the sociology of art: any discussion of specific art works' (Becker et al.

2006, 1). While the humanities tend to emphasize the text over practice, the social sciences tend not to include the text, or the product, in the analysis. There are exceptions, and some media industry research has addressed questions about the impact of particular modes of production on what is actually produced, for example, David Bordwell, Janet Staiger and Kristin Thompson's seminal study *The Classical Hollywood Cinema* on the organizational conditions as well as the stylistic and storytelling structures in Hollywood until 1960 (Bordwell et al. 1985). Studies like Thompson's *Storytelling in the New Hollywood* (1999) or Bordwell's *The Way Hollywood Tells It* (2006) have constructively argued how particular modes of production influence storytelling strategies with much more detail on particular products than will be offered here. This book does take an interest in the development of specific series, but the product as such is not thoroughly investigated for formal-aesthetic qualities.

The focus of this book is on a certain mode of writing and producing television drama. Building on the work of previous scholars, the goal is to provide more detailed analysis of the actual writing and production process, emphasizing the value of production analysis of creative collaborations to further understandings of how new television works come into being. Production analysis can take many forms and range from macro to micro levels, from political economy to professional routines (Newcomb and Lotz 2002). Most production analysis operates with several levels of analysis simultaneously to capture the complexity of the production process. Specific case studies are often central to the analysis, as Horace Newcomb has discussed (1991) comparing three classic examples of television case study research with different approaches (Cantor 1971; Elliott 1972; Gitlin 1983). Questions regarding the degree of creative freedom and the organizational and financial framework are central in all of these three classic studies, as is the case in more recent research (e.g. Levine 2001; Lotz 2004). As Newcomb has noted, the driving question in most production studies, then as now, is to make sense of the cultural industries with the many problems related to 'creativity and constraint in industrial settings' (2007, 129).

Most studies of film and media production are reconstructions of past events based on interviews and document analysis rather than observations or conversations during productions. An example is film scholar Robert L. Carringer's book *The Making of Citizen Kane* (1996), which among other things explores the complicated relationship between the young Orson Welles and the experienced screenwriter Herman J. Mankiewicz, leading to Mankiewicz not receiving a credit on the film until The Writers Guild looked at the matter. Much can be learned from this kind of retrospective data gathering, but it is hard to gain a nuanced understanding of the specific nature of the creative collaborations and processes from this approach. Behind-the-scenes publications on legendary productions can offer insights, like Steven Bach's account of his time as a producer with United Artists during the making of the famous failure *Heaven's Gate* (1980) (Bach 1985), but books like these are of course written from an insider's perspective. They offer back story details from the process of production, but without academic analysis to nuance the understanding of choices and events.[1]

The complexity of studying production leads Newcomb to argue for what he terms 'synthetic media industry research', comparing media work to a dance, where one has to focus on 'movement, fluidity, and choices, both strategic and tactical, in any situation', since the processes are marked by 'constantly shifting involvement and engagement of individuals and groups who are always exceptionally aware of both the structures in which they work and the degrees of agency they hold' (Newcomb 2009, 269). The question is, of course, how to study this kind of fluid process, where practitioners make choices based on their assessment of many different parameters in specific situations. This book follows researchers such as Robert E. Stake, who has emphasized the value of specificity and particularity when doing qualitative case studies in natural settings (2000, 2005) and when trying to interpret what is sometimes described as 'meaning in action' (Jensen 2002, 236). A fundamental challenge is how to design a research framework suited to break down the complex processes, when practitioners are choosing special paths and not others for the projects at hand.

Production as problem finding and problem solving

One way forward can be found in the work of David Bordwell, who has insisted on not forgetting the social practice and individual choices related to film and media production. Together with Noël Carroll, he has proposed a problem-driven, 'middle range' approach to film scholarship, where one defines a problem within the domain of cinema non-dogmatically and sets out to solve it 'through logical reflection, empirical research, or a combination of both' (Bordwell and Carroll 1996, xiv). As John Thornton Caldwell has argued, one can regard this approach as 'workmanlike, specific, delimited, and local', drawing on a pragmatic and process-driven perspective (2008, 25).

Bordwell has suggested that a fruitful strategy for conducting this kind of scholarship is to focus on the many choices by practitioners in the process through a problem/solution frame of inquiry 'granting a role to the artist's grasp of the task and of her own talents as well as to the possibility of errors, accidents (happy or unhappy), unintended consequences, spontaneous and undeliberated actions, and decisions made for reasons not wholly evident to the agents' (1997, 150). Bordwell places special focus on the decision-making processes of film and media practitioners, along with the idea that decisions are made in social situations with specific demands. As he points out: 'The artist's choices are informed and constrained by the rules and roles of artmaking. The artistic institution formulates tasks, puts problems on the agenda, and rewards effective solutions' (1997, 151). Furthermore, he discusses how artists draw on traditions and certain norms in their present time as the starting point for creating something new.

Bordwell's problem/solution framework of inquiry shares many similarities with influential theories from the field of creativity research. Cognitive studies of creativity have often regarded creative work as a form of problem solving. A problem can be defined as 'a situation with a goal and a hindrance' (Runco 2007, 14). If one has a clear cut problem, one can move on to problem solving immediately, but in many artistic processes choosing the problem to actually solve will often be central to the process. What painting should one paint? What film should one make? As the American philosopher John Dewey has famously stated, 'a problem well put is half solved' (Dewey in Campbell 1995, 48). A number of creativity scholars have focused on problem finding in artistic processes to investigate why and how an artist decides to focus on one problem and not another (e.g. Csikszentmihalyi and Getzels 1976). The studies highlight the importance of the often underestimated phase of defining what problem to actually solve, which in the context of this book can be regarded as the important stage of conceptualizing what series to write and how to go about it before the actual execution of the plans.

Scholars coming from the school of Creative Problem Solving (CPS) have offered numerous models for how to understand creative processes in an attempt to clarify the movement from the mess-finding, data-finding and problem-finding stages of defining a problem through the idea finding to the solution and acceptance-finding stages of a task at hand.[2] I have previously used models from CPS (Isaksen and Treffinger 2004) to break down the stages of development, writing and production in feature filmmaking when doing detailed production studies of the nature of each stage and exploring what makes the diverging ideas of each stage converge and move on to the next stage (Redvall 2009, 2010a). The case studies of this book are not structured around the stages outlined by CPS, but aspects of CPS are referred to, when for instance analysing the amount of time spent in the early stages of a problem-finding effort during research and development or differences in the approach of writers and producers as to when they expect solution finding and acceptance finding in terms of a script.

From the problem/solution framework suggested by Bordwell and ideas of creative processes from CPS, one can derive a picture of television production as marked by individuals making choices in a collaborative work process; choices that are marked by the works already produced as well as by the different types of constraints surrounding the process. This approach insists on the ever-present importance of the social as well as institutional context when dealing with creative work.

Studying creativity in context

Most definitions of creativity focus on the ability to produce something that is new (e.g. original, unexpected) and is of a high quality and appropriate (e.g. meets task restraints) (e.g. Weisberg 1993; Sternberg and Lubart 1999). The concepts of 'novelty' and 'value' are thus central to this understanding of creativity (Mayer 1999, 449). Whether something has value or not is in many definitions linked to the outside recognition of the work produced and thinking about the relationship between issues of novelty, quality and appropriateness is useful for analysing the negotiations of what one intends to produce in a film and media context.

Early understandings of artists and their processes were based on mystical or religious explanatory frameworks with creative individuals often being regarded as geniuses (Sternberg and Lubart 1999, 5). Either you were blessed with the gift of creativity or you weren't. The 1920s saw a shift from discussing the idea of the genius towards discussions of different degrees of giftedness in the attempt to study whether one could find specific personal traits or patterns of thought in especially talented or intelligent people (Ryhammar and Brolin 1999, 261). The research of the psychologist J. P. Guilford is normally defined as the starting point for the scholarly field of creativity research (e.g. Sternberg 1999). His approach was to study whether specific personal traits characterize creative individuals. This psychometric perspective and the focus on the individual and cognitive aspects of creativity were dominant until the

1980s, when both a social-psychological and a systems approach of cre-ativity emerged, often termed 'confluence approaches' (Sternberg and Lubart 1999, 10).

The work of the Hungarian/American psychologist Mihaly Csikszentmihalyi embodies this move towards including contextual ele-ments in the understanding of creativity. His systems view of creativity is based on the conviction that creativity cannot be studied by isolating individuals and their work from the social and historical surroundings. Explaining the emergence of his so-called 'systems model' of creativity, Csikszentmihalyi has described how his early research focused on indi-vidual thought, emotions and motivations. Gradually, the task became more frustrating since it turned out to be to explain particular aspects of his data. As an example, he mentions how one of his studies concluded that the female students in an art school showed the same creative potential as their male colleagues. However, 20 years later none of the women had earned the recognition as outstanding artist to the same degree as their male counterparts (1999, 313).

Observations like these prompted him to design a systems model for creativity, building on the notion that creativity is never the result of individual actions alone, but:

> the product of three main shaping forces: a set of social institutions, or field, that selects from the variations produced by individuals those that are worth preserving; a stable cultural domain that will preserve and transmit the selected new ideas of forms to the following gener-ations; and finally the individual, who brings about some change in the domain, a change that the field will consider to be creative.
>
> (Csikszentmihalyi 1988, 325)

According to Csikszentmihalyi, creativity is thus the result of an interplay between these three forces, which he visualizes as follows (Figure 1.1).

The domain is to be understood as a formal system of symbols based on information that can be regarded as 'a set of rules, procedures and instructions for actions' (Abuhamdeh and Csikszentmihalyi 2004, 33). If one does not have access to the information within a certain domain, one is unable to contribute with new knowledge. As an exam-ple, Csikszentmihalyi mentions the difficulty of composing a symphony with no prior knowledge of music or of being acknowledged as a gifted mandarin chef without knowing anything about the Chinese cuisine (1988, 330). Some domains have a structure, which makes them hard to

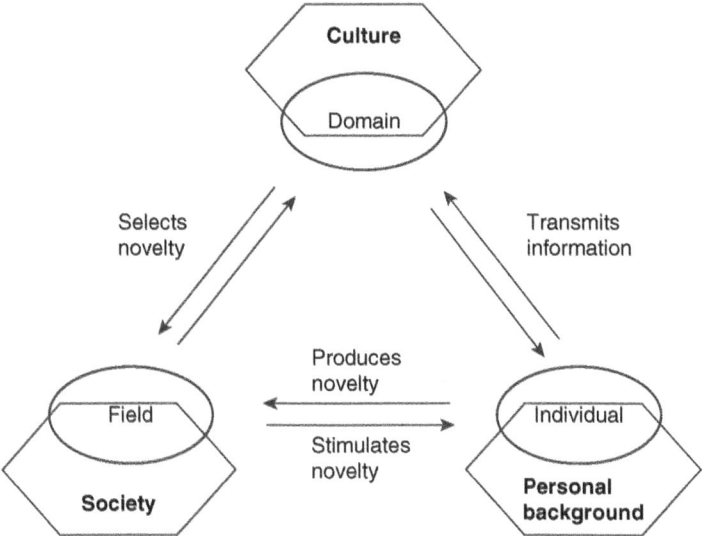

Figure 1.1 The systems model by Mihaly Csikszentmihalyi[3]

enter and renew, while others are more accessible. Within the domain of film and media production, there are, for instance, particular understandings of best practice, such as classical storytelling strategies, which one will be measured against when proposing a new variation. Moreover, existing works within the domain shape the understanding of quality among the individuals wanting to create new variations as well as among the experts assessing their value.

The field is the social aspect of the model and encompasses the individuals who function as gatekeepers by deciding whether a new idea or a product should be included in the domain (1999, 315). In a screenwriting or television drama context, screenwriting and production teachers, critics, journal editors, script editors, commissioners or network executives are examples of people in key positions, enabling them to choose which works deserve to be produced or recognized, broadcast and remembered. The individual is the third element in the system. According to Csikszentmihalyi, one can speak of creativity when a person uses the symbols in a specific domain, gets an idea, sees a new pattern or creates something new, which by the appropriate field is found worthy of being in the relevant domain. Based on this systems approach, he defines creativity as 'any act, idea, or product that changes an existing domain, or that transforms an existing domain into a new one. And the definition of a creative person is: someone whose thoughts or actions change a domain or establish a new domain' (1988, 28). In relation to this definition, Csikszentmihalyi stresses that it is impossible to change a domain without the explicit or implicit consent of the field responsible for it, and the experts thus hold great power in terms of selecting certain examples of novelty at the expense of others.

This approach to creativity shifts the focus from the traits of the creative individual towards a broader understanding of creative work. As Csikszentmihalyi notes, whether one's work is recognized is not only related to talent or giftedness but also to 'chance, perseverance, or being at the right place at the right time' (1988, 29). Personal traits are relevant, but since creativity is based on the interaction of person, domain and field, there is much more to creating a novelty with an impact on the domain. Csikszentmihalyi has compared his model to classical models of evolutionary processes, where evolution occurs when an individual organism produces a variation, which is chosen by the environment and carried on to the next generation (1999, 316). He suggests that this process of mutation, selection and transmission can be regarded as a form of creative evolution.

According to Csikszentmihalyi, the systems model can be useful for trying to answer questions about whether a society generally values and encourages creativity, whether there is a social and economic openness towards change, as well as the degree of mobility or complexity (1999, 322). Issues like these bring studies to the macro level of analysis, and as a psychologist, Csikszentmihalyi also raises quite detailed issues related to the background and personality of individuals. As with most conceptual models, the systems model naturally gives rise to debates about particular elements, such as whether it is constructive to, for instance, separate individuals and their personal background from society as such. However, the model's overall framework for thinking about creativity and creative processes as happening between different shaping forces is a useful way of outlining the complexity of most film and media production, which can thus be regarded as a complex interplay of the talent producing new series; of the conceptions of best practice in the domain of television drama; and of the experts or institutions with the power to select which ideas should be given the opportunity to move from pitch to production. Based on the structure and the basic understandings of the systems model, this book thus proposes a Screen Idea System for how to approach the writing and production of television drama.

The Screen Idea System framework

The Screen Idea System is an attempt to bridge ideas from media industry and screenwriting studies with the more process-oriented conceptions of creative work from the field of creativity studies, emphasizing how things happen in a constant and dynamic interplay between different forces on several levels. The Screen Idea System is thus the conceptual model behind the structure of this book, which starts by discussing larger issues related to studying series from one particular broadcaster (DR) (Chapter 2), the development of particular managerial 'dogmas' for production (Chapter 3) and the training of talent from one particular film school, The National Film School of Denmark (NFSD) (Chapter 4), before moving into case studies of how this framework of a specific production culture is crucial to include in the understanding of the work of practitioners within DR as well as of the nature of the series produced.

Timothy Havens and Amanda D. Lotz have recently proposed 'The Industrialization of Culture Framework' for explaining the operation of media industries (2012). Their framework constructively emphasizes how one always has to take the social trends, tastes and traditions in a specific culture as well as the mandate of a specific media institution (for instance commercial vs non-commercial mandates) into account when analysing the conditions for media industries (such as technology, regulation or economics), the day-to-day practices of organizations and individuals, the texts produced and the meeting between the public and the texts (2012, 4–5). The framework thus stresses the importance of the different contexts surrounding all media production, leading to discussions of the work of practitioners as different degrees of circumscribed agency (2012, 15). In this framework, three main forces are considered to be moulding the work of individuals into 'socially sanctioned forms', namely 'the general culture itself, formal and informal professional expectations, and specific organizational practices and norms' (2012, 15). The framework by Havens and Lotz points to the vastness of trying to understand the complexities of media industries with the work of, for instance, screenwriters as but one tiny element in an enormous machinery.

The Screen Idea System shares the industrialization of culture framework's interest in the forces that shape the work of individuals, but singles out the importance of individuals in this process, arguing that the writing and production of television drama starts and ends with a screen idea. Similar to how Csikszentmihalyi insists that creativity does not exist in a vacuum (1999, 315), a screen idea does not come out of nowhere. It builds on or rebels against notions of best practice for screenwriting and on the existing tastes, trends and traditions for television drama in the domain. Moreover, ideas are shaped by meeting the field where institutions have a specific mandate for production and a management looking for particular kinds of product, and where money for financing the development, writing and production of new variations is always an issue.

In the field of screenwriting research, the idea of understanding the process of screenwriting as structured around a screen idea comes out of the work of Ian Macdonald (e.g. 2003, 2004, 2012). Building on a term used by Philip Parker to describe the start of a script's development (1998, 57), Macdonald has outlined how to think of a screen idea as 'the core idea of anything intended to become a screenwork, that is "any notion of a potential screenwork held by one or more people. Whether it is possible to describe it on paper or by other means"' (2012, 113). This definition highlights how ideas exist before 'pen is set to paper', and how development of ideas is based on what Macdonald describes as 'the norms of the screen industries' (2012, 113). The context of the screen idea is given great importance, and Macdonald has studied how certain notions of quality are used when assessing screen ideas, pointing to 'realisability, an appropriate structure, a clear thesis and some aspect of originality' as four common goals (2012, 113). These goals share similarities with the previously mentioned definitions of creativity focusing on quality, originality and appropriateness, but also point to the importance of what in the DR Fiction framework is often discussed as a clear 'premise' rather than 'thesis'.[4]

Based on the concept of the screen idea, Macdonald has pioneered the idea of the Screen Idea Work Group, emphasizing how screen ideas are developed in flexibly constructed groups organized around specific projects (2010). The Screen Idea System is an attempt to encompass how these work groups, consisting of individuals with special talent, training and track record propose new, original variations in a constant interplay with the ideas of quality and appropriateness in the domain and the field (Figure 1.2).

Mirroring the structure of the systems model, the Screen Idea System proposes a dynamic understanding of the processes where the existing knowledge in the domain informs the choices of individuals as well as the conceptions of quality when the field assesses suggested new variations. If found to be original, of high quality and appropriate by the field, the ideas of individuals can be produced and acknowledged

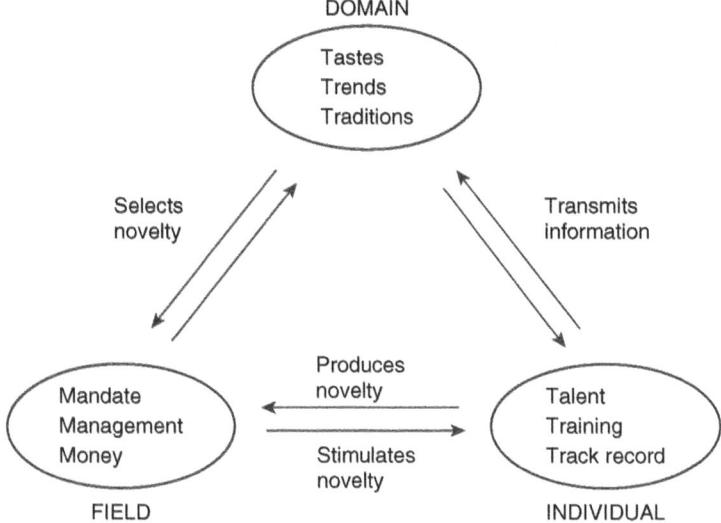

Figure 1.2 The Screen Idea System

as creative, and thus end up being included as new variations in the domain. However, the field not only has a gatekeeping function but can also have a positive impact on individuals by creating a framework that stimulates novelty.

Translated to the topic of this book, one can approach the writing and production of television drama in Denmark as a system where writers with an individual talent, training and track record propose ideas for potential TV series. These ideas build on the trends, tastes and traditions in the domain and have to find acceptance by the experts in the field, where projects are assessed based on the mandate, management and money of the institution involved. In this book, series are thus proposed to an institution with a non-commercial, public service mandate, with a management having certain 'dogmas' for production and with a budget for producing only a few high-profile drama series every year. Most individuals have trained at the same institution, the NFSD, which has focused still more on teaching not only screenwriting for film but also television writing since the 2000s. These individuals have been encouraged to develop original ideas for series, and rather than focusing on the existing traditions in the national realm, they seem to have been drawing still more on their personal tastes and the latest trends in international quality television.

As will be addressed in later chapters, what one can call the domain of Danish television series has changed dramatically since the late 1990s with a new kind of product finding both national and international acclaim. This change is of course related to the ideas of certain writers, but it is also highly influenced by new approaches to scripted fiction within DR as well as by developments on the international television scene. This book deals with a number of aspects related to this complicated interplay, based on an understanding that the emergence of an impressive streak of successful series from DR has to do with a number of elements, which have to be addressed from different perspectives. The Screen Idea System is helpful in visualizing this interplay and in emphasizing how the emergence of new television series is based on highly collaborative and contextual processes.

Issues of authorship: Auteurs, authors and visions

One of the consequences of approaching television writing as a highly collaborative endeavour is the blurring of traditional conceptions of individual authorship. However, a major change in the approach to television writing and production at DR since the 1990s has been the emergence of the concept of 'one vision', singling out the creator of the series as the person with the guiding vision for a project all the way through production. This concept of one vision is addressed in all chapters of this book, and it is thus worthwhile to briefly introduce particular ideas of creative collaborations and processes as the basis for further discussions of individual vs collective authorship.

As Steven Maras has noted in relation to the auteur theory coming out of France in the 1950s and 1960s, few topics provoke 'as much emotion in screenwriting discourse' (2009, 97). The explanation for this is that many interpretations of the auteur theory have emphasized the importance of the director at the expense of the screenwriter. Consequently, the screenwriter has tended to be marginalized, both in the film and media industry and in academic scholarship. Some have fought this, like film critic Richard Corliss formulating a 'Screenwriter's Theory' on 'author-auteurs' (1974) as a response to Andrew Sarris translating the thoughts behind *la politique des auteurs* (Sarris 1962) and publishing an 'auteur-bible' (1968).[5] The focus on the director and on individual authorship is still prevalent in some film scholarship, even though a film scholar like John Caughie, writing about recent theoretical developments, has found that ' "the delirium of auteurism" has been sanitized by common sense' (2008, 408), and there generally seems to be more discussions about the potential pitfalls of auteurism such as the risk of not acknowledging the complex work flows of art as collaboratively produced (e.g. Aitken 2008, 36; Schatz 2009, 50).

Television studies has in many ways been trying to position itself against the auteurist discussions of film studies (Kraszewski 2011, 168). Similarly, most discussions of media industry studies challenge ideas of individual authorship when arguing that industrial production and patterns of mass production is based on a group effort (e.g. Holt and Perren 2009; Havens and Lotz 2012). Based on extensive criticism of the traditional notion of singular authorship, television and media industry scholar Michelle Hilmes has acknowledged that there can be some advantages in singling out an individual, but this approach often works against understanding the complexity and interdependence of the process (2009, 26). She finds that instead of letting the focus on one individual distort the realities of media authorship, one should foreground the problems related to this and 'bring the struggle into productive analysis' (2009, 26). One of the intentions of this book is exactly to foreground this complex interplay of many different collaborators and workflows to create a nuanced sense of how to think of authorship and agency in relation to television series coming from DR with a one vision brand.

Several scholars have argued that one needs to know more about the actual making of media works if one wants to constructively address issues of their authorship (e.g. Tybjerg 2005; Schepelern 2005; Gray and Johnson 2013). One can't merely look at their list of credits. Coming from a philosophy of art perspective, Paisley Livingston and Berys Gaut have constructively been writing about different types of authorship related to questions of creativity and intentionality during the process of creation (e.g. Gaut 1997; Gaut and Livingston 2003; Livingston 1997, 2007). There are now several theories challenging the notion of singular authorship with ideas of for instance 'multiple authorship' (Gaut 1997), 'collaboration analysis' (Carringer 2001), 'collective authorship' (Sellors 2007) or 'joint authorship' (Livingston 2009). The issue of 'sufficient control' (Gaut 2010; Livingston 2009) will be raised in Chapter 5 when analysing how to think of the concept of one vision in the DR production framework in relation to the role of the showrunner in the US television industry.

'Why should one care?' one could argue, since it can seem like an overly academic exercise to debate delicate aspects of authorship, but issues like these also have implications for the world outside of academia. In screenwriting, issues of credits and copyright are central and they are often related to conceptions of who contributed to what extent and who can be regarded as having a major impact on the work produced. In the DR context, the idea of one vision can sound like a way of treating the creator of a series like an almighty auteur with complete creative control. It is worthwhile studying how this idea of one vision functions in the everyday work of writing and producing television. This is not a minor matter, as the concept of one vision has turned out to be quite influential in recent industry debates where for instance the Norwegian television industry has had fierce discussions about the lack of one vision in relation to the national production and has debated suggestions of copying what is perceived as successful work methods from the Danish framework (e.g. Iversen 2010; Kåset and Ødegårdstuen 2010). As argued by former Head of Drama at DR, director and screenwriter Rumle Hammerich, one can't import a concept without knowing its actual meaning (Hammerich 2010), and concepts on paper can take on very different forms in practice. Studies of concrete production processes thus not only furthers current academic debates about screenwriting, authorship, creativity and media production, but also allows for a better understanding of the actual proceedings, which ought to be of value to practitioners in the industry.

Theorizing collaboration

Collaboration permeates production, but it is a somewhat neglected area. Analyses of production often stress the impact of different types of constraints, but production processes are also marked by enabling elements and collaborations, which further the work of individuals. Based on the Screen Idea System as the overall framework for understanding the processes at hand, a crucial question is, of course, how to then study television writing and production and how to embrace constraints as well as collaborations along the way. This book has found inspiration in other writings on specific creative collaborations and on different stages when approaching the task of creating a new product. Studies of group theory and group skills often highlight that mutual goals, social interdependence and trust are important in group interaction (e.g. Johnson and Johnson 2006, 66–68), as are aspects of having differentiated roles and integrated norms (2006, 15). As already described, not only film and media studies but also creativity studies tended to focus on the individual for quite some time, but the past ten years have seen more studies of collective creative work (e.g. Paulus and Nijstad 2003) as well as bestsellers on the strength of creative collaboration (Sawyer 2008).

Whereas Ian Macdonald's concept of the Screen Idea Work Group is one way to think of the creative collaborations around potential moving image narratives, another fruitful way to think of production as a collective endeavour is to approach these collaborations as different kinds of what Vera John-Steiner has called 'thought communities'. John-Steiner developed the idea of thought communities based on studies of remarkable intellectual and artistic collaborations, where she found that 'generative ideas emerge from joint thinking, from significant conversations, and from sustained, shared struggles to achieve new insights by partners in thought' (2000, 3). Based on the Russian psychologist Lev Vygotsky's theories, John-Steiner stresses the importance of a dynamic dependence of social and individual processes, leading to a 'co-construction of knowledge, tools, and artifacts' (2000, 5). Focusing on issues of having a shared vision and aiming for shared growth, she introduces four patterns of partnerships as different forms of thought communities, which are defined as different from cooperating teams in the way that 'their members take emotional and intellectual risks to construct mutuality and productive interdependence. Their objectives are to develop a shared vision as well as achieve jointly negotiated outcomes' (2000, 196). There is thus a sense of personal investment and risk-taking involved in the work of thought communities.

John-Steiner's four patterns of thought communities consist of the distributed collaboration, the complementary collaboration, the family collaboration and the integrative collaboration. Distributed collaboration is common and involves everyday conversations in professional contexts, for example, at conferences, in electronic exchanges or among artists sharing a workspace. Participants are linked by shared interests, but their roles are informal and voluntary (2000, 197–8). According to John-Steiner the complementary collaboration is the most common and is characterized by 'a division of labor based on complementary expertise, disciplinary knowledge, roles, and temperament. Participants negotiate their roles and strive for a common vision' (2000, 198). The family collaboration is defined by a mode of interaction where roles are flexible or can change over time, as when participants help each other in changing roles from, for example, being a novice to a level of more expertise (2000, 201). In family collaborations, participants are normally linked to each other during a longer period of time.

A longitudinal collaboration is also central in the integrative collaboration, which thrives on 'dialogue, risk taking, and a shared vision. In some cases, the participants construct a common set of beliefs, or ideology, which sustains them in periods of opposition or insecurity' (2000,

203). According to John-Steiner integrative partnerships are motivated 'by the desire to transform existing knowledge, thought styles, or artistic approaches into new visions' (2000, 203), and one of her main points is that the integrative collaboration seems to be the best for the emergence of new patterns of thought or new art forms. An explanation for this is that it is hard to handle the burden of disciplinary and artistic socialization on your own.

This approach to understanding creative collaborations is interesting in relation to studying television writing and production, which is normally a highly collaborative endeavour. There are few examples of team writing in Danish feature filmmaking, but the nature of television writing in the DR production framework has gradually become to have head writers collaborating with episode writers on new series. This kind of 'writing by committee' is often discussed in rather negative terms (e.g. Caldwell 2008) and primarily understood in relation to sheer logistics like the volume of what needs to be produced at a high speed in the television context. However, it is also worthwhile to explore the potential creative benefits of having this kind of dialogue between writers about how to create a new work. The screenwriting collaborations investigated in this book have thus been approached as different kinds of thought communities with the Screen Idea System offering a conceptual framework for understanding and analysing these kinds of longitudinal, complex processes in relation to not only the individual production processes but also to the crucial context.

Accordingly, the following chapters are structured to contribute with insights on all the 'P's in production, but with a particular focus on the work processes of screenwriters. Whereas the earlier chapters deal more with the people and the press in a macro context (drawing on interviews and document analysis as the main sources), later chapters focus more on the production processes and the gradual development of the products (drawing primarily on interviews and observational studies). Before focusing on the current state of affairs, however, Chapter 2 provides a crash course in Danish television drama, setting the scene in terms of the traditions in the domain and of the particular mandate related to producing public service television for a small nation market.

2
Danish Television Drama: A Crash Course

Introduction

In Denmark, as in many other countries, local scripted drama is among the most popular content on television. Since the late 1990s, new series from DR have continuously had impressive audiences on Sunday nights at 8 pm. Some reruns of older series also attract large audiences. In the autumn of 2012, the legendary family chronicle *Matador* (1978–1981), which was originally broadcast as four seasons, received its seventh rerun on Saturday nights at 8 pm with audience figures that forced the competing channel TV 2 to move their prestigious talent show to 9 pm. Even the national football team couldn't compete, seeing the little over half a million viewers watching a game on 8 September beaten by more than a million viewers for the rerun of the first episode of *Matador* in spite of the fact that 3.6 million DVDs of the series had been sold by the spring of 2012 (Figure 2.1).[1]

The possibility of reaching large domestic audiences is of course one of the reasons why TV series are generally popular with broadcasters despite their high cost and the challenge of finding the right material. Moreover, series can help to brand stations, as a US cable channel like HBO has effectively shown with their original series that are now famous worldwide as 'not being TV'. The rerun potential is another contributing factor. While sport events and many reality formats are live shows, scripted drama has the potential of making a comeback and, in some cases, also of having a long life on the screens in other countries, maybe even as remakes.

Even though TV series are now recorded and 'stacked', watched on DVD and available on other platforms, they are still very much 'appointment viewing' in the national television landscape, where many viewers

Figure 2.1 Mads Skjern (Jørgen Buckhøj) and his son in the legendary family chronicle *Matador* (1978–1981) on life in the small town of Korsbæk in the years 1929–1947. Photo by Rolf Konow. Courtesy of DR

plan to watch the new series when they are shown for the first time. The series can be regarded as bringing the audience together in what David Morley has called 'a constructed national family' when writing about the mediated nation as symbolic home (2004). Issues of how TV series can provide public value to a nation are critical in many discourses of public service television, such as in Trisha Dunleavy's studies of public service television and television drama in New Zealand (2010, 2012).

This chapter provides a crash course in the history of Danish television drama and some of the central discussions and concepts related to understanding TV series from a small nation public service broadcaster like DR. While there are obvious similarities in the development of television between many countries – related to the same kind of technological innovations or international trends – there are also a number of more nation-specific issues and challenges that are important for understanding the writing and production of television drama in a certain context.

Based on the Screen Idea System for production, this chapter sets the scene for the later focus on the development from *The Kingdom* (1994) to *The Killing* (III 2012) and for the case studies of current practice, by establishing the traditions in the national domain and by introducing crucial considerations around the fact that DR has a non-commercial, public service mandate. The chapter presents the development of drama from DR in terms of a strong realist tradition and traces the emergence of more genre fare when moving away from a TV theatre tradition towards serialized content leading to the current focus on mainstream character-driven one-hour family or crime series based on original content rather than adapted material. Finally, issues related to competition and collaboration in terms of production and financing are addressed.

Public service fiction

In many small national production cultures, the production of drama series is linked to ideas of public service television. This fact should not be underestimated when discussing TV series coming from a public service broadcaster like DR. Audience figures definitely matter still more for public service broadcasters in the competitive television landscape of today, but drama series are also a crucial part of a public service obligation to represent a variety of national stories in the native language on the small screen. As Tom Stempel has discussed when studying the development of US television writing, one can think of television writers being 'storytellers to the nation' (Stempel 1992). Whereas the rare

Danish blockbuster at the cinemas might sell around half a million tickets, a regular episode of a drama series from DR on Sunday nights at 8 pm is, according to current Head of Drama Piv Bernth, expected to find an audience of no less than 1.3 million people and a quality rating of at least 4 out of 5 (in Nielsen 2012b).[2] The content of the TV series are widely on the public agenda with media headlines ranging from discussions of complicated political cases in *Borgen* (2010–2013) to whether detective Sarah Lund got on the right trains in the Copenhagen transportation system when delivering ransom money in the second episode of *Forbrydelsen III* (2012). TV series from DR have always been intended to have a broad appeal, but the overall idea of what kind of fiction a public service broadcaster like DR should offer to the nation and how it should be produced has changed dramatically over the years.

DR was founded as a state-owned institution in 1925 (as 'Statsradiofonien') and started broadcasting television, one hour three times a week, in 1951. However, it took a while before people had a selection of programmes to watch and were actually watching. In 1955, there were only 3,000 people paying licence fees; by 1958 there were 100,000; and by 1965 the number reached one million (Søndergaard 2006, 29). Television in Denmark has always had to deal with the fact that the number of viewers is limited, making certain types of expensive content, like drama series, hard to finance. In 2010, there were 2.4 million registered licence payers. In 2012, the licence fee per household amounted to DKK 2,352 (around EUR 310) for access to radio and television.[3] In 2012, DR's 'mother channel' DR1, which airs the drama series, was the second most viewed TV channel in Denmark with a market share of 28 per cent (DR 2013).

In a history of Danish television, Stig Hjarvard stresses the fact that from the beginning, TV – and radio – was organized as a national monopoly and thus naturally came to function as both the creator and mediator of a shared national experience and consciousness (2006, 8). TV became an important element in the social welfare project and, as in many other countries, the TV medium became part of building the nation (see e.g. Buonanno 2012 on Italian television drama). The intention was not only to make television for the people but also to make television to educate the people. The early years of television was marked by what Danish television scholar Ib Bondebjerg has called an ideology of cultural unity, building on the notion that all Danes had the same sense of culture and of quality as the cultural elite (1991, 151). This gradually changed as the concept of public service television became more about securing the existence of a plurality of expressions and cultural diversity as well as about public enlightenment and educating citizens for the common good.

Much has changed for DR since its establishment as for all other European public service broadcasters. Among the important developments beyond borders and traditional barriers are the major technological changes in the form of communication satellites as well as the regulatory change in the form of the integration of the inter-European television market jurisdiction, which took place in the 1980s and early 1990s (e.g. Collins 2004, 34). In a Danish context, a crucial change was the coming of the competitive, national channel TV 2 in 1988, offering a great amount of international programming to Danish audiences. From the outset, TV 2 focused on sport, news and debate formats while fictional content was primarily popular American and British films and series (Agger 2005a, 147). Today, TV 2 is producing Danish-language fiction of its own, as is the satellite channel TV3, which is owned by the Viasat Corporation.[4]

While a number of things have thus changed quite a bit over the years, DR is still a publicly funded institution, expected to 'serve the people' and to assume a number of societal and cultural obligations (DR 2012). As described in the Act of Parliament, DR is to secure the existence of a wide variety of programmes and services ranging from news and education to art and entertainment, focusing on quality, diversity and multitude in its approach to programming; Danish language and culture is naturally to receive special attention (Ministry of Culture 2011). A main obligation is to offer what the market-driven players are not providing, yet – as stated in the mandate description on the DR website – DR is also expected to compete on creativity and quality within all kinds of programmes. This means that DR is about producing programmes for the few and for the many (DR 2012). The Media Agreement for 2011–2014 (Ministry of Culture 2013), a political agreement on quality and diversity in radio and television, can be regarded as a strengthening of DR and of public service values, and it shows that in spite of the constant, public debates about what defines public service television and how to go about it, there is still a strong support for the concept across political parties.

As discussed by Danish television scholar Gunhild Agger, it has sometimes been hard for television fiction to find its place in a public service mind set, where ideas of enlightenment and entertainment have often been regarded as two very different things (2005a, 146). Up until 1989, scripted fiction was produced in two different departments with the Theatre Department ('Teaterafdelingen') producing plays and more serious drama, and the Entertainment Department ('Underholdningsafdelin-gen') producing comedies and lighter fare. With the establishment of a TV Fiction Department in 1989, one can say that there was an ambition to bridge the divide, but when it comes to drama production and audiences the emphasis has definitely been more on popular content than on programmes for the chosen few since the late 1990s. This has led to a focus on the high-profile series for Sunday nights at the expense of most other formats like one offs, mini-series, everyday dramas or more experimental fare, a fact which is currently debated both inside and outside of DR in relation to the public service obligations and to opportunities for new talent in less prestigious genres and slots (Bondebjerg and Redvall 2011, 103).

Early television drama

Fictional content was present on the Danish television screens from the very first night of broadcasting on 2 October 1951. Part of the first transmission were three scenes from Johannes Allen's play *Harlekins Tryllestav/The Wand of Harlequin* (performed at The Royal Theatre earlier the same year), and early television drama was characterized as 'television theatre' (Bondebjerg 1991, 151). The TV medium was primarily used to transmit stage performances, and the repertoire of the theatre of the time naturally influenced the development of television fiction (Agger 2006, 145). One obvious explanation for this was that the live transmissions made performances of plays good content. DR could not tape material until 1959, and it was easier to convert live performances from the stage to the screen than trying to create a whole new form. Many scholars have focused on this 'liveness' as a quintessential property of television.[5] The TV theatre was sometimes referred to as 'the theatre of the people', as one could think of the TV theatre as the largest stage of the country (Agger 2005b). The transmissions of plays were popular and the strong link between television and theatre continued well into the 1970s. However, there were different trends over the years, the transmission of more modernist plays rather than a repertoire of canonized classics being one of them (Bondebjerg 1991, 151).

DR started taping television drama from 1962, but the tapes were expensive and in the first years of taping they were often reused and productions thus lost (Agger 2006, 151). Gradually, new technology, offering the opportunity to move away from the defining liveness, started changing the modes of production. This led to television aesthetics moving closer to those on the cinema screen and to the development of more independent and media-specific modes of expression. Gunhild Agger has outlined three major strands in the television drama of the 1960s and 1970s. A realist strand, a modernist strand and a genre-oriented strand, aimed at making national versions of popular international genres like crime stories, comedies and historical drama (Agger 2006, 152). Agger defines the period from 1964 to 1980 as marked by both a popular and modern break-through on Danish screens, followed by a period marked by the intention to produce quality fiction with a certain Danish touch (1980–1988), based on discussions of what defines national fiction in a time of increased international competition. After the establishment of TV 2 in 1988, there emerged a new focus on audience success and an ambition to use popular genres and a more energetic and cinematic storytelling for making series of relevance to the nation.[6]

Realist dramas

Realist dramas have, in particular, had a strong position over the years, as in several other European television cultures. As discussed by John Ellis when comparing cinema and television (1992), John Caughie when contrasting the realist and the modernist drama (2000) or Birger Langkjær when writing about realism and Danish cinema (2012), the notion of realism is a complicated concept with many different interpretations and connotations. Defining the realist tradition as the strongest in the history of Danish television drama, Gunhild Agger has argued that this realist tradition is defined by an intention of making the storytelling strategies invisible – as in classical Hollywood filmmaking – having continuous motivations for the development of the action and using continuity editing. Moreover, she stresses that the realist tradition has a focus on the recognizable with a sense for detail, and it has a notion of time that mirrors time in ordinary life and what she calls an 'everyday experience structure' at the core (2005, 292–3). It is worth emphasizing how the more serious everyday realism described by Agger is continuously highlighted as the most defining attribute in accounts of the history of Danish television drama (Schepelern 1986; Bondebjerg 1993; Agger 2005a).

Within this tradition, the television plays by Leif Panduro from the late 1960s through the 1970s are the most influential. Panduro has given name to what is sometimes referred to as 'the Panduro formula', which can be regarded as a serious approach to telling realist, mainstream stories with a social-psychological core based on principles of classical narration.[7] There has also been a long tradition for comedy in everyday settings with the most famous example being Erik Balling's series *Huset på Christianshavn*/'The House in Christianshavn' (1970–1977). With its 84 episodes on the ups and downs of everyday life from the point of view of a particular neighbourhood, the series has been regarded as a Danish take on the still-running soap *Coronation Street* (ITV, 1960–present) (e.g. Agger 2006, 157).

One can list several reasons why realism has been a popular strategy for Danish television drama, as in many other European production countries with the British televisual social realism as a prominent and internationally known example (e.g. Rollinson 2011). The public service obligation generally makes representing national life and current conflicts of the people a natural choice and working on limited budgets creates an obvious inclination to turn the gaze towards real or naturalist settings rather than building expensive sets. There have been many popular works within the realist strand, but the realist tradition has often been criticized in debates of the local output in the national sphere. When film scholar Peter Schepelern analysed the state of Danish television drama in the 1980s, concluding that it was 'all-penetratingly boring' (1986, 57), the focus on psychological or historical realism was blamed. Schepelern found that while cinema and theatre had been given the role of telling the unique and adventurous stories, television drama because of its focus on simple stories with a clear relation to reality had a tendency to become trivial. In his opinion, a stereotypical or didactic approach was among the dangers of choosing that path (1986).

Similar discussions of different degrees of realism and the genres chosen can still be found, but in recent years there has been remarkably less criticism despite the fact that almost all DR series since the 1990s have had a realist contract with the audience though working within the confines of genre. There are only a few notable exceptions working to overturn or disrupt this realist paradigm, like Lars von Trier's *Riget*/*The Kingdom* (1994), which inventively blurred the boundaries between the supernatural and reality, or the low-budget thriller series *De udvalgte*/ 'The Chosen Ones' (2001), which followed a group of young people in a haunted Copenhagen apartment. Following that, only the original 'depression comedy' *Lykke*/*Happy Life* (2011–2012) is an example of a long-running series challenging realism as the mode of representation. *Happy Life* in many ways marks a break with the series of the past years, using both musical sequences, an exaggerated acting style and recurrent dream sequences as dynamic comedy tools to move its satirical portrait of everyday corporate life and a Prozac-medicated nation forward (Figure 2.2).

Figure 2.2 The 'depression comedy' *Lykke/Happy Life* (2011–2012) about the ambitious Lykke (Mille Lehfeldt) challenges the realist tradition in series from DR by including, for instance, musical sequences. Here, the staff of the medical company Sanafortis is momentarily dancing, headed by actors Louise Mieritz and Lars Brygmann. Photo by Agnete Schlichtkrull. Courtesy of DR

The serialized format

What is regarded as the first Danish TV series *Regnvejr og ingen penge*/Rainy Weather and no Money (1965) is based within the realist strand, as were several other of the early attempts with the serialized format (Bondebjerg 1993, 93). Literary classics were also split into several parts for television, and a number of Danish novels have been serialized for the small screen.[8] However, during the 1960s, the serialized form was also used for new genre productions like crime stories. Leif Panduro wrote *Ka' de li Østers?*/Do you like Oysters? (1967), which was followed by other crime stories in several episodes.

Danish audiences have been able to watch foreign series on national television since the late 1950s. In the beginning, it was mostly British crime fiction like *Fabian of the Yard* (1954), but the 1960s saw a greater variety of series with the arrival of, for example, American western series and sitcoms (Bondebjerg 1991, 151). In the 1980s, soaps like *Dallas* (1978–1991) and *Dynasty* (1981–1989) made the social melodramas popular, and foreign fare has been a source of inspiration for a number of national productions. In this sense, though there has been much talk of internationalization since the 1990s (e.g. Bondebjerg and Redvall 2011; Bondebjerg and Redvall forthcoming 2014), there has been a susceptibility to international genres and storytelling strategies for a much longer period of time. Early attempts to marry a social-realist portrayal of everyday life with the genre conventions of, for instance, crime or comedy series was received with a certain scepticism, but some series like the six-episode police series *Een gang strømer.../Once a Cop...* (1987) proved to many critics that new hybrid forms could work and that action scenes were also possible on Danish grounds.

The question of whether national series should copy American style and content or produce alternatives of a different kind is often part of debates on television drama in smaller nations. These debates are in no way unique to television. When discussing British cinema, film scholar Andrew Higson has outlined the ever-present national cinema dilemma of whether to product simulate or product differentiate when trying to compete with the dominating US product (Higson 1995). The strategy of DR since the late 1990s can be regarded as a successful way of simulating many aspects of the visual style and storytelling strategies from popular international genres, yet differentiating the series by rooting them deeply in a Danish reality and targeting a broad mainstream audience with the intention of giving them public service value for their money. The idea of 'double storytelling', described in Chapter 3, has been important in this regard, with its insistence on a public service layer of storytelling underneath an entertaining plot.

The two most influential and still remembered TV series before the 1990s are the already mentioned *Matador* and *Huset på Christianshavn*. Both series were produced by the major production company Nordisk Film for DR, in contrast to the production framework of the past many years where all long-running drama series have been in-house productions by DR Fiction. Even though DR has a long tradition of working with comedy, for instance, with the work of Erik Balling, scripted comedy has almost disappeared at DR since the shaky attempts to do Danish sitcoms in the 1990s. However, the 2000s have seen the rise of some innovative satirical formats on the sister channel DR2, targeted at content with a more niche appeal.[9] While comedy has thus not played a part in the recent development of DR series, the impact from *Matador* and the historical drama is still alive.

Historical dramas

Matador (1978–1981) is a historical drama about life in the small town of Korsbæk in the years 1929–1947. The series tells of both major social, societal and psychological developments during a period of change and a world war through the 24 episodes, which were broadcast as six episodes each year. Journalist and author Lise Nørgaard conceived the series based on her personal experiences, but the series share similarities with a British series like *Upstairs, Downstairs* (1970–1975), which had been broadcast in Denmark in 1976–1978. *Matador* is the most famous example in a long tradition of scripted historical television drama, which Agger has analysed as operating within five different genres: TV-versions of literary classics, current interpretations of the past (like *Matador*), the drama documentary, the historical adventure drama and the biographical series (Agger 2005a, 328).

Adaptations of literary classics dominated the early years of Danish television, but in the later years the preferred strategy has been to do current interpretations of the past or to use the past as a setting for more thrilling adventures. *Bryggeren/The Brewer* (1996–1997) offered a 12-episode take on the development of the Carlsberg Breweries, focusing on a conflict between father and son as the dramatic engine. While *Matador* was all fictional characters, *Bryggeren* thus combined a biographical approach with a portrait of a family drama at a certain point in the development of Danish society. The tradition from *Matador* has been most clearly continued in the extremely popular historical series *Krøniken/Better Times* (2004–2007), which took over where *Matador* had left off by portraying Denmark in the years 1949–1972. The series used the coming of television and the radio and television factory Bella as the original framework for telling an epic story about four young people fighting to find themselves in a world of change during the 25 year time span. The series reached still overwhelming audience figures (2.7 million people watched the last episode), and according to statistics from 2009, 18 of the 22 episodes were still on the list of the 25 most watched programmes since 1992.[10]

While family series or what one could even call 'society series' like *Matador* and *Krøniken* have also found large audiences in the other Nordic countries, the series have not travelled internationally. One of the few examples of a historical series winning international acclaim is the two-episode mini series *Unge Andersen/Young Andersen* (2005, produced by Nordisk Film for DR) about the formative boarding school years of fairy tale writer Hans Christian Andersen (1805–1875), which won an Emmy for best international mini-series in 2005. However, the production of historical series has been very limited since the 2000s. Besides *Better Times* and *Young Andersen*, the five-episode mini-series *Album* (2008, produced by Fine & Mellow for DR) dealing with recent history when following how the life of three families intertwine from the 1970s to the 1990s is the only historical series of the 2000s.

Mini-series

During the 2000s, the mini-series also all but disappeared. One of the rare exceptions was Per Fly's six-episode series *Forestillinger/Performances* (2007), which has been defined as 'the work of an auteur' (Piil 2008, 722) and is remarkably different from other productions of the decade. Set during the artistically and emotionally tumultuous making of a theatre production, the series ambitiously tracks the same chain of events in each episode, but each time from a new character's perspective. The series won critical acclaim as an original approach to television drama, but it clearly showed how the Sunday evening audiences want more traditional content. Airing in the same slot the week after the first season of *The Killing* (2007), which had an average of 1.7 million viewers, the first episode of *Performances* was seen by 800,000 viewers, but it got the lowest quality ratings ever measured for a Danish television series (3.3 out of 5) and the audience steadily declined to only 350,000 viewers for the last episode (Piil 2008, 726). *Performances* was deemed too challenging and an example of how the mainstream audience now expects a certain kind of prime-time drama from DR. As film scholar Peter Schepelern explained to the Danish newspaper *Information*, this was to be expected when showing a 'narrow', 'high end' 'intellectual melodrama' for 'ordinary Danes' wanting more 'entertaining and moving' series (2005, 726).

Since *Performances*, *Album* has been the only other primetime mini-series produced by or for DR. However, a new high-profile series in eight episodes is on its way. In 2010, DR received an out of the ordinary extra DKK 100m (app. EUR 13m) from the Minister of Culture to produce a historical series. Following fierce discussions about this kind of commissioning and competition between several projects from external production companies, Miso Film landed the contract with the series *1864*. With a budget of DKK 173m (app. EUR 23m), *1864* tells the story of the 1864 Battle of Dybbøl, where the Germans seized a third of Denmark's territory. The series is based on two books by Tom Buk-Swienty and written and directed by Ole Bornedal. The cultural director of DR, Morten Hesseldahl, commented on the selection by stressing the quality of the project and the tremendous significance of the period it will cover (from the Three Year's War of 1848–1851 until 1864), arguing that '1864 is not only about the fatal war but also about the Danish nation's self-understanding' (in NFTF 2011). The historical drama is thus planned to make a strong comeback, since politicians have allocated special money to ensure its return on the small screen with a high-concept profile. This way of politicians commissioning a particular kind of national product has not been seen before and naturally gave rise to discussions of potential violations of the arm's length principle, meant to secure a distance between politicians and art commissioners, when the Minister of Culture took an interest in the projects being pitched (Elkjær 2011).

As described above, the history of Danish television drama has seen a number of different approaches and genres. However, it is worth noting three major points related to the series produced when it comes to the drama series since the late 1990s. First of all, DR has focused almost exclusively on the long-running, character-driven family or crime series of an hour at the expense of one-offs, mini-series or other formats. Secondly, the series have targeted the prime-time mainstream audience, meaning that more experimental fare, like *Forestillinger*, has basically disappeared and that the budgets have been spent on offering high-profile series for Sunday nights with no money left for making less popular products for other time slots. Thirdly, the productions have been original series developed by writers at DR for DR, rather than attempts to adapt other material, like the massive number of crime novel television adaptations coming from Sweden in recent years. These points will be discussed in more detail in Chapter 3, focusing on the changes in the framework for production since the 1990s and the dogmas for DR Fiction formulated in 2003, putting the writer at the centre of production based on the concept of one vision (Figure 2.3).

Competing genres and channels

When reflecting upon the genres and formats chosen for series at DR in the past years, it is also worth noting that other broadcasters have offered Danish-language series in a wide variety of genres in the same period of time. The number of competing productions is quite limited and generally marked by smaller budgets, but DR has faced competition from TV 2 since the late 1990s when *Strisser på Samsø/Island Cop*

Figure 2.3   Per Fly's *Forestillinger/Performances* (2007), consisting of six episodes tracing the same events from the perspective of six different characters, has been one of the few series from DR in the 2000s to go against the mainstream. In the photo, the director Marko (Dejan Cukic) and the actors Tanja (Sonja Richter) and Jakob (Mads Wille) discuss how to best approach the adaptation of the poem *Venus and Adonis* by William Shakespeare at the fictional Copenhagen theatre in the story. Photo by Per Arnesen. Courtesy of DR

(1997–1998) on a big city cop as fish out of water in a small community proved that TV 2 could attract large audiences for television drama if it made the right kind of series.

However, TV 2 has not had other series with the ability to rival DR to the same degree, and the following drama series like *Morten Korch* (1999–2000), reviving the melodramas of author Morten Korch (1876–1954) in 26 episodes, or the 60-episode *Hotellet/At the Faber* (2000–2002) with a family hotel as its arena did not find a similar appreciation among either critics or audiences. Instead of going up against DR in the more serious character-driven drama genres, TV 2 has mostly produced other kinds of drama like the first Danish law series (*Forsvar/Defense* 2003–2004), a popular attempt at Danish comedy-drama (*Lærkevej/Park Road* 2009–2010) and a range of comedy/sitcom formats with *Langt fra Las Vegas/Far from Las Vegas* (2001–2003) and *Klovn/Clown* (2005–2009) as the biggest hits.[11]

Since 2008, there have been new opportunities for television drama coming from other broadcasters than DR, with the establishment of the so-called 'public service scheme', financed with public money through the Media Political Agreement and administered by The Danish Film Institute. The official aim of the public service scheme is to support development and production of different kinds of programming, among them television series 'which in content, form and mode of expression represent originality, substance and quality' (DFI 2012).[12] The scheme is regarded as a financial supplement to the current output on Danish television and the aim is to secure the existence of ambitious and well-produced scripted drama, with no limitations as to genres or formats. Broadcasters reaching more than 50 per cent of Danish households can apply, and the productions, which have to be produced by an independent production company, must be shown in prime time no later than 24 months after receiving support (DFI 2012).

So far, TV 2 has been the most successful applicant of the scheme, receiving support for productions like the crime series *Den som dræber/Those Who Kill* (2011), *Park Road* (2009–2010) and the five-episode mini-series *Blekingegade/The Left Wing Gang* (2009–2010) for the main channel. Some critical voices regard the scheme as a deliberate attempt to channel licence money to TV 2, while others stress its importance for creating opportunities for production outside of DR, such as Gunhild Agger arguing that the scheme has helped TV 2 get back on the 'quality drama band wagon' after having had a hard time competing with DR since the late 1990s (Agger in Ludvigsen 2011).

The establishment of the public service funding scheme does seem to have led to more ambitious drama productions from both TV 2 and TV3. Together with the romantic/musical series *Store drømme/Big Dreams* (2009), *Blekingegade* and *Park Road* were part of a major investment in drama production intended to brand TV 2 as 'the largest community in Denmark'. Then Head of Programming for TV 2, Palle Strøm, argued that since TV 2 had found it hard to compete with DR for some time, they had decided to move in a new direction. He described the new strategy as aiming for something more modern and forward thinking than the traditional 'heavy' drama (Strøm in Steffensen 2009). *Park Road* found an audience and was later the basis of a feature film, but both *Big Dreams* and *The Left Wing Gang* failed to find the large audiences wanted.

Subsequently, Head of Fiction Katrine Vogelsang from TV 2 discussed particularly *Big Dreams* as 'a brave failure', which proved that one should probably not move too far away from the beaten track, since the audience 'wants the same, just in a new way' (Vogelsang in dramatiker.dk 2011, 40–2). According to Vogelsang, TV 2 thus decided to return to more 'safe genres' rather than trying to experiment with genre hybrids (2011, 40–2). TV 2 had previously found a fair amount of success with three seasons of the police series *Anna Pihl* (2006–2008), and TV 2 seems to have refocused on crime series, even trying to compete quite directly with DR by programming *Those Who Kill* in the classical DR Sunday night slot in 2011. In terms of viewers, the series did not provide the numbers that TV 2 wished for with audiences fading over the course of the season, but it marked a new ambition to compete in DR territory and has since been shown in the UK (on ITV3 in 2012) and sold for a US remake starring Chloë Sevigny.

The next crime series from TV 2, *Dicte* (2013–), broadcast on Monday nights at 8 pm, became a bigger hit with a steady audience of more than a million viewers, and a second season is set for 2014. *Dicte* is based on the crime novels by Danish author Elisabeth Egholm. Contrary to the strategy of building on original material by DR, TV 2 has thus finally found a prime-time drama series with the mainstream appeal by adapting bestselling content. However, TV 2 seems to be aiming for both adapted material and original content. Another popular TV 2 series is the original drama series *Rita* (2012–) about a teacher with many issues in the classroom as well as in her private life. The series has moved into its second season and the US cable network Bravo has made a remake as one of their first scripted drama pilots with Anna Gunn in the title role.

Concurrently with TV 2 trying to renew their approach to television series in the late 2000s, TV3 launched their hitherto most ambitious drama production, *Lulu & Leon/Lulu and Leon* (2009). Head of Programming at TV3, Morten Mogensen, explained the new investment in Danish drama as an attempt to reach a wide audience, since Danish language-drama is what the viewers want (Mogensen in Steffensen 2009). According to Mogensen, TV3 didn't deliberately try to differentiate themselves from DR, but their approach to a family crime story with *Lulu & Leon* can be seen as a quite different take on the genre. Until then, TV3 had primarily produced comedy and soap such as the romantic *Bridget Jones*-like series *Nynne* (2006) and long-running soaps like *Hvide løgne/White Lies* (1998–2001) and *2900 Happiness* (2007–2009).

Both TV 2 and TV3 have thus invested more money in television series in the wake of the public service support scheme, but DR has publicly had a calm attitude towards the intensified competition. As Ulla Pors Nielsen, Head of Programming for DR1 2005–2010 commented following the new focus on drama at the competing channels DR only gets better from getting competition (Nielsen in Steffensen 2009). She described DR as having 'a genre of its own' with the Sunday series (Steffensen 2009). However, with the appointment of former DR producer Katrine Vogelsang as Head of Fiction in 2011 and the temporary hiring of veteran DR producer Sven Clausen in 2012, changes seem to be happening in the TV 2 approach to producing drama, and it is likely that DR will see still more competition in the years to come – also within the high-profile drama genre, which DR would like to consider their own.

International collaboration

In terms of financing, the increased domestic competition does not seem to be a problem. Series from DR are mainly financed by licence money in combination with some co-financing from other Nordic public service broadcasters and top financing from The Nordisk Film & TV Fond. According to Head of DR Fiction Nadia Kløvedal Reich, only 4–5 per cent of the financing comes from outside sources (Reich 2012). The other Nordic countries have been an important market for a number of years, where viewers watch not only the crime series but also the family fare (Bondebjerg and Redvall 2011, 109). The Nordic languages share similarities, but they are too far apart for series not to be subtitled when leaving their native country. However, cultural similarities and a tradition of Nordic collaboration have been a great advantage for the production and distribution of series, and the collaboration between Nordic public service broadcasters has been institutionalized for more than 50 years through the organization Nordvision.[13] Nordvision was founded in 1959 to create an institution for co-ordinating collaboration, primarily based on cultural rather than economic incentives, and the Nordvision Fund, which was established in 1988, is an important source of financing for major drama productions (Rowold 2009, 9).[14]

Only the crime series have enjoyed substantial interest from non-Nordic viewers until the political and personal dramas of *Borgen* found wider international audiences. As a consequence, only the crime series have been able to attract international financing, particularly from the German market where ZDF has been influential in co-financing DR series, thereby securing some extra money for production. At the European TV Drama Series Lab in 2012, Peter Nadermann from ZDF highlighted this involvement in the series from DR as a successful collaboration, emphasizing the value of working with a trusted partner and describing the production model of DR as 'vivid' and marked by 'freedom and professionalism' (Nadermann in Redvall 2013, 61–2). The current structure of the DR production framework will be discussed in Chapter 3, but as for the overall approach to production it is worth noting that the DR series does not have substantial international financing and are thus not influenced by a number of different stake holders, which has sometimes been the case in Danish feature filmmaking since the 1990s (e.g. Brandstrup and Redvall 2005; Bondebjerg and Redvall 2011).

In the wake of the success of series like *Borgen* and *The Killing* on the international scene and following the launch of new digital video-on-demand services like Netflix and HBO Nordic on the Danish market in 2012, DR Fiction has been approached by HBO about the possibility of co-producing series with Danish and American actors, but set in Denmark. According to Head of Drama Piv Bernth one of the reasons why HBO takes an interest in co-producing with DR is that they want 'the extra public service layer' (Bernth in Thorsen 2013). So far, writer of *The Killing* Søren Sveistrup has been hired to come up with a potential idea for a collaboration, and it will be interesting to see how outside financing might influence the national production culture in the years to come. The global, multiplatform television landscape of today does put many of the established strategies of both commercial and non-commercial broadcasters under pressure, and as discussed by several Scandinavian scholars the basic structures for production and distribution are challenged in several ways, not only with regard to television drama (e.g. Bruun 2010) but also with regard to some of the fundamental principles for public service television in general (e.g. Lund et al. 2009).

As for satisfying national audiences, the series from DR still appear to stand up to the increased national and international competition from the new players and platforms. The domestic series still find large audiences, and according to the 2011 Annual Report of DR 70 per cent of Danes find that the Danish series are the best within their genre (DR 2011, 46). As this chapter has outlined, this has not always been the case, and Chapter 3 will address the major changes in the production framework at DR since the 1990s, which are an important part of understanding the recent success of series like *Borgen* and *The Killing*.

3
Dogmas for Television Drama: Changing a Production Culture

Introduction

There have been major changes in the approach to writing and producing television at DR since the mid 1990s. This chapter introduces how Lars von Trier's *Riget/The Kingdom* (1994) was an important source of inspiration to people in the film and television industry and brought the two worlds closer together by marrying cinematic imagery with episodic storytelling and by showing that one could create productions that were eclectic and artistic as well as popular for the small screen. The hiring of two film directors as Heads of Drama in the mid 1990s further strengthened the meeting between film and television, and with the building of new studios and the creation of so-called 'production hotels' the spaces of production facilitated the making of long-running series as flagships for DR.

Taxa/Taxi (1997–1999) became the first series in a new strategy to mirror American production frameworks based on a notion of creating quality within well-known genre conventions. Following its first International Emmy Award for best drama series in 2002, DR Fiction formulated 15 so-called dogmas for production, defining that productions should be marked by the concepts of 'one vision', 'double storytelling', 'crossover' and 'producer's choice'. These concepts are still central to the DR Fiction production framework of today, which is outlined at the end of this chapter.

The chapter thus addresses how new managerial ideas within DR have changed the production culture for television drama remarkably since the late 1990s. Not only by putting the writer at the centre of the process and by copying work methods from the US industry but also by changing the spaces of production and by creating new connections between the film and television industry, having screen idea work groups connected to projects from the early stages of their development, rather than working with the same full-time employed staff for most productions. These changes grew out of new executives wanting to create a new kind of product for the domain, and from a Screen Idea System perspective these decisions at the management level have had a major impact on the series produced by creating a certain outlook and framework for production. With the formulation of in-house production dogmas, the previously tacit knowledge in this specific production culture was put down on paper, making the fundamental ideas of DR Fiction transparent, and at the same time establishing concepts, which could be used and discussed in everyday work processes. The ideas of how to organize production among experts in the field changed greatly in this period of time, having numerous consequences like the establishment of writers' rooms and the implementation of a head writer/episode writers structure for making series. This will be further explored in the chapters on one vision and the writing of *Borgen* (2010–2013) and *Forbrydelsen/The Killing* (2007–2012).

Breaking the rules with *The Kingdom*

It was somewhat surprising when a mini-series by the art house film director Lars von Trier came on screen in 1994 with an appeal to viewers and critics alike. *The Kingdom* was produced by Zentropa for DR after executive producer Svend Abrahamsen encouraged von Trier to try his hands at television. Lars von Trier wished to do a ghost story and, together with screenwriter Niels Vørsel, he quickly settled on the biggest hospital in Denmark, Rigshospitalet in Copenhagen, as the perfect setting. Rigshospitalet (also known as 'Riget', which means 'the kingdom') became a space populated with the spiritualist patient Fru Drusse, a spooky foetus, a phantom ambulance, strange echoes in the elevator shafts, quirky doctors and a pair of dishwashers with Down's syndrome in the basement to provide a Greek chorus. Lars von Trier has described the process of writing the series as almost 'automatic writing', since there was a deliberate decision to write fast rather than spending a year and a half on a script (in Schepelern 2000, 169). Moreover, von Trier has called *The Kingdom* a hack work, saying that the ambition was to not hold themselves back in the service of what is regarded as good taste (2000, 178).

However, what was intended as an unpretentious and entertaining television series turned out to be a turning point in his career as well as on the Danish television screens. Before *The Kingdom*, von Trier had directed the television film *Medea* (1988) for DR and his feature film 'Europa trilogy', consisting of *The Element of Crime* (1984), *Epidemic* (1987) and *Europa* (1991), which had gained him international recognition. *The Kingdom* became his national breakthrough to a wider audience and created an awareness around his persona, not the least because he appeared at the close of each episode, wearing legendary film director Carl Th. Dreyer's tuxedo and asking audiences to be prepared 'to take the good with the evil'. The series had a share of 50 per cent and around one fifth of the population saw the four episodes, whereas only 12,000 people saw *The Kingdom* when it was later released in a cinema version (Schepelern 2000, 178–9). Individual episodes were reviewed in the daily newspapers, and several characters and expressions from the series are still present in the collective national consciousness, like the cursing by Swedish doctor (Ernst Hugo Järegård) yelling out his frustration with the Danes over the rooftops of Copenhagen (Figure 3.1).

The Kingdom was unlike anything previously produced for Danish television in its mystical content, its dark humorous tone and its imagery and sound. To a large extent, the special look of the series was based on pragmatic production decisions. To save time von Trier decided to

Figure 3.1 The end credits of *Riget/The Kingdom* (1994) where Lars von Trier advises audiences 'to take the good with the evil'. Framegrab. Cinematography by Eric Kress. Courtesy of DR

use natural light alone, and only scenes with ghosts – calling for double exposures – were filmed in a traditional manner (Schepelern 2000, 171). The camera work mostly has a sense of reportage, and the decision not to respect the traditional optical axes of action when editing and the use of jump cuts created an unconventional look. According to Peter Schepelern, part of the inspiration for the stylistic decisions came from US crime series *NYPD Blue* (ABC 1993–2005) and *Homicide* (NBC 1993–1999), which built on extensive use of handheld cameras in order to create the sense of being live on the spot (2000, 174).

The series thus broke several classical rules of filmmaking, creating a unique look, but audiences and critics proved completely capable of dealing with the innovations. They appreciated the fresh breath of air, and the series went on to a second season (1997), to win international acclaim and to be remade in the US as *Kingdom Hospital* (initiated by Stephen King and directed by Craig R. Baxley, ABC 2004).[1] What was meant as a fast potboiler ended up having a very different public life, and it also had an impact behind the scenes. New generations of film-makers saw that television could be a place for highly personal works and concurrently a window to larger audiences (as discussed by directors in Hjort and Bondebjerg 2003).

Ole Bornedal's *Charlot and Charlotte* (1996) was another critically acclaimed mini-series with a wide appeal, but since then director-driven one-offs or mini-series have been almost non-existent. Instead, the meeting between the worlds of film and television has primarily taken place in the form of directors working as episode directors on long-running series and through the exchange of central crew members, which has been an important part of the production framework at DR since *Taxa* (Figure 3.2).

Television series as flagships: *Taxa*

The early 1990s had seen the production of some longer television series for DR. In-house, DR had produced the soap *Ugeavisen*/'The Weekly Newspaper' (1990–1991) with a small local newspaper as the arena for Monday night dramas. Also in the genre of more everyday, emotional drama, the production company Nordisk Film made the family series *Landsbyen*/'The Village' (1991–1996). The first six episodes aired on TV 2, but the series was then bought by DR and ended up as 44 episodes.[2]

The series was written by the brothers Peter and Stig Thorsboe, who later became the head writers of some of the most influential series to be made by DR in the 2000s. Tom Hedegaard directed all episodes of

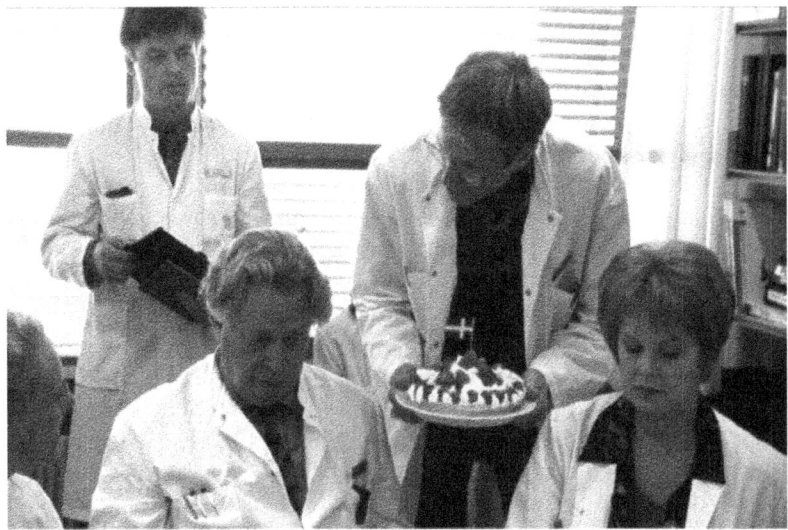

Figure 3.2 Swedish doctor Stig G. Helmer (Ernst-Hugo Järegård, sitting on the left) has a hard time among the Danes in *The Kingdom*. In this instance, he suffers at one of the notorious morning meetings with Rigmor Mortensen (Ghita Nørby) by his side. Photo by Eric Kress. Courtesy of DR

the first three seasons, but during the fourth season (from episode 19) decisions were made to experiment with having both episode writers and episode directors for the first time. According to Stig Thorsboe this proved to be hard, since he found that too much time was spent on trying to make the new writers go in the same direction as the material (Thorsboe 2012), but producer Sven Clausen finds that important lessons were learned on this series as to possible new ways of organizing production (Clausen 2010).

Clausen was also the producer of the historical series *Gøngehøvdingen*/'The Gønge Chieftain' (1992), which was the most expensive series produced by DR up to then. *Gøngehøvdingen* was criticized for not having the quality expected from a high-cost series and led to major discussions about what to aim for with drama series from DR. When film director Ole Bornedal was hired as Head of Drama 1993–1994 – before going off to Hollywood to direct his 1994 Danish thriller-hit *Nattevagten* as the *Nightwatch* (1997) – he publicly announced that it had become modern to hate DR, since there was a lack of bloodthirstiness and of challenging oneself (in Nordstrøm 2004, 15). He took on the job with a call for television drama to become more popular and less elitist (in Rasmussen 2007).

Film director Rumle Hammerich, who followed Bornedal as Head of Drama in 1994, shared his predecessor's critical thoughts on DR drama productions. He stressed that it was not self evident that DR should have in-house production. The department needed to make itself indispensable, and the ambition was to become the most productive entity in the Danish world of audio-visual fiction with the help of the raised budgets for television drama in the licence agreement of 1994 (Nordstrøm 2004, 16). Hammerich has described DR at the time as an organization with a weak identity. One possible way to change this, he found, was to produce a long-running series, which could become 'a flagship' week after week rather than the shorter series, which – with *The Kingdom* as the remarkable exception – quickly disappear from the screens as well as from the public awareness (Hammerich 2011). Today, major television series are often intended as 'must-see television' or 'tent-pole' events (Cornea 2009, 115; Clarke 2013), but at the time there was no deliberate branding of the series from DR, and no structured attempt to create a special hype around them.

Hammerich decided to aim for what he has called 'quality within a genre' and targeted original material intended for television rather than trying to adapt existing works from other media (Hammerich 2011). The inspiration was American quality television series of the time, and the ambition was to make a popular series, which respected but renewed a well-known genre. According to Hammerich, the idea for the first attempt to create this came from an open idea competition, which Bornedal had launched during his brief time as Head of Drama. A journalist had suggested a sitcom with a small taxi company as the main setting. Hammerich liked the arena, but thought it was better suited for more dramatic material. He contacted the author and television writer Hanne-Vibeke Holst and together they discussed how to use the taxi arena as a setting for a series, which should be able to run for 100 episodes, into the 2000s. Conversations centred on questions about what the Danes ought to bring with them into the next millennium, and they settled on the notion of charity or caring for the other as the intended theme of the series. Another guiding decision was to say that contrary to many drama series and soaps where secrets and their revelation is the main motor for the story engine, this series should be more interested in solutions and people dealing with their problems. As Hammerich says, this was the case, since 'that is what life is about – and that is what TV series can mirror, the real life' (Hammerich 2011). There were, thus, deliberate genre ambitions, but with a sense of having

Figure 3.3 The cast of *Taxa* (1997–1999), which launched the careers of several actors, such as Trine Dyrholm and Anders W. Berthelsen, standing next to each other under the sign of the taxa company. Photo by Ulla Voigt. Courtesy of DR

aspects of the everyday life at the core as well as considerations of wider social or societal points for audiences (Figure 3.3).

Hammerich hired two other writers and the now three writers tried to develop the series together. However, Hammerich did not feel that the material met his expectations, and this got thoughts going on the importance of ownership. He found that the writers were working on his vision, trying to make him happy, instead of making the material their own and taking ownership. He decided to fire the writers and start all over with Stig Thorsboe as the main writer with carte blanche to turn the material into his own. For Hammerich, the development story of *Taxa* is an example of the importance of one person being in control of projects and ideas coming from writers, rather than producers trying to think up good concepts for series (Hammerich 2011). This idea of one vision will be discussed later in this chapter and particularly in Chapter 5 focusing on how one vision in practice comes in many different shapes.

The building of studios

Whereas the content focus of the mid 1990s moved in the direction of genre productions as known from US television, major changes in the production framework were also inspired by work methods from the US television industry as well as from strategies in other European production cultures. Among the changes were the building of new studios for drama production at DR, the creation of so-called 'production hotels' and the move towards a 'relay' mode of production ('stafet') with head writers in charge of series, which are shot in blocks of normally two episodes with changing episode directors for each block.

When Hammerich became Head of Drama there were no DR studios for drama production. According to the Director General of DR from 1994 to 2004, Christian S. Nissen, it was a time marked by some confusion about how to think of television in relation to theatre and film. He has described the hiring of Hammerich as important for the drama production finding its own 'artistic standpoint' (Nissen 2007, 158). According to Nissen, Hammerich's initial idea for the drama department was to remove it from the rest of DR to create a more 'Klondyke-like place', where a new production culture could emerge (2007, 159). Contrary to this, Nissen would like to have productions as part of the everyday life of the broadcaster, so that one could meet people in costumes in the canteen and get a sense that things were going on in this regard. The outcome can be seen as a compromise, with the building of studios for television drama creating new spaces for production, but having the studios at the site of the rest of the DR production, TV Byen ('The TV Town') in the Copenhagen suburb Søborg.

Before the building of new studios, productions were shot at Det Danske Filmstudie ('The Danish Film Studio') in Lyngby outside of Copenhagen. According to Hammerich, shooting in those studios was expensive and created a problematic split of productions between Lyngby and TV Byen. He wanted studios for DR Fiction and worked hard to come up with a building proposal, which would cost the same as four years of renting (Hammerich 2011). When a reasonable price was reached, DR decided to invest in what was DR's first building project in many years (Nissen 2007, 159). Hammerich finds that building studios not only facilitated production but also created a new respect in the industry and an increased self-confidence within DR Fiction. DR used to be the guests in the production environments of the film industry, but now DR was the host and could decide when and how to shoot.

One of the central players in the Nordic television industry, former Head of Drama at Norwegian public service broadcaster NRK, Hans Rossiné, has pointed to the existence of studios for in-house productions as an important reason behind the success of Danish television series (in Bondebjerg and Redvall 2011, 103). With the building of the expensive new headquarter for DR, DR Byen ('The DR Town'), which was ready to be used in 2006, DR Fiction later got more studio facilities in the new location at Amager. However, the new house turned out to be unfit to house all the productions of DR Fiction, which is now split between TV Byen, where, for instance, *The Killing* and *Arvingerne/The Legacy* (forthcoming 2014) was shot, and DR Byen, where *Borgen* was shot.

This division of the department is currently considered as a problem, as some people find that the split has complicated communication between people and productions. Some people at DR have a strong sense of identity with one place rather than the other; for instance, writer Søren Sveistrup, who finds the rather shabby TV-Byen more suited for his mindset when writing and producing *The Killing*, than the glass offices in the new buildings (Sveistrup 2012). Producer Camilla Hammerich argues that having 'two addresses' is currently a big problem (Hammerich 2012), and *Borgen* researcher Rikke Tørholm Kofoed explains that a lot of knowledge is lost because of this. As Kofoed says, communication not only between people on the same production but also between productions is essential, and it 'can't be formalized, since no one has the time for that. It has to happen by itself' (Kofoed 2012). The infrastructure of production thus currently seems to be challenging certain aspects of communication and collaboration, on specific productions as well as within DR Fiction, and it was one of the topics discussed during the departmental day of DR Fiction in October 2012.

Production hotels as sites of synergy

Besides the building of new studios, one of Hammerich's principal ideas in the 1990s was to facilitate this kind of communication and knowledge exchange through what he calls 'production hotels'. As a director, Hammerich had spent six years making television for public service broadcaster SVT in Sweden. He describes himself as a great admirer of the Head of SVT Drama from 1986–1996, Ingrid Dahlberg, who, according to him, managed to get substantial funding for television production while allowing a great degree of creative freedom (Hammerich 2011). In Sweden, production had been organized as production hotels, an idea which Hammerich decided to import at DR. The basic concept is to have all people working on the same production physically in the same space rather than having production personnel divided depending on their expertise, like all production designers being in one location and all costume designers in another. Hammerich explains:

> That's not how filmmaking works. It works exactly by a cinematographer talking to a production designer and a director. They sit together and they meet all the time. Thus we created these production hotels where all people would move in as a team. In this way we created short ways of communication, since I believe that this is the core of filmmaking: communication.
>
> (Hammerich 2011)

Film scholars analysing the emergence and organization of the US studio system have pointed to the division of labour as a central element (e.g. Bordwell et al. 1985). According to Janet Staiger, this division led 'to the separation of the planning phase and the execution phase' (1979, 18), and in screenwriting studies questions around this division is often discussed as a traditional divide between the conception and execution stages (Maras 2009). As is the case with most major production units, the DR Fiction framework for production is based on a clear division of labour and different degrees of specialization. However, since the establishment of the first production hotels, facilitating communication between professions seems to have been a managerial focus, not only during the stages of execution but also during the stages of conception.

Whereas the division of DR Fiction in TV Byen and DR Byen is currently creating a physical distance between productions, the idea of production hotels for individual productions is still prevalent. *Borgen* thus has an area of its own in the new buildings in DR Byen, with both the location of the writers' room, the producer's office and the desks of other production people such as the line producer, the production designer and the costume designer in an open work space, where they can easily get a hold of each other or have coffee and lunch. This is regarded as a great advantage, not only for production but also for the writing process with the writers being able to open the door and ask inspirational, fact-checking or production questions to the many qualified people just outside the four walls of the writers' room. *Borgen* producer Camilla Hammerich believes the presence of the writers in the midst of the production framework to be a great asset (Hammerich 2012), and Rumle Hammerich, who has been back at DR as episode director of *Borgen* (episodes 3 and 4), regards the *Borgen* set up as a an example of how the idea of production hotels is still used and remains an important element in effectively functioning production (Hammerich 2011).³

Whereas film and media studies have taken an interest in the spaces of execution, limited attention has been given to the spaces, which are not part of the actual shoot.⁴ In relation to new Danish cinema, Mette Hjort has discussed how the collectivist nature of many projects by Lars von Trier and the structure of his production company Zentropa's so-called Filmbyen ('The Film Town') in the Copenhagen suburb of Avedøre seems to have facilitated collaboration on many different levels as what she has called 'a site of synergy' (2005, 20). What has been going on behind the scenes at DR can be regarded as an attempt to create sites of synergy, where practitioners can have on-going and informal discussions during development, writing and production, rather than being spread out in different departments and only brought together for formalized meetings. The importance of inhabiting the same space has continuously been brought up in interviews, and whereas most other Danish television production takes place in rather isolated companies spread out over Copenhagen, DR is one of the few places in the industry with the physical capacity to bring people together in the same space, and the financial capacity to actually keep them there for substantial amounts of time.

Relay production

Through building studios and the creation of production hotels, the spaces of production underwent great changes in the 1990s, as did the approach to the actual production framework. To gain new inspiration for both content and production strategies, producer Sven Clausen was sent on a research trip to Sweden, England and the US to study the work methods in other production cultures. Together with writer Stig Thorsboe, he had previously heard an inspiring presentation by *NYPD Blue* writer and producer Steven Bochco, and when director Anders Refn managed to get access to Fox Studios in Los Angeles, the production of *NYPD Blue* became an important source of inspiration for how to organize and shoot new series.

On the practical side of television production, the approach to lighting in the studio and working with a two camera set-up was studied and later imported when Anders Refn was the conceptualizing director of *Taxa*. In terms of organizing the work days, Clausen describes how the American crew would work at least ten hours a day for eight days to produce one episode (Clausen in Nordstrøm 2004, 54), which would not work in a Danish work context because of union rules and a different tradition for production. Instead, what can be termed a 'relay model' for production was created where one could make production more efficient by shooting blocks of two or three episodes together, thus saving time by shooting all scenes in a certain location for several episodes together. Moreover, the idea was to have changing directors for the different blocks, which is now common in many production cultures and is generally regarded as a great advantage at DR. Having directors come and go allows for several directors working at different stages in the process at the same time. Moreover, Hammerich argues that this relay of directors provides a new energy for the team compared to the same director doing a similar thing in episode after episode (Hammerich 2011). Clausen finds that the model also contains a constructive competitive element between directors (Clausen 2010).

However, in a traditionally director-driven film culture with directors having final cut, a production model where directors come and go naturally leads to the question of who then has the final word and the vision for the series. Clausen highlights the research trip to the US as the time where the idea of one vision became established in the Danish production framework, creating a clear sense of the different roles in production (in Nordstrøm 2004, 55). Discussions of US quality television since the 1980s have focused on how certain series had a sense of authorial signature in spite of their highly industrial context (e.g. Caldwell 1995). In terms of the production of the US series, which the DR observers admired at the time, the head writer was interpreted as the person with the vision for the series and the one making major decisions. This idea was imported as the concept of 'one vision', putting the head writer at the centre of production and making him or her involved in all parts of the process, from writing or developing the visual concept and casting, to the final decisions in the editing room. Clausen describes the use of one vision as both expensive and time consuming, but the best way to produce prime-time quality drama series (in Nordstrøm 2004, 55).[5]

The ideas of shooting with several cameras, organizing production as a relay between directors and insisting on the head writer as the person with the vision for a series have been implemented in the DR production framework since the making of *Taxa* in 1997. At first, there were no clear-cut concepts or more formalized definitions among people in the department of the new nature of production, but following the award of an Emmy for *Rejseholdet/Unit One* (2000–2004) in 2002, this tacit knowledge was put down on paper in 2003 by Head of Drama (1999–2012) Ingolf Gabold and his staff.

Dogmas and double storytelling

Gabold has described inheriting a department which was functioning well, where he focused on taking the position of being 'in charge of' rather than 'in control of' the processes by having the overall responsibility for production and the important communication with the broadcaster, but delegating the creative control of new projects to their head writer and producer once he had been part of the initial development and greenlighting process (Gabold 2013). The idea of being in charge of and not in control is part of the so-called dogmas, which also describe his role as Head of Drama as a coach to the producer, while the producer is the coach for his or her key staff (Figure 3.4).

Figure 3.4 The cast of the popular police series *Rejseholdet/Unit One* (2000–2004) with Ingrid Dahl (Charlotte Fich, at the centre) as the one in charge. On the far right is actor Mads Mikkelsen, who later went on to achieve international fame. Photo by Miklos Szabo. Courtesy of DR

For many people the word 'dogma' has a rather negative connotation as a rigorous belief system dictating a definite doctrine with little flexibility or openness to change. In the Danish film and media culture, however, the word has a special status by referring to the Dogma 95 Manifesto, which gained national and international recognition with the success of the first dogma films *Festen/The Celebration* (1998), *Idioterne/The Idiots* (1998) and *Mifunes sidste sang/Mifune* (1999). The 15 dogmas for DR Fiction (see Figure 3.5) address both more concrete and content-related issues for production – such as the idea of one vision or the need for several layers in the storytelling – and more general organizational issues in the department, like collaborating with the Media Research Department or aiming for long-term planning.[6]

The idea of one vision will be discussed in more detail in later chapters, when analysing how this concept can be interpreted in numerous ways and take on various forms in the hands of different writers and producers. A number of the dogmas are rather self-explanatory and some will be addressed at later stages in the book. However, some deserve immediate attention as being decisive for the writing and producing processes of new series, with the definition of concepts like 'double storytelling', 'crossover' and 'producer's choice'.

Dogma number two emphasizes that the public service obligation of DR leads to demands of series not only containing 'a good story' but also a story with ethical or social connotations. In this book, this is referred to as 'double storytelling'.[8] According to Rumle Hammerich the idea of double storytelling has been around since his time as Head of Drama, but he refers to it as 'the philosophical layer' (Hammerich 2011). In the interviews for this book, some writers and producers have referred to this as 'the public service layer' (e.g. Ilsøe 2012; Rank 2012). Some writers find the concept to be rather silly, since good stories should always contain several storytelling layers and have a larger, contextualizing premise than what is immediately perceived through the dramatic action. Screenwriters Stig Thorsboe and Hanna Lundblad suggest that it is more fruitful to think in terms of a good premise, referring to a sentence distilling the essence of a series.[9] However, they find that it can often take a long time to actually know what the exact premise of a series might be, whereas it is easier to define different storytelling layers earlier in the process (Thorsboe 2012; Lundblad 2012).

Head of DR Fiction Nadia Kløvedal Reich describes double storytelling as crucial to creating series, which can stir debate, mirror relevant issues of our times and create insights into different values, cultures and ways of living (Reich 2012). However, she also lists having a strong premise

DR Fiction – 15 dogmas to guide our productions

1. The author is – to DR Fiction – a prerequisite for the existence of this department. Here, 'the author' does not necessarily mean the screenwriter in the usual sense – the author could also be (in fiction genres other than the 'traditional drama') the editor, the director or somebody else. What is essential is that the author is the one with the vision to drive the fiction onwards when it comes to a particular project by DR Fiction. The author is treated with respect in relation to the term 'ONE VISION'. The author develops his/her scripts in close collaboration with DR Fiction, so that our expertise with regards to development can clearly impact on the final product. In terms of its plans for production, DR Fiction has a certain number of 'in-house screenwriters'. Between productions, they can be hired on a monthly salary to develop new series.
2. DR's public service status demands that our productions contain – besides 'the good story' – an overall plot with ethical/social themes. In other words, we must always have a dual narrative. The weight of each of these two narratives in relation to one another will always depend on society's historical-cultural discourse.
3. There will be a crossover between the writers and directors from the industry and those from DR Fiction.
4. There will be a crossover between the production staff from the industry and those from DR Fiction.
5. DR Fiction producers must have a clear sense of the director's intentions in relation to the head writer's intentions.
6. The Head of Drama delegates his/her responsibility for any individual production to its producer.
7. Taking DR Fiction's total finances, resources and staff into account, the producer must be offered as much choice as possible.
8. The Head of Drama acts as a coach in his relationship with the producer – just as the producer acts as a coach to his/her key staff. Our motto as leaders is: *not in control – but in charge.* This attitude does not encourage consensus decisions.
9. By ensuring the best possible planning – including the delivery of scripts on time – the production staff will be ensured reasonable working conditions.
10. In order to achieve the best possible synergy between the production, the medium and the audience DR Fiction strives to develop its productions with an eye on this triangle of communication.
11. There must be a clarified relationship between the Senior Editorial Board and DR Fiction when it comes to choice of content.
12. There is an ongoing long-term plan for content and finances between the Senior Editorial Board and DR Fiction: Adult TV fiction five years, Children's fiction three years, Radio drama two years, Youth drama – ongoing.
13. There is ongoing contact between DR's media research and DR Fiction with regard to gathering research for the department's different productions, including various tests/trials.
14. DR Fiction focuses on innovation in repertoire, production processes and staff through collaboration between the Senior Editorial Board and HR.
15. DR Fiction spends an annual 2 per cent of its overall budget on developing new drama.

Figure 3.5 The DR production dogmas[7]

as one of the four central concepts for producing series in DR Fiction of today in combination with double storytelling, one vision and producer's choice (Reich 2012). According to Reich, the premise should be the guideline for all creative decisions on a series. As an example she mentions the premise for *Borgen* – 'Can you hold on to the power and still hold on to yourself?' – which signals that it is not a series about politics, but a series about the relationship between people and power. Some premises are later used as taglines in the public sphere, like the now classic premise for *Unit One* stating that one hunts a beast and captures a human being. Based on the reading of early drafts and on observations during the development process of the new series *The Legacy*, an important task of the head writer seemed to be to capture and formulate the essence of the family drama as a premise. A broad selection of very different versions were on the table along the way, leading to several talks about the core of the series between the writer, the producer and the DR Fiction executives to try to ensure that everyone was heading in the same direction.

Previous Head of Drama Ingolf Gabold and producer Sven Clausen both place great emphasis on double storytelling as well as clear-cut premises (Clausen 2010; Gabold 2011). In relation to American mainstream cinema of the 1980s and 1990s, Justin Wyatt has written about high concept filmmaking as based on films, which can be condensed into one simple sentence (Wyatt 1994). He quotes Steven Spielberg for saying: 'If a person can tell me the idea in 25 words or less, it's going to make a pretty good movie. I like ideas, especially movie ideas, that you can hold in your hand' (Spielberg in Wyatt 1994, 13). It is of course always good to have a clear pitch or a tagline, but the idea of a premise or of double storytelling should not be confused with the ideas of high concept filmmaking. Rather than stating an attractive or easily digested one-liner, most premises for the public service DR series are questions or statements about rather large societal or ethical issues. Some premises, like the one for *Unit One*, have been suited for selling the series to the public, but many of them are merely intended to be the common thread through all episodes during the writing and production, rather than something, which can be used in a marketing campaign. In the case of *The Legacy*, finding the right premise centred on defining the nature of the material in the writers' room and in conversations about the project. In this regard, working with formulating a premise was more a creative tool for the writers linked to the idea of double storytelling than an attempt to devise an easily marketable selling point.

Producer's choice and Screen Idea Work Groups

The concepts of producer's choice and crossover are related in that they both mark a break with the tradition of working with the same full-time employed staff from production to production. The ambition is to give the producer the liberty to hire his or her first choices for the different positions on a production rather than having to work with a staff on a steady payroll. This structure has led to DR Fiction currently consisting of 35 full-time employed staff members, while all others, according to Head of DR Fiction Nadia Kløvedal Reich, are hired on freelance contracts for individual productions (Reich 2012). As an example, whereas DR used to have a number of script editors and readers, these disappeared in the early 2000s, since writers according to then Head of Drama Ingolf Gabold complained about their work and he thus decided to create 'a dramaturge-free space' for production (Gabold 2013). Instead, producers should now have the responsibility for the dramaturgical discussions around a project after an initial 1:1 meeting between Gabold and the writer (Gabold 2013). This has led to talk of 'creative producers' in the DR framework, and the absence of in-house dramaturges at DR Fiction has sometimes been considered an important 'de-bureaucratization' of the script process in Nordic industry debates (e.g. Rosenlund 2012).

The concept of producer's choice is not only used in relation to television drama in DR Fiction. It is linked to major reorganizations in DR as a whole – sometimes discussed as the 'producer's choice-model' – where the idea was to rethink DR having its primary identity as a broadcasting entity, focusing on scheduling and the relation to the audience, rather than as a production entity (Bruun 2010, 150). Accordingly, the structure of DR was changed to have a central commissioning entity, DR Medier, ordering individual programmes from different production units within DR, one of them being DR Fiction. All series from DR Fiction are thus pitched to DR Medier. In principle, DR Medier can commission television drama from external production companies rather than drawing on the in-house expertise, but it is in everybody's interest at DR to have series growing out of DR Fiction. Not the least to legitimize having an in-house production unit specifically for television drama.

Within DR Fiction, however, the concept of producer's choice is most widely used to refer to producers on specific projects being in a position to hire specific crews for each production. This has allowed for building semi-permanent 'Screen Idea Work Groups' around an idea, similar to the structure that Ian Macdonald has outlined for feature filmmaking

(2010). Thus, there are no longer any in-house dramaturges or script editors, a fact which has been brought up in Norwegian discussions of NRK series, where script editors have been partly blamed for the lack of a one vision system similar to the one in Denmark (Rosenlund 2012). However, dramaturges or script editors can be brought in if the head writer feels the need for it, and they can then be hired to fit the specific needs of the writer and the project at hand. During the making of *The Legacy*, several different directors or consultants were thus asked to help crystallize and concretize the vision of the first-time Sunday night head writer.

There are obvious creative advantages in being able to tailor a unique team for each production, but of course this also creates conditions of what is often discussed as the precarity of work in the creative industries (e.g. Deuze and Elefante 2012). The producers are the only steadily employed people among the key positions in production, but some writers have been at DR for very long periods of time. Writers Stig Thorsboe (*Taxa, Krøniken/Better Times, Lykke/Happy Life*), Peter Thorsboe (*Unit One, Ørnen/The Eagle, Livvagterne/The Protectors*), Søren Sveistrup (*Nikolaj and Julie, The Killing*) and Adam Price (*Borgen*) have been hired not only to write series; they have also been given paid sabbaticals in between productions while figuring out what to do next. Having worked almost exclusively for DR for many years, these writers can be regarded as examples of the in-house head writers mentioned in the first dogma. Directors and other members of the crew do not have the same kind of privileges. Several episode directors have been attached to more than one series since *Taxa*, but there is no sense of in-house directors.

The pay for writing for DR seems to be generally regarded as good among both head and episode writers, and compared to the insecurity of developing, writing and financing productions in the film industry, one can be relatively certain of one's work actually coming to the screen in the DR framework.[10] In the last few years, the film industry has complained about television stealing the best screenwriters in Denmark. Being able to offer decent pay and longer periods of employment are considered to be major reasons for this (Redvall 2010a). Among practitioners working at DR Fiction there is some criticism of labour issues related to a concept like producer's choice, but there also seems to be a general agreement that it is the best creative choice for production.

Crossover and cinematic collaborations

The concept of crossover has been hailed as fruitful for both the film and television industry, among practitioners as well as in academic studies (e.g. Hjort et al. 2010). Crossover refers to hiring people from the film industry to work on television series. When becoming Head of Drama in 1994, Rumle Hammerich was keen to have talented film people as part of the productions to give the series from DR a more cinematic look (Hammerich 2011). Several directors, directors of photography and other crew members as well as actors have been going back and forth between film and television since the making of *Taxa*, bringing the two industries closer together over the years. The television series have gained a more professional and cinematic look from talent from the film industry bringing their experience to the small screen. Concurrently, new talent from the film industry took the opportunity to gain valuable experience and a steadier income.

Director Ole Christian Madsen has explained how the TV series have contributed significantly to the professionalization of Danish cinema, since they have functioned as a kind of 'boot camp' for several young directors (in Hjort et al. 2010, 169).[11] Agreeing with the boot camp line of thought, Madsen's colleague Niels Arden Oplev has argued that the series have offered young directors a good opportunity to function as the boss of large teams (in Hjort et al. 2010, 211).[12] This can be quite frightening for less experienced talent, and according to Oplev, the speed of television production makes one act in a more instinctive way 'instead of all this nerve-wracking nonsense, where you ponder everything 117 times more than you should before making a decision' (2010, 212). He has polemically argued that prior to this opportunity for younger talent, 'filmmakers never became routinized in this way until they were so old as to be virtually incontinent' (2010, 212). Young directors have thus found it valuable to be able to practice their craft in the television industry.

Moreover, many directors highlight the joy of knowing that they are directing something, which will most likely find a large audience. Madsen has described 'the fantastic experience' for directors in 'the fact that people actually wanted to see the things we produced' (2010, 169). However, while there have been many benefits for the film industry in the new approach of DR Fiction, Niels Arden Oplev also addresses several dangers. Among them is the danger of how the speed of television production might make you lazy or prompt you to settle for easy solutions. Oplev also blames the speed of television for having undermined the number of shooting days for filmmaking and finds that cinema has aesthetically come to resemble TV series still more (2010, 212). Crossover is not only debated in terms of production strategies but also in terms of the aesthetic consequences for film and television, respectively.

When thinking about one vision, television and authorship, some interesting statements from directors about DR series are about the pleasure of entering somebody else's vision, and how working with an established framework 'takes some of the responsibility off your shoulders' (2010, 211). There is already a script and a cast in place and you then have to do your best within that framework. As noted by Oplev it was liberating for him 'not to be responsible for everything, and to know that if something went wrong the director wouldn't automatically be blamed' (2010, 211). There is, however, a great difference in the work of an episode director and a conceptualizing director, who is part of finding the cast and settling on the visual concept for a series. Starting out as an episode director on *Taxa*, Oplev later went on to be the conceptualizing director of *Unit One* and *The Eagle* (2004–2006), and he compares the latter role as more comparable to the work of a director in feature filmmaking.[13]

Peer-to-peer training or family collaboration?

In spite of the fact that the basic ideas of the dogmas were developed in the late 1990s and put down on paper in 2003, they are described as an important reason behind the current success of the DR series and still regarded as the main guiding principles for production. In the 2010s, the dogmas left the in-house realm to become part of the public sphere. When Head of Drama Ingolf Gabold was interviewed for the Nordvision annual report of 2011, the dogmas were published to accompany what the headline of the article described as a story of 'success that just won't go away' (Hartmann 2012, 49). In interviews for national and international media the concepts of one vision, double storytelling, crossover and producer's choice have been brought up repeatedly, and there is now an official story of the DR way of doing things, which has for instance been much discussed in the Scandinavian trade press (Iversen 2010; Pham 2012) and in international publications (Gilbert 2012; Collins 2013). The dogmas are now part of the corporate storytelling of DR Fiction, and one of the goals in later chapters is to take a closer look at the extent to which the central concepts of the dogmas can be regarded as influencing the writing and production routines. As an example, it is worthwhile exploring how a managerial definition of one vision as the first, guiding principle for production manifests itself in the work of different writers at DR.

As described above, the current framework, which is now presented as an example of best practice at both industry events and in the press, did not appear overnight. Many people have worked for several years on developing the current structures around writing and production. In terms of the structures for writing, screenwriter Hanna Lundblad finds that the developments are an example of 'on the job' or 'peer-to-peer' training (Lundblad 2012). Even though productions have been marked by producer's choice, many people have had the opportunity to build on the experiences from one production to the next, and especially among writers there is a food chain of 'growing up' within the DR framework when moving from episode writer to head writer of a series based on one's own idea. There has been an opportunity to learn from more experienced colleagues and practice one's skills in a similar way to what Vera John-Steiner describes as a family collaboration where participants over time help each other in changing roles from being newcomers to taking on more experienced roles (2000, 201).

There has been a remarkable consistency in the names of producers and writers making the Sunday series during the 2000s, and in spite of a sense of a generational handover in the 2010s, the current structure of DR Fiction is still marked by people who have been working at DR for several years. New Head of Drama from 2012 Piv Bernth has been employed at DR since 1998, producing series like *Nikolaj and Julie* (2002–2003) and *The Killing*. She is expected by industry observers to continue the current framework of production (e.g. Andersen 2011) and has announced that the plan is to continue 'the winning recipe', but also to take it further (Bernth in Pham 2012). Head of DR Fiction since 2008 Nadia Kløvedal Reich has stated that the intention is 'to go with our current set up and continue to work with writers, because writers are where it all starts' (Reich in Pham 2012). The statements show how there is an official narrative about DR and speaks of a specific best practice recipe within the DR Fiction framework in the 2010s.

DR Fiction in the 2010s

DR Fiction has the largest in-house television drama production of the Nordic countries (Reich 2012).[14] When several productions are up and running, there might be 300 people employed, but as mentioned only around 35 of these are working full time in the department. That number can be seen as an example of the difficulties of distinguishing between DR and 'the industry'. Nadia Kløvedal Reich likes to think of this structure as the industry working at DR, and repeatedly makes this point if DR Fiction is the target of criticism from external production companies wanting to see more outsourcing of series.

DR Fiction is a programme-producing unit within DR, pitching series to DR Medier. The repertoire of DR Fiction is made in collaboration between the Head of DR1 and DR Fiction building on an ambition of four year planning. In spite of DR Fiction being based within DR, Reich insists that the department is always in competition, not only with other national productions but also with the international industry. As Head of DR Fiction, she has no influence on the programming decisions of DR. She describes her job as making the product that DR Medier wants, otherwise they will buy it somewhere else. The model of commissioning is called 'the BUM model' ('BUM-modellen', 'bestiller-udfører-modtager-modellen' or 'the commissioner-provider-receiver-model'), which is also known from other areas of public management and is marked by a division of the commissioning and producing entities. DR Fiction invests in developing possible series and then pitches them to DR Medier to get a greenlight for production. Some series never make it. *Borgen* was considered to be too narrow in its political focus the first time around, but after further developing the series was re-pitched and commissioned.

As part of DR, DR Fiction is financed by licence fees. The budgets can differ from one year to the other. In 2012 it was estimated to be DKK 120m (app. EUR 16m) (Reich in Pham 2012). According to DR's Public Service Contract for 2011–2014 with the Minister of Culture, DR is obliged to produce at least 20 hours of Danish drama, not counting satire, theatre productions, or short and feature films (2011, 8). In the current contract, the four main purposes of public service broadcasting is defined as (1) strengthening the citizens' ability to act in a democratic society; (2) uniting and reflecting Denmark; (3) stimulating culture and language; and (4) furthering knowledge and understanding (2011, 5). Reich describes how DR Fiction is thus obliged to unite 'the Denmark family' and target mainstream production. There has to be a balance between trying to be cutting edge and having a wide appeal. As an example, she mentions how a series like the conversation-based psychotherapy drama *In Treatment* (HBO 2008–) would have a much too narrow appeal to be made at DR.

DR Fiction produces around 20 episodes of Sunday night drama every year; these are the high-profile series at the core of this book. The Sunday series thus fulfil the hours of drama demanded in the Public Service Contract, but DR Fiction is also involved in other productions. The current Public Service Contract calls for more focus on drama for children, and DR has recently produced in-house children/family series like *Mille* (2009) and *Limbo* (2012). For a number of years, DR Fiction has been trying to also move into production of less prestigious drama series for week night slots (as discussed by former Head of Drama Ingolf Gabold in Redvall 2010c), and according to Reich the first example of such a series is finally set to premiere in 2014. Moreover, DR Fiction produces around 30 hours of original radio drama a year and satire for DR2.

A rather peculiar, but highly cherished, tradition among viewers is the advent calendar genre, which in 2012 celebrated its 50th anniversary with the writing/directing duo Michael Wikke and Steen Rasmussen's family drama *Julestjerner*/'Christmas Stars' (2012). Having an advent calendar consisting of one episode a day from 1 December to 24 started as more of an educational project with the first advent calendar from 1962 consisting of small stories from around the world (Monggaard 2012). Over the years, the genre has become a popular family event throughout December, with TV 2 and DR taking turns producing new fare every second year, and the series now focus on dramatic and entertaining content with some sort of Christmas angle. *Julestjerner* was among the most watched programmes in December 2012 with more than one million viewers for the airings at 7.30 pm.[15] With the many different productions, the output of DR Fiction adds up to around 40 hours of television drama annually (Reich 2012).

As outlined in the previous chapter, the financing of product from DR is primarily based on national government funding and some money from other Nordic public service broadcasters, the Nordisk Film & TV Fond and Nordvision. The crime series have had German ZDF co-financing, and with US players like HBO suddenly showing an interest, DR is currently looking at increasing co-production and co-financing. However, Nadia Kløvedal Reich stresses that DR will never go into co-production where 'we do not have the control of the creative process and we will never jeopardize the "one vision and producer's choice thinking"' (Reich in Pham 2012). The concepts of the dogmas are thus discussed as crucial to production, even if other partners were to be involved.

As for budgets of individual series and episodes, no one at DR is eager to put specific numbers on the table. External production companies sometimes complain that there is too little knowledge about the actual cost of production at DR (e.g. Hansen 2009). Reich insists that the price per minute is lower than production at external production companies, even if she adds 35 per cent for the use of in-house facilities, which the industry regards as a benefit of 20 per cent. She explains that DR does not publish their numbers in order to avoid spending too much time discussing them with the industry. However, some figures are announced publicly. According to Reich, an episode of the third season of *The Killing* cost DKK 4–5m and was shot in 14 days. She argues that one of the secrets of producing at a reasonable price is to keep content and production close to each other, thus securing the best conditions for a constructive meeting of 'art' and 'the machine' (Reich 2012). As will be further explored in Chapter 5 on the writing of *Borgen*, an advantage of working with production hotels – besides facilitating communication and collaboration – may also be that is brings the stages of conception and execution close together, so that discussions about the actual cost of things are integrated in the process at an early stage.

With regard to issues of creativity and control, Reich describes how she as Head of DR Fiction officially has final cut, but no intention of using it. Across all interviews conducted for this book, only one instance of a major disagreement regarding final cut has been brought up repeatedly. The disagreement was about a pair of shoes worn by a right wing politician in the first episode of *Borgen*. The shoes were perceived as potentially ridiculing, and Reich and then Head of Drama Ingolf Gabold were afraid that they could lead to criticism of a biased portrayal of the character and allegations of taking a political stand, while the writers and the director of the episode wanted the shoes to stay. The shoes did stay, but according to Reich in a form where they were not as visible. This is seemingly the only instance of taking a disagreement to executives outside of DR Fiction, but the case study of *Borgen* shows how there are notes and comments from both the producer and the Head of Drama for the head writer to consider during the writing of each new episode. The somewhat paradoxical explanation for why Reich as the Head of DR Fiction has final cut, is that then the writers and directors do not have it; in her opinion this ensures the possibility of discussion. Whereas final cut is thus officially in the hands of DR Fiction, the observations and interviews for this book point to the head writers actually having the freedom to make the final calls, but these are made after listening to many opinions along the way.

New generations and national audiences

DR Fiction has been marked by a generational shift in the 2010s with Ingolf Gabold and Sven Clausen retiring and veteran writing teams like Stig Thorsboe/Hanna Lundblad and Peter Thorsboe/Mai Brostrøm now producing for other broadcasters. In terms of audiences, there are also talks of focusing more on the younger generations. When Piv Bernth and Nadia Kløvedal Reich talk about continuing the current framework, they add the need to target younger audiences and to change 'the recipe before viewers realise there is a recipe' (Bernth in Pham 2012). The attempt to target younger audiences is linked to the introduction of a television drama slot on weekday nights, while a younger generation of head writers and episode writers are in charge of forthcoming series like *The Legacy* (Maya Ilsøe) and *Follow the Money* (Jeppe Gjervig Gram).

Whereas the official mission statement by DR Fiction is thus to continue a production framework, which has been refined since the 1990s, it is likely that there will be changes in genres, choices of content and storytelling strategies in the years to come, when moving beyond the high-profile series and trying to appeal to a younger crowd. However, the focus is still on the national audiences in spite of the international success. Piv Bernth and Nadia Kløvedal Reich have repeatedly made it clear in the press that international acclaim is fantastic, but that the mandate of DR Fiction is to produce Danish television drama (e.g. Reich in Thorsen 2013). The public service mandate gives priority to the national audiences, and it will be interesting to see how the international interest in series from DR might influence the ways of production or the series themselves in the years to come.

The following chapters explore the nature of the current framework in more detail, drawing on the main points of this chapter about the managerial approaches to creating a structure for the best working practices and the best public service series. While observing meetings at DR during 2011 and 2012, it has been interesting to learn how concepts from the dogmas were also used by the commissioning executives outside DR Fiction, as when *The Legacy* was pitched at an early stage in development and interpreted as a perfect example of double storytelling. Coining concepts within the production framework facilitates a mutual understanding of the guiding principles for production as a sort of mission statement for the creation of series, among practitioners as well as in conversations with commissioners.

At the European TV Drama Lab, discussions of current challenges in the European television industry repeatedly pointed back to writers, producers and broadcasters not speaking the same language when discussing ideas and stories (Redvall 2012a, 7). At DR this does not seem to be the case. A major reason for this can be traced back to the simple fact that all people involved in the process are under the same roof, even if they are separated into commissioning and producing departments.

However, the deliberate effort to create a shared language also plays a major part, and even though concepts like one vision or double story-telling can be granted different levels of importance and interpreted in different ways, their mere existence help to create a certain mindset for what characterizes a series from DR. The case studies of individual productions and processes aim to provide a more nuanced understanding of how this works in practice.

4
Training Talent for Television: DR and the 'TV Term'

Introduction

Almost all writers and the younger producers at DR are alumni from The National Film School of Denmark (NFSD). As two examples, all writers of *The Killing* and all the episode writers of *Borgen* have an educational background in the Screenwriting Department of the School. The vast majority of talent behind recent series thus come from the same educational institution with which DR has had a steady collaboration since the late 1990s. As part of the Screen Idea System perspective on writing and production, this chapter analyses the ideas of best practice being taught to the new talent at the Film School, and traces how teaching writing for television gradually became an established part of the curriculum during the 2000s. This partly happened due to new developments in the domain, where US quality series convinced people at the School that it was worthwhile to also take television seriously in an art school environment after years of focusing exclusively on film. However, central experts in the field from DR also played a major part in this development by encouraging collaboration, sharing their knowledge and taking an interest in the students to help ensure the emergence of strong television writers.

The collaboration was established at a time when DR experienced an acute lack of talent in terms of writers with an interest in television series and with knowledge of how to collaborate as part of a head writer-episode writer structure. The collaboration began with introductory teaching on television writing and meetings between students and DR producers, but since 2004 it has been institutionalized through the so-called TV term where student writers and producers at the School spend half a year developing a potential series particularly for

DR together with production designers from the School of Design. The series is developed based on ideas about the nature of 'a good series' as outlined in the 'TV dummy paper' (see Appendix), and at the end of the term the series is pitched to DR Fiction executives and other industry players in order to get constructive criticism from a real-life perspective.

Head of Drama at DR Piv Bernth has called the collaboration between the two institutions one of the secrets behind the recent success of DR (in Pham 2012). Based on interviews with writers and producers from the School and a case study of the 2012–2013 edition of the TV term, this chapter investigates the nature of this collaboration, where DR Fiction has actively engaged in training talent for future series. This has provided the opportunity to teach students a certain approach to television drama – based on a public service mandate and concepts like one vision and double storytelling from the production dogmas – as well as the opportunity to scout for new writers in a film school framework.

Television writing in a film school context

In a small film and television industry like the Danish, there are few places to train for the job as writer or producer. In fact, the NFSD is the only official training ground for these professional roles. Some alternatives, such as the filmmaker-driven, independent film school Super 16 has emerged, training directors and producers since its start in 1999, and since 2011 also including screenwriters in their programme. However, a look at the educational background of the writers at DR since the late 1990s reveals that a significant number of these are alumni from the NFSD. They have been through the same curriculum and know each other from their school days, while only a few writers, like *Borgen*-creator Adam Price, are self-taught or have other educational backgrounds.

Academic interest in a career or a film culture most often starts after the formative years, although some film historical discussions have emphasized the importance of certain institutions and student collectives over time. Discussions of the 'Movie Brat' directors, counting names like Martin Scorsese, Steven Spielberg, George Lucas and Francis Ford Coppola, is one example of a discourse where the directors' training as part of the first 'film school generation' in American film is regarded as significant to their approach to filmmaking at that certain point in time (e.g. Pye and Myles 1979). This chapter argues that the series from DR in recent years have been marked by the emergence of what one can regard as the first generation of trained television writers and that it is worthwhile investigating the kind of training offered before entering the industry as well as the relation between the structures around the training of individuals and the structures of production in particular film and television cultures. Compared to larger countries, there are of course remarkable differences in the size and structures of the training grounds in a small nation television industry like the Danish, yet there are still points of relevance beyond borders in terms of how to think of exchanges and collaborations between educational institutions and the industry.

In the past few years, research on training for filmmaking has been revitalized through several studies on film schools. From a European perspective, Duncan Petrie has explored the historical development of film schools and analysed the often complicated relationship between theory and practice when training future filmmakers (2010, 2011, 2012). His research addresses a movement from film schools as art schools to film schools being perceived more as 'training providers' marked by market-driven imperatives in the global film industries demanding certain skills more than others (2010, 43). The education at film schools – as at universities – is now often discussed in more instrumentalist terms, focusing on the right skills needed for working in the creative industries rather than artistic arguments. There seems to be great value in investigating these developments in the educational framework of different film and television cultures, not only to better understand the impact of education from artistic perspectives but also to discuss the consequences of a more industry-oriented conception of art schools in relation to broader discussions of cultural policy and creative industries. The two-volume anthology *The Education of the Filmmaker*, addressing a range of different issues related to film education throughout the world, is a ground-breaking publication in this regard (Hjort 2013a, 2013b).[1]

The NFSD has been the topic of substantial research in recent years, but the focus has been exclusively on the training for filmmaking. The School has been given an important place in the development of what has been called the New Danish Cinema (Hjort 2005; Hjort et al. 2010) with its implementation of working with creativity under constraint – often seen as the basis for Dogma 95 and films like Lars von Trier and Jørgen Leth's playful *De fem benspænd/The Five Obstructions* (2003) (Hjort and MacKenzie 2003; Hjort 2007) – and its insistence on creating a shared language of storytelling between professions (Philipsen 2005; Redvall 2010b). This chapter focuses on the School's impact in the domain of television drama by training future writers and producers and being part of the establishment of certain concepts of best practice and quality product. However, before moving on to the nature of the collaboration with DR and a study of the TV term specifically, the chapter establishes how the School has been influential for screenwriting in the Danish film and television culture in general through the Screenwriting Department challenging the traditional auteur approach to the creation of new products.

From industry training to diplomas

The establishment of the NFSD in 1966 was based on new conceptions of film as an art form, calling for a place where new talent could explore the nature of film art instead of training in the industry, which had been the case until then.[2] As argued by Ib Bondebjerg, in the years 1930–1960 the Danish film culture was dominated by a studio system similar to the American where a number of production companies worked with regular film teams and directors (2005, 56–7). Peter Schepelern has documented how only six writers wrote more than half of the 350 sound films produced in those same 30 years (1995, 19). These writers were craftsmen who could deliver original scripts as well as adaptations on a regular basis. However, this 'classical' film culture was challenged by a number of developments around 1960, which led to changes in the structure of the industry and the understanding of the film medium as such. Among the changes was how the influence from the French New Wave and a new modernism in European film led to a focus on the individual artist or the privileged position of the director.

Danish director Palle Kjærulff-Schmidt has described the New Wave as an inspiration to move from a view of film as being pure entertainment to a view of film as a medium where new realizations could be explored. He has argued that this led to abandoning 'the old rules of the craft' and instead trusting that a form would emerge if the content was vital enough (in Bondebjerg 2005, 85). This new conception of films being regarded less as factory products and more as individual works of art challenged the position of the skilled screenwriters behind the popular films and established the idea among many directors that they should write their scripts themselves or at least that their scripts should be based on their personal ideas for a story. Since then, the modern Danish film culture has been based on the understanding that a film springs from the vision of a director. Contrary to the more producer-driven American film culture where studios and producers often buy the rights to finished scripts and later get a director attached (Taylor 1999; Wasko 2003), there are still almost no 'spec scripts' in the

Danish industry and screenwriters are traditionally regarded as crafts-men structuring the thoughts of directors on paper rather than artists in their own right.

However, the position of the screenwriter has gradually changed dur-ing the 2000s because of the emergence of strong screenwriters and a new respect for screenwriting as a craft (Redvall 2010a). Some screen-writers have found international recognition; among them Anders Thomas Jensen, who has been called 'one of the finest script craftsmen in world filmmaking today' by film scholar David Bordwell (2007, 17).[3] Others are less prominent in the national and international audience and academic awareness, but the impact of talented screenwriters on Danish cinema is now widely recognized. As for television, the writ-ers are enjoying a completely different position than in the world of film with the head writers now in the media spotlight. This new posi-tion is interesting to track in relation to the developments at the NFSD, where it took many years to include screenwriting in the curriculum and later great effort to make the directors interested in the work of the Screenwriting Department.

The auteur and the screenwriting tradition

The early years of the NFSD was marked by what one director has called a time of 'storytelling blindness' (Redvall 2010b). Topics like story structure and dramaturgy were not on the curriculum. There was a widespread suspicion of classical 'Hollywood principles', and screen-writing was not something that was taught during the first decade of the School's existence. Henning Camre, who became Head of the School in 1975, has described how the absence of a screenwriting edu-cation was striking: 'There was not an actual education in the work with screenplays, that was something the director – as auteur – was expected to already have mastered' (2006, 24). Camre hired Mogens Rukov as a screenwriting tutor, and together they established regu-lar screenwriting courses, which were met with both resistance and indulgence, since 'something as fundamental as dramaturgy and screen-writing didn't exist at that time. And it was presumably the dominant opinion that teaching it wasn't feasible' (Camre in Wivel and Bro 1991, 11). Rukov has explained that the teaching of screenwriting started at a bad time, because it was a time of moving from subjectivity being 'the law' together with the idea that nobody could teach anybody anything, towards an acceptance of the possibility of basic elements in screenwrit-ing being something that could actually be learned (1991, 39).[4]

At the time when the first screenwriting students graduated in 1982, the screenwriting courses lived a parallel life of their own, separate from the rest of the students at the School. However, around the same time a new awareness in the industry was emerging: that one might actually be able to learn something about telling stories. Former Head of Drama at DR Ingolf Gabold has argued that there was a minor revolution in the Danish film and TV world when the Swedish dramaturge Ola Olsson came to the NFSD in 1979. Olsson introduced ideas about story structure and terminology which, according to Gabold, created the possibility of a shared language between screenwriters, directors, production designers, directors of photography and the rest of the team: 'Ola Olsson gave us a film and TV dramaturgy that let the stuffy air out of that room, which a lot of film and TV people had kept hermetically closed, believing that their creations could not be put in a formula or be discussed in a professional language beyond judgments of taste by their colleagues and the audience' (2006, 9). The ideas of Olsson were taught and implemented at DR as part of the so-called TV-Sum courses.[5] The courses also had several international guests emphasizing the value of working with certain dramaturgical models (Bondebjerg 1991, 152).

As a directing student at the NFSD and afterwards as a screenwriting student (graduating 1982) before later becoming Head of Drama at DR, Rumle Hammerich has described how the introduction of storytelling structures was a revelation, since until then the students had been 'floating around in a magical darkness regarding screenwriting' (2006, 97). The brothers Peter and Stig Thorsboe (graduating 1984), who became the most used head writers at DR in the 1990s and 2000s, participated in one of the early short courses and later applied for the longer screenwriting course. Peter Thorsboe has stated that there was no prestige in writing films at the time; for most people screenwriting was something they would do over a summer break outside their official careers in literature or journalism (2006, 144–5).

Peter and Stig Thorsboe both had an interest in television, but TV series were not part of the curriculum at the time. They were inspired by the teachings of the British screenwriter Neville Smith, who had a background in writing for television, but focused on film while at the School. During a study trip to England they met another British screenwriter, Troy Kennedy Martin, who had written *Z Cars* (1962–1978), which they admired. After finishing the regular screenwriting course, they convinced Camre to invite Troy Kennedy Martin over for a workshop, focusing specifically on television. According to Peter Thorsboe, this turned out to be his best experience at the School. Martin divided the students into groups and sent them out into real life settings. Peter and Stig Thorsboe were sent to a police station where they observed the work and listened in on conversations. Peter Thorsboe describes how it was a great gift to learn how to use reality in one's writing in this way. Another gift from the meeting with Martin was his introduction to the writings of Joseph Campbell and Christopher Vogler, whose thoughts on using myths as the basis for storytelling Peter Thorsboe still draws on today (Thorsboe 2012). The 1980s was thus marked by dramaturges putting certain ideas of storytelling on the agenda, both at the NFSD and at DR, while British television writers were influential by being sources of inspiration through their work in the domain and by being the first to actually teach the writing of television at the school.

The Screenwriting Department

Whereas the early courses in screenwriting attended by Peter and Stig Thorsboe were a part-time undertaking, a full-time screenwriting education was established from 1988. According to Lars Kjeldgaard, who was hired as a teacher together with Rukov, there were numerous problems with the screenwriting courses up through the 1980s (Kjeldgaard 2007). Indeed, one possibility was eliminating them all together, since they did not have much to do with the teachings at the rest of the School. However, it was decided to dramatically rethink the design of the courses before establishing an independent department for screenwriting with the intention of fighting the strong focus on literature in Danish cinema, to which Rukov and Kjeldgaard attributed the depressing state of the national films in the 1980s.

Until the establishment of the Screenwriting Department there had been many novelists among the students, but now a deliberate attempt was made to attract new people from advertising agencies, artists or actors. The basic idea was to 'teach people to surrender themselves to film' instead of having a literary approach to writing films (Kjeldgaard 2007). 'Show, don't tell' became a mantra and, as a supplement to in-house lecture notes about directors ranging from Buñuel to Cassavetes, American screenwriting manuals like Syd Field's *Screenplay* (1979) were introduced. According to Kjeldgaard, the fundamental principle was to identify with 'great storytellers, no matter where they were' (2007). However, because of the introduction of terms like 'acts' and 'genres' some students, according to Kjeldgaard, felt that the teaching was too influenced by thoughts from Hollywood filmmaking.[6]

Nikolaj Scherfig, screenwriter of, for example, *Bron/The Bridge* (2011–), was among the first students. He was thrilled by being introduced to basic and concrete thoughts about fundamental storytelling concepts like plot, character, scenes and conflicts, but he also states that the notion of a *real* director at the time was still that he wrote scripts himself, or wrote them together with a famous novelist (2006, 158). Scherfig has described how directors felt threatened by screenwriters, since they were convinced that they in fact wanted to become directors; the idea of anybody actually wanting to be a screenwriter was too absurd (2006, 159). This attitude has been regarded as changing with the directing students of 1993 who took an interest in the screenwriters (Philipsen 2005). Director Thomas Vinterberg has explained that while the School was previously dominated by the cinematographers this changed by his class of directors putting the actors and the story at the centre of attention (Vinterberg and John 2006, 180).[7] Since then, there have been steady collaborations between students of directing and screenwriting, and even if these have not been without problems, the relation between directors and screenwriters is now well established (Redvall 2010b).

The coming of teaching for television

Even with an independent education for screenwriting, it took a while to gain the interest of the directors, and it also took some time for the screenwriting education to embrace the television medium as an integrated part of the teaching agenda. Mai Brostrøm (graduated 1996), screenwriter of *Rejseholdet/Unit One* (2000–2004), *Ørnen/The Eagle* (2004–2006) and *Livvagterne/The Protectors* (2008–2010) for DR, was part of the first group of students together with Nikolaj Scherfig. Inspired by the work of Dennis Potter and series like *House of Cards* (1990), she came to the School with an interest in television, but found that there was no teaching of television writing (Brostrøm 2012). Discussions of whether teaching the writing of film vs television is based on the same principles or rather two different disciplines has been on-going for several years. As argued by screenwriter of *The Killing*, Søren Sveistrup, one can regard television writing as fundamentally based on the same storytelling principles as films or even novels (Sveistrup 2012). He found a strength of the School to be how it focused on storytelling as such, for any medium, rather than trying to differentiate between specific demands of different media.

Today, however, film and television are described as based on different storytelling strategies by the current Head of the Screenwriting

Department, Lars Detlefsen. He defines film as the journey into the unknown and television as the aquarium, which is to be understood as based on the everyday, recognizable stories of life in a small town or at the work place. Characters develop differently in works for film and television, and the School now spends a great amount of time addressing these differences by teaching storytelling for film and television individually, while still insisting on certain traits for all kinds of stories (Detlefsen 2012). Whereas some in the industry have argued in favour of having two separate programmes for teaching film and television writing, Detlefsen does not see this as the right approach in a small industry like the Danish with a limited output of both feature films and TV series. He believes that there is both logistical and artistic value in learning both kinds of writing and in being able to move back and forth between film and TV. This reflects the idea of crossover from the DR dogmas, based on the wish to bridge the worlds of film and television rather than keeping them apart (Figure 4.1).

Mai Brostrøm and Michael W. Horsten (episode writer of *The Killing*) were part of the first course on television writing in January 1996, which was organized following the regular screenwriting education as an additional offer (Brostrøm 2012; Horsten 2013). Head of DR Fiction Rumle Hammerich, producer Sven Clausen and screenwriters Hanna Lundblad

Figure 4.1 Dejan Cukic as the fictional screenwriting teacher Selkoff talking about circular dramaturgy in Jacob Thuesen's feature film *De Unge År/The Early Years – Erik Nietzsche Part 1* (2007), based on a screenplay by Lars von Trier inspired by his time at the Film School (1979–1983). Framegrab. Cinematography by Sebastian Blenkov

and Peter Thorsboe were among the teachers. The course led to making television writing an integrated part of the screenwriting curriculum. This happened in the fall of 1997, and according to Sven Clausen DR took great interest in this initiative, since the new focus on long-running series in the wake of *Landsbyen*/'The Village' (1991–1996) and during the development of *Taxa* (1997–1999) 'disclosed an acute lack of Danish episode writers with experience in writing for the medium and the genre – and an enthusiasm for the format'.[8] The teaching at NFSD was seen as a possibility 'to secure future deliveries by being visible – not the least as a source of inspiration – already at the level of education'. One of the assignments during the first term was to write a scene for *Taxa*, and the collaboration between the School and DR led to some of the students being hired shortly after graduating, for instance, Søren Sveistrup and Dunja Gry Jensen.

Television thus became part of the screenwriting curriculum concurrently with DR Fiction developing a new focus on long-running drama series, but it took some time before the teaching developed into the now institutionalized TV term for writers, producers and production designers. Detlefsen finds that the early interest in television was met with some resistance at the School. One reason why this resistance gradually faded was a shared sense of a change in the nature of television series with a number of international series becoming popular and well respected (Detlefsen 2012). Changes in the domain thus helped create a new sense of a need to also focus on television. Moreover, a number of students found their first employment in television, and this labour aspect also justified the value of taking television seriously within the school framework.

The first TV term

Detlefsen developed the first TV term together with the Screenwriting Department coordinator Charlotte Omann. They wanted the term to be built around a specific assignment, and Detlefsen thus approached DR about a possible collaboration, because 'DR were the best at the time' (Detlefsen 2012). Head of Drama Ingolf Gabold and producer Sven Clausen found the institutionalized term to be an excellent idea, and the Head of the Producer's Department at the NFSD Ole John also wanted to have his students take part and suggested including students in production design from the School of Design. This led to the creation of the first TV term in 2004, which was organized around groups of writers, producers and production designers spending four to five months developing a potential series for DR. Since then, the term has been running every two years, more or less in the same format as the first (Detlefsen 2012). Following the first term, Gabold praised the initiative in the press, since he found that there was still a 'shocking lack of writers' for television drama and that the TV term could hopefully change that (in Redvall 2005).

The screenwriting alumni now working at DR all place great emphasis on the establishment of the term. The fact that you get to pitch for the actual decision makers at DR is highlighted as extremely motivating by writers (Ilsøe 2012; Gram 2012), and both writers and producers describe the value of getting a concrete sense of how the role of the writer and producer is different in film vs television (Larsen 2012; Rank 2012). Jeppe Gjervig Gram finds that the TV term is the time at the School, which mirrors what he terms 'virtual reality' the most, in the sense that you have an assignment that might actually be real and allows you to meet the people with the power, whom you want to impress (Gram 2012).

For Gram and his writing colleague Tobias Lindholm, their suggested series led to being hired by DR as episode writers of the family series *Sommer/Summer* (2008) straight after the School. However, so far none of the series pitched have made it to the screen, all though some are said to still have the possibility of making it into development at some point. In that regard, the TV term is more about getting the opportunity to work with a set assignment and pitch your interests and skills to a broadcaster, than about selling a project for production. Similarly, the School continuously stresses the fact that the term has to be regarded as a school assignment with an overall educational purpose, rather than as a pitch opportunity for a future job (Detlefsen 2012). Studying the most recent TV term there was, however, a clear sense that DR uses it to scout for both talent and ideas, and the term in the autumn of 2012 consisted of developing a very specific kind of product for DR rather than the more open assignments of earlier years to produce any kind of drama series.

The structure of the TV term

The TV term is the third term out of four in the two-year education of screenwriters at the NFSD. Whereas directors, producers, cinematographers and editors spend four years at the School, the screenwriting education is half the length, and the normally six screenwriting students accepted every second year are busy. Besides the teaching and writing of their personal projects, they collaborate with directors on their midterm and final films, and during the TV term they are at the centre of the process during the development of an idea for a new series. This happens in group constellations of two writers, two producers and one or two production designers, who work together through the process of conceiving an idea from the beginning of the teaching in August to the delivery of the completed assignment before Christmas.

Before the actual teaching starts in the autumn, each group is given a so-called 'inspirational box', or as Lars Detlefsen paraphrases 'homework', before the summer break. The box consists of a number of TV series, Lee Goldberg and William Rabkin's book *Successful Television Writing* (2003) and scripts for national and international series. In 2012, the box contained the first seasons of *2 Broke Girls* (2011–), *Bored to Death* (2009–2011) and *In Treatment* (2008–) as well as the second season of *Forbrydelsen/The Killing* (2007–2012). The scripts were the first episodes of *Mad Men* (2007–2013) seasons one to five, the third episode in the second season of *The Killing* and the first episode of *Boss* (2011–2012). Detlefsen describes the box as a tool to 'tune into making television series' (2012), and the students are also given what Detlefsen terms 'a dummy' or 'a recipe' for a TV series concept (Detlefsen 2012, see Appendix 1). The dummy lists a number of things to include when thinking about new series, ranging from considerations of genre, theme and premise over issues of characters, arenas and storytelling strategies to presentations of casting and crew choices, budgets, mode of production, time slots and target groups. The dummy specifies how each group is to produce a project presentation consisting of not only pitches for the first six episodes but also of full scripts for the first and last episode and ideas for a second season.

The TV term of 2012 was the first with Head of DR Fiction Nadia Kløvedal Reich and Head of Drama Piv Bernth representing DR as commissioners in the process. They decided to give the students a set assignment asking for a week-night comedy or comedy-drama series of 28.5 minutes targeting younger audiences rather than a Sunday night drama series.[9] Since DR is hoping to create a new slot for this kind of programming in the near future, they would like to get ideas from the film school generation of talent. The strict genre and format definition of the assignment was met with scepticism by some students, but they all accepted the challenge. Former students interviewed about the TV term commented that they felt sorry for the students of 2012 when they learned that the genre was defined as comedy, since comedy is not for everyone (Ilsøe 2012; Larsen 2012). Moreover, as screenwriter Maya Ilsøe stated, if the idea of DR is to go with the one vision of the writer, one should allow the writers to explore their desires rather than forcing them in a certain direction (Ilsøe 2012). Other writers find that the idea of working with less prestigious series than the high-profile Sunday series can be a good idea since they can be more easily approached (Larsen 2012). From a DR perspective, Reich argues that it was interesting to get ideas in a genre and format, which has not been produced in-house for quite some time (Reich 2012). The intention of moving into week-night series has been present for a long time (as discussed by Gabold in Redvall 2005), and the TV term was a way to get inspiration in this regard.

Based on the observations from the final pitch of the projects developed, all projects seemed to build on the individual interests of the writers, even if these were framed within the comedy genre and the week-night time slot. No one commented on problems related to developing this kind of series, and having certain parameters for the process can be regarded as helpful when having to move through the mess-finding, data-finding and idea-generating stages in a short time span.

Teachers and tutors from DR and the industry

The TV term is marked by a combination of teachers from the School and professionals from DR providing input on how to write and produce TV series. The teachers responsible for screenwriting (Lars Detlefsen) and production (Ib Tardini) at NFSD make a curriculum together with the teacher responsible for the production designers (Jakob Ion Wille). This always marks a logistical challenge, since the School of Design has a different system of teaching and grading than the film school and a changing number of students (Wille 2013). However, all teachers find that it is crucial to have the production designers attached during the entire process. Detlefsen describes how it is often strange for the production designers in the beginning of the process, where there is yet nothing to design, but from a film school perspective it feels important for the process that they know how thoughts emerged and what the central choices for a project is based on (Detlefsen 2012). The production designers are thus invited to take part in the initial mess and data finding.[10]

Another strength of this approach is to create the sense of being a team and make everyone a part of the exploration (Detlefsen 2012). As Detlefsen states, the work of the early, diverging stages of a process is never a waste, since there is a value in exploring different paths before settling on one. Once a path is chosen, the designers will be busy bringing life to the arena and characters at the core, but before that they are also an important part of visualizing the yet fragile idea. Each group has a production room of its own, where ideas can gradually be externalized and evolve on posters and white boards. There is not a sense of a production hotel since only the producers, writers and designers are present, but having a physical space for the project and the collaboration is regarded as important to the process.

During the TV term there are classes on TV series for all writers and producers (taught by Detlefsen), and since the term began the previous script editor for DR and now screenwriter Hanna Lundblad has given all students an introduction to storytelling for television and to the specific demands for series made for DR. During the three days the students are asked to analyse the major turning points in all scenes of individual characters in an episode or to study classic season openings. The teaching also consists of discussions of good arenas or main characters and encourages the students to present interesting arenas or characters from their own lives, which are then mixed when the class tries to collaboratively come up with the most intriguing combinations. According to Lundblad, a big difference from teaching in 2012 vs the earlier TV terms is how the students are now familiar with most series and quite fluent in basic storytelling terms and traditions (Lundblad 2012). Former students have described how the TV term was a revelation in creating a new awareness around television (e.g. Rank 2012), but quality television series now seem firmly established in the minds of the students, and the teaching is more about exploring their desires and emphasizing how one can do a range of things if one is completely aware of what one is doing – and able to explain the choices made to broadcasters when they ask.

Each term has tutors attached for the different professions involved. In 2012, former DR producer Sven Clausen, Zentropa producer Louise Vesth and screenwriters Hanna Lundblad and Karina Dam were student consultants together with the *Borgen* production designer Knirke Madelung. The teaching schedule started in mid August and included one week at DR in September where the students got to follow productions and talk to people in production. Later in the process, the students also got to meet the in-house media researchers. At the January pitch of the final projects, several groups referred to having consulted the researchers on issues related to the main audiences of certain time slots etc., and in the eyes of DR the groups seemed to have the right sense of the potential audience of their suggested series in terms of both gender, age and background in relation to content and air time. This kind of reflection is encouraged by the dummy paper from the beginning and was addressed not only by producers but also by writers and designers when pitching the final projects.

In mid-October there was a so-called 'paramount meeting', where the students pitch their initial ideas to DR, followed by an evaluation the next day.[11] In 2012, the paramount meeting led to one group splitting into two, since the screenwriters could not agree on an idea and based on the DR feedback decided to go in separate directions. Using a term like 'paramount meeting' brings a sense of international industry lingo to the process, and the many English terms used and the amount of references to international series was remarkable when television was taught or discussed by the students. As is the case with the content of the summer box, the inspiration for producing series is the state of the art in the international domain, and the students are well aware of new series, trends or terms and continuously discuss their series in comparison with what they perceive as the best product from abroad.

The teaching of collaboration and one vision

According to Detlefsen, the TV term is not only about making a TV series; it also focuses on the art of collaboration (Detlefsen 2012). The term is the only time at the School where writers work in pairs, and for Detlefsen it is very much about learning to write together with some-one else and working closely together with a producer. It is important to learn how to collaborate with colleagues of one's own profession as well as with others in relation to working with all sorts of drama, and Detlefsen thus highlights how the term does not put the writing of film on hold, but also adds important lessons to working with film. As he states, it is always worthwhile finding out how to get one's ideas through, when to compromise or not, what sacrifices are needed or how to best collaborate with other creative people (2012).

Whereas there is traditionally little teaching on the potential chal-lenges of collaboration in the school framework (Redvall 2010b), the TV term is regarded as contributing with instrumental lessons in this regard through the making of a specific project between not only film students but also the design students from another school. In 2012, the creativity coach Thea Mikkelsen gave a lecture and was attached as an advisor, but Detlefsen finds that the students should not be nursed too much in this regard. He argues that it is crucial to learn the way back to the work after things have gone wrong. Accordingly, he tries to allow for things to go off track, since 'you learn more from your mistakes and disasters than from being guided through so that everything is smooth and fine' (Detlefsen 2012). The splitting of one group was accepted after two months of disagreements, but the producers and the designer then suddenly became very busy when having to work with the ideas of two writers at once. With the inclusion of experts like Mikkelsen, the School seems to nurture a better understanding of creative processes and collaborations, but it is not an attempt to avoid challenges or conflicts as such, since the handling of these are regarded as important lessons.

The question of the individual and the group is not only about learning how to collaborate but also about how to create collaborative projects with one vision. The concept of one vision was continuously brought up in interviews about the TV term and marked several discussions at the project evaluations. Whereas the professional roles of head writer and episode writers are more given in an industry context, trying to maintain a shared vision as two writers with equal footing can be quite a task. The project evaluations were not marked by discourses of major challenges in terms of collaboration in the two groups that had stuck together. Members of both groups described a good process, but the evaluation of one of the projects was met with concerns from DR that the collaborative process had created confusion about the core of the idea. As an example, Reich commented how the premise for a series was presented as centred on romance, but all A-plotlines for episodes dealt with professional conflicts while the B-plotlines were about romance. This muddled the premise, and in the following discussions the students commented on the challenges of wanting to take the project in different directions along the way and maybe sometimes settling on compromises rather than having one clear vision. Another project was praised for the consistency in the way in which all aspects supported the main idea of the individual writer, one of the two writers going rogue.

The concept of one vision was part of many of the discussions in the evaluations even though the basic framework for the film school assignment can be said to challenge the nature of the concept to a large degree by asking several people to develop an original idea together and by dictating the genre and format for the series. Forcing a certain assignment upon the students can be regarded as a fundamental clash with the one vision notion of ideas originating from the desire of writers to tell something, and there can be many challenges in making writers work together. However, one can argue that the assignment of 2012 only defines a genre and a format rather than any sort of content or a certain arena, similar to if the writers were to develop a one-hour Sunday night drama series with a mainstream appeal, which has been the case of previous terms. The students of the 2012 term were thus free to invent any sort of comedy series and the four projects proposed were very different in content, setting and style.

Pitching to the industry

The two-day pitch session in January was marked by a friendly atmosphere with constructive criticism from DR representatives Reich and Bernth and producer Louise Vesth as well as shorter comments from the consultants or teachers. Each group had around one hour to present their project based on the concept, scripts, production plans and designs, which had been handed in before Christmas. After a short break, there was an hour and a half for feedback, where Reich and Bernth commented on all aspects of the projects from a DR Fiction perspective, while Vesth from a producer's perspective would specifically address the proposed mode of production, the cast and crew or the budget. Having coached all groups on how to best pitch their projects, Vesth would also evaluate their presentational skills. All groups presented artwork for the series by the production designer and one group had also found time to shoot a scene, thereby giving a sense of the imagined acting style and the nature of the comedy in the material.

One of the remarkable things in the pitches was how all groups made an effort to communicate why their project was not only of high quality, entertaining and timely but also had a larger societal relevance. The idea of double storytelling was foregrounded many times, and Reich and Bernth often commented on projects with an emphasis on their public service aspects related to the larger themes behind the immediate story on the page. The social and ethical connotations are thus not only at stake in relation to drama series but also when it comes to comedy, and the comedy series were interpreted as dealing with big issues like unemployment among young people, the financial crisis or how traditional Danish values are changing in the face of globalization. The feedback was generally encouraging and positive, but there were always concerns about certain aspects, whether it was the quality of the writing, the depth of certain characters or more logistical points addressing the number of location shifts in a day related to the proposed cost of shooting or the use of shooting on location vs studio. It was a pitching context marked by the sense of an exam and an eagerness to impress the industry panel, but the pitch was happening in an educational spirit with Detlefsen constantly referring to his students as his 'children' and making brief introductions to the process of each group. The pitch took

Figure 4.2   Students pitching their projects to the industry experts and teachers at the end of the TV term. Photos by Jakob Ion Wille. Courtesy of Jakob Ion Wille, The School of Design and The National Film School of Denmark

place at the School rather than at DR, keeping the school context ever present, and the room was not marked by a sense of DR commissioning series or hiring certain writers even when the feedback seemed very positive (Figure 4.2).

Even though the TV term is centred on developing a potential real life project with continuous input and feedback from industry players, the process is fundamentally approached as a learning process from both the NFSD and the DR perspective. Nadia Kløvedal Reich describes the TV term as a great opportunity to meet the new talent (Reich 2012), rather than a place for discovering the next golden idea or picking up potential series. Detlefsen stresses that the term is not about developing a series for DR, but about 'playing that we are developing something for them; it is after all still a school process' (2012). In his opinion it is a process of giving the students the best opportunity to become as accomplished as possible so that they can later get a job working for DR, should that be their desire.

Since the term of 2010, the NFSD has also had a two-week collaboration with TV 2. It is based on a set assignment for the screenwriting students only, where each writer individually develops an arena, characters and a synopsis for an episode of a new series. Carrying out this task in such a short time span is only possible since the students have previously been through the TV term. Detlefsen describes the first experience with this collaboration as positive and exciting 'since it is a completely different world than DR. It is like coming to another planet. Everything is different' (Detlefsen 2012). According to Detlefsen the difference is particularly in the one culture focusing on public service values and the other focusing on 'selling tickets', but there is also a difference in DR drawing on a long tradition in comparison to TV 2 (2012). Whereas for the past many years, the students have thus only been working with developing series for a broadcaster with a public service mandate, there is now also a focus on learning to work with a more commercial mandate – even if this assignment has a very different place in the overall curriculum.

Learning by doing

The TV term is highlighted as an important initiative for talent development by DR Fiction as well as by teachers and former students from the NFSD. Several people stress the value of having this opportunity for gaining industry-like experiences while still in the safe context of a school and point to the problem of gaining further training in the industry after their student years. Since the DR output of series is rather limited, few writers get the chance to work as episode writers in the DR framework, and writers, producers and broadcasters all argue that it is better to have the opportunity to train in other formats than the Sunday night drama series as a recently graduated writer. Screenwriter Maja Jul Larsen describes how she is grateful that it took some years before she became an episode writer of *Borgen*, since she needed other writing experiences before feeling ready for that task (Larsen 2012). Other writers agree that you are far from ready to conquer the DR drama series straight out of school (Ilsøe 2012; Mosholt in Redvall 2005). The question is where to gain that experience in a small nation industry, where the main broadcaster has decided to almost only produce the high profile one-hour drama series.

As discussed in Chapter 2, the competition when it comes to domestic series is quite limited. Head of Fiction at TV 2 Katrine Vogelsang argues that the limited output makes it hard for young writers to gain the necessary experience to become head writers and for broadcasters using the same experienced writers are thus the safe bets (in Danske Dramatikere 2012, 40). The lack of training opportunities also relates to producers. *Borgen*-producer Camilla Hammerich describes her experience on TV 2's *Hotellet/At the Faber* (2000–2002) as jumping five classes ahead in school, and many writers and producers have gained valuable experiences early in their careers with soaps like *Hvide Løgne/White Lies* (1998–2001) and *2900 Happiness* (2007–2009) for TV3. These series do not travel and are not held in high regard by critics, but they are a crucial part of moving up the ladder in the industry.

At the European TV Drama Series Lab in Berlin, several writers and producers stressed the need for better training opportunities in the

European television industry (Redvall 2012a). Not only in the form of basic courses in television making within traditional educational institutions but also as more specific courses teaching writers about production to prepare them for taking on the role of being showrunners (2012a, 29) or as mentoring programmes (2012a, 35). The collaboration between the NFSD and DR was highlighted as an exciting initiative. The collaboration is most visible through the institutionalized TV term, but there are also other more informal collaborations between the two institutions. When being asked about 'the wonderful relationship with the Danish Film School' in an industry interview, Head of Drama Piv Bernth agreed that the collaboration is 'vital for us' and 'also one of the secrets of our success' (in Pham 2012). This is not only in the form of the TV term. Bernth mentions how she, as a producer, had five student cinematographers on the set of the third season of *The Killing* for three weeks. People at the NFSD and DR know each other well and there is a mutual interest in teaching students the ways of the industry across different professions.

The collaboration between DR and the NFSD has also caught the eye of film schools in Norway and Sweden, where the structure of the TV term has been copied. In 2010, Sven Clausen helped organize a first edition of a TV term at Lillehammer University College, home of the Norwegian courses in practical filmmaking. The plan is to also establish a TV term at Dramatiska Institutet (DI) in Stockholm, and there were observers from both the Swedish public service broadcaster SVT and DI during the final pitch of the Danish TV term in 2012 to learn from the process before implementing a similar structure in the Swedish curriculum. According to Clausen a term like this can hopefully help bridge what he perceives as a big divide between the film and television industry in the Swedish context.[12] From the NFSD perspective, Detlefsen is only happy that the TV term can be exported, but he warns about expecting immediate effects of new initiatives such as these, which often take ten years to really catch on – as was the case with the TV term, which is now well respected at the School as well as in the industry (Detlefsen 2012).

At the NFSD, the TV term and the close collaboration with DR is not seen as conflicting with being an art school. On the NFSD website, the School is presented as 'an art school which means that the teaching aims at developing and supporting each student's unique talent'.[13] However, the very next sentence emphasizes that the school concurrently places great emphasis on students learning 'the craft of filmmaking to ensure their future employment in the professional film- and media industry'. As discussed in the above, the TV term is clearly grounded in the school setting and discussed as a learning process even though the industry is involved. The output of the term is not only about producing a concept for a potential series but also about learning storytelling for television and about collaborating with colleagues of the same or other professions.

From a DR Fiction perspective, the term has turned out to be an excellent platform for teaching students the DR public service approach to TV series and for scouting for new talent. Head writers like Maya Ilsøe and Jeppe Gjervig Gram thus established a relationship with DR already during the TV term, and almost all head writers and the vast majority of episode writers of DR series in the past are alumni from the School. The School has thus had a major impact on the talent writing the DR series. How this talent works when at DR will be explored in the coming chapters.

5
Writers, Showrunners and Television Auteurs: Ideas of One Vision

Introduction

Television production is a complex process with input from many people along the way. The collaborative nature of the workflows is generally acknowledged as the nature of creating new series, and in television studies there has been remarkably less interest in singling out the individual contributions behind specific productions than among scholars focusing on the film medium, traditionally found to be the place for more individual, artistic expression. Within the extensive 'how-to'-literature for film and television writing, the collaborative process is often addressed from the very outset of books on writing for the small screen. Whereas classic 'how-to books' for film often address the singular writer and rarely comment extensively on the mode of production as such, several books on writing for television start by emphasizing the collective nature of the process. In *Writing the TV Drama Series*, Pamela Douglas states that 'if you go on to write for television, you'll never work alone. Series are like families, and even though each episode is written by one writer, the process is collaborative at every step' (2007, 11). Moreover, many screenwriting manuals for television address the industrial context, stressing how television writing is not only about being good at storytelling but also about the industrial rules of the game.

In their book on successful television writing Lee Goldberg and William Rabkin underline the importance of understanding the interplay of the concept for a series, its characters and narrative structures, which is what you see on screen. However, another important part of the process is 'the business behind the camera, the unglamorous stuff that shapes, and reshapes, what you write more than anything else. It's where reality collides with creativity' (2003, 7). As a television writer, one collaborates with a number of people from the very outset of a process. Film scholar Kristin Thompson has noted how the amount of plot needed for series in the American context necessitates a group effort, meaning that the idea of the singular writer creating a series on his or her own – thus winning 'the awed admiration' of their peers – is an exception (2003, 39–40).

Despite the widespread agreement about television writing being a highly collective process, the concept of one vision in the DR production dogmas singles out the head writer as the one person with the vision for what is to be produced from start to finish. As already discussed, this does not imply that the head writer has to write everything on his or her own, but that his or her vision should permeate all aspects of production. This chapter explores this concept of one vision by investigating its gradual implementation in the production framework since the late 1990s as well as the current conceptions of its meaning among practitioners working at DR Fiction.

Within the Screen Idea System, experts in the field can introduce different managerial ideas, thus creating a certain framework for what is likely to find acceptance by the gatekeepers at that point in time. The question is, however, how these ideas are implemented in practice, and how they work in the interplay with the individual talent and the ideas of what should be produced for the domain of Danish television drama. As discussed in the previous chapter, the concept of one vision is regarded as originating in the intention of copying work methods from the US industry, and the chapter opens with an introduction to the current interest in the role of the showrunner in the US television industry.

Recent research on the role of showrunners (e.g. Cornea 2009; Mann 2009; Perren 2011, 2013) and on writers' rooms (Caldwell 2008; Henderson 2011; Phalen and Osselame 2012) show a renewed interest in the divisions of labour in the US television context and in how to understand the contributions of individuals in a context where one professional role is now identified as the most important for the process as a whole. In the public realm, writings on specific showrunners are also getting still more common, and some even discuss particular creators of series as 'TV auteurs' (Molloy 2010).

Based on interviews with writers, producers and executives at DR, the chapter traces how to understand one vision in the DR mode of production since the 1990s. The analysis points to how there were initial problems with establishing a head writer/episode writers structure, since neither head writers nor episode writers were accustomed to this kind of division of labour in terms of the writing process. The chapter focuses on the gradual development of the one vision concept from the work of Stig Thorsboe and Hanna Lundblad (e.g. *Taxa/Taxi*, *Krøniken/Better Times* and *Lykke/Happy Life*), Peter Thorsboe and Mai Brostrøm (e.g. *Rejseholdet/Unit One*, *Ørnen/The Eagle*, *Livvagterne/The Protectors*), Søren Sveistrup (*Nikolaj og Julie/Nikolaj and Julie* and *Forbrydelsen/The Killing*) and Adam Price (*Borgen*) to the upcoming head writers Maya Ilsøe (*Arvingerne/The Legacy*, forthcoming 2014) and Jeppe Gjervig Gram (*Follow the Money*, planned for 2015). The analysis stresses how the idea of working with one vision comes in the shape of many types of collaborations depending on the head writer and with producers, directors, actors and other crewmembers involved to different extents. The process of writing during production is highlighted as essential to allowing this input to influence the text.

The chapter ends by discussing how to understand the concept of one vision in relation to the role of the 'showrunner'. Interestingly, the increased focus on showrunners in the US production framework seems to have created a renewed interest in understanding the actual processes behind the scenes. What does a showrunner actually do? What is the nature of the different contributions when major series are produced? As an example, when a series like *Banshee* for premium cable network Cinemax (2013–) is presented as being from the creator of *True Blood* (HBO, 2008–) Alan Ball, it makes audiences link the new series to his famous name and successful track record. However, the series was conceived by the less famous writers Jonathan Tropper and David Schickler with the director Greg Yaitanes, known for *House* (Fox 2004–2012), as part of the executive producing team. High-profile American series have many people taking credits, and as with other series it is often hard to decipher the input of different individuals behind the many layers of writers and producers, especially since the current corporate storytelling of several cable networks is to present showrunners as brands in their own right. In a smaller, national production context like the Danish there aren't as many 'cooks' on the credits, but a number of people have still contributed behind the scenes. The nature of these collaborations are worthwhile exploring if one wants to gain a nuanced understanding of the specific mode of production and be able to compare strategies between production cultures (Figure 5.1).

Figure 5.1 Ida Nørregaard (Anne Louise Hassing) and Erik Nielsen (Ken Vedsegaard) during a romantic moment in the historical drama series *Krøniken/Better Times* (2004–2007), taking its point of departure in the year 1949 and following four young Danes through the next 25 years of history. Photo by Mike Kollöffel. Courtesy of DR

Showrunners and 'sufficient control'

The term 'showrunner' is normally used to describe the role of one individual who has the overall responsibility for a show. In a recent competency analysis of showrunners, a showrunner is defined as 'the chief custodian of the creative vision of a television series. The showrunner's primary responsibility is to communicate the creative vision of that series – often from pilot episode through to finale' (CHRC 2009, 4). The report concludes that typically showrunners are 'successful TV writers who have risen through the ranks, gaining the necessary skills in production' needed to be in charge of television series (2009, 4). 'How-to books' on television writing and production often define the showrunner as the executive producer (e.g. Sandler 2007) who 'defines the course of a show and supervises all aspects' (Douglas 2007, 255). Some describe this responsibility in more detail. When writing about how to produce one-hour drama series, Robert Del Valle thus stresses how the showrunner is 'the creative force behind a series': 'This is the writer/executive producer who created the series and who oversees the writing staff. He/she is also ultimately responsible for delivering the completed episodes to the studio and network within the required creative, budgetary, and scheduling parameters' (2008, 403). This definition regards the showrunner as the creator of the series and explicitly links the job of the showrunner to the writing staff as well as to many other responsibilities around production.

Alisa Perren has traced the use of the label showrunner back to the industry trade publication *Variety* in 1990, and it was first used in *The New York Times* in 1995 (2013, 1). However, she points to how the position rather than the label has a much longer history, highlighting how classic studies of the role of the producer (e.g. Cantor 1971; Newcomb and Alley 1983) have sometimes interpreted producers as exercising artistic agency within the industrial structures of television production (2013, 2). Perren refers to how 'an individual or team has assumed the showrunner's responsibility' related to what is described as the hiring, inspiring and firing of a series' staff and crew, dealing with network and studio executives, organizing the writing staff and fleshing out the long-term and episodic stories of a show (2013, 1–2). Perren suggests to think of showrunners as 'intermediaries', engaging with a wide variety of professions during the course of making and marketing a series (2013, 4). This intermediary function can have wide-ranging implications, as discussed in the work of Denise Mann in relation to showrunners for major shows like *Lost* (ABC 2004–2010). She finds, that in 'today's blockbuster-style television production circumstances' in the US, the showrunner is not only in charge of running the writers' room but also in charge of managing a series as a multi-platform transmedia franchise (2009, 100). She mentions one insider talking about a shift away from the single showrunner to 'a six-pack of executive producers', and constructively discusses how allocating authorship is difficult with the many different 'authors' involved on a show like *Lost* (2009, 100). In a similar vein, Alisa Perren has provided examples of the concrete work experiences of showrunners through conversations on creativity in the contemporary cable industry (2011), opening for fruitful discussions about the nature of production and for more scholarly debates of for instance individual vs collective authorship.

The use of the term 'showrunner' in relation to writers, producers or creators is not common in the European television industry, but the term is gaining more ground. Christine Cornea has discussed the gradual introduction of the term in the UK in relation to series like *Doctor Who* (BBC 2005–), where she regards 'the assigning of an

American-style showrunner role to Russell T. Davies' as a 'signifier of the BBC's intended "quality" status for the series' (2009, 116). Since then, successful US showrunners have been imported for major European productions like *Borgia* (Canal Plus 2011–, Tom Fontana) or *Hunted* (BBC 2012–, Frank Spotnitz). However, as remarked by Frank Spotnitz when telling the German television industry about working as a US showrunner in Europe, the idea of having a showrunner mostly makes sense when one has many hours of fiction to produce (Redvall 2012a, 16). Often the rather small-scale production in many European countries makes the need for a showrunner to be in creative control of the entire production obsolete. The European way of producing drama series has traditionally been based on an individual writer working on his/her own with script editors commenting later in the process rather than having writers' rooms creating material during production under the supervision of a showrunner.

As argued by social anthropologist Georgina Born when discussing the idea of the 'single authorial voice' in her study of the BBC (2005, 235), there has, for instance, been a widespread scepticism towards team writing in the UK (2005, 237). The lack of team writing has also been brought up by industry analysts, complaining about the marginalization of European screenwriters in the wake of the auteur theory (Finney 1996). This seems to be gradually changing in some European production cultures, and at least in the Danish framework a collaborative structure of a head writer working with several episode writers on high-profile television drama was introduced in the mid 1990s when decisions were made to focus on one-hour character-driven drama series based on original content and driven by one writer's vision.

According to the institutional narrative of DR Fiction, one vision refers to singling out the writer as the most important person in the process based on the intention to build on his or her original idea and granting him or her creative control all the way through production. Speaking about directors in filmmaking, Thomas Schatz has argued that one can only talk about authorial designation, if one person has been actively involved from the writing all the way to post-production and has thus had creative control over a film from start to finish (2009, 50). This element of control has been fiercely debated in discussions of cinematic authorship with the concept of 'sufficient control' emerging as one of the more constructive ways to think of the relationship between different contributions (e.g. Perkins 1972; Livingston 2009; Gaut 2010). As argued by Gaut, 'the sufficient control strategy' does not mean that an artist needs to be 'someone who has total control, but merely sufficient control over the artwork. Sufficient control displays itself not just by the artist's direct personal input into his work, but also in the fact that he uses others' talents, absorbing them into his own work' (2010, 112). This understanding of cinematic authorship opens for acknowledging the value of contributions by collaborators while still attributing singular authorship to the director who 'controls a film not just by what he himself invents, but also by what he allows actors, cameramen and others to do' (2010, 112). In this way, as pointed out by Livingston, productions can be collectively produced without having been collaboratively or jointly authored (2009, 72–6).

Analyses of cinematic authorship can get into quite theoretical and philosophical discussions of intentions, agency and control both with regard to art house directors, such as Ingmar Bergman (Livingston 2009), or the possibility of single authorship in mainstream films (Gaut 2010). In this context, it suffices to highlight the relevance of thinking about concepts such as 'sufficient control' in terms of the collaborative writing process of television and the idea of one vision. Not only for more theoretical or analytical purposes focusing on tracing lines between works or arguing in favour of one specific author with a special agenda for a work. In the world of screenwriting and production, it is also a pragmatic matter of credits and pay related to questions of who can be said to have influenced a product to what extent.

When analysing issues of control and creative visions, an obvious question is of course how to gain knowledge about these issues on specific productions. Robert Carringer has argued in favour of grounding authorship discussions in collaboration analysis, consisting of two stages. In the first stage, one temporarily suspends the usual focus on individual authorship, while researching the constitutive elements behind the creation of a new work. In the second stage, 'the primary author is reinscribed within what is now established as an institutional context of authorship' (2001, 377). According to Carringer, this allows for a more nuanced understanding of authorship at stake than automatically granting one person a privileged position in the process. Paisley Livingston has outlined different ideas of joint authorship, focusing on whether there is equal footing and a sense of shared responsibility along the way (2009, 73). Both Carringer's and Livingston's approaches to understanding authorship call for concrete knowledge about the actual production processes, and this is what has always complicated discussions of film and media works. Case studies are needed if one wants to say something more specific about the authorship of an individual product. The same goes for theories like Vera John-Steiner's ideas of creative collaborations and thought communities (2000). Empirical data needs to shed light on the nature of the creative collaborations and the ways in which new ideas and products emerge.

In relation to series from DR, an interesting aspect in terms of authorship and one vision is the relation between the head writer and producer in the process. Television has traditionally been regarded as the producer's medium (e.g. Newcomb and Alley 1983) and film as the director's medium, even though Hollywood studio productions have also been discussed as works where producers should be included in understandings of authorship (Schatz 1996). From a screenwriting perspective, it seems fruitful to ask where a writer with one vision fits into these understandings. The concept of one vision puts the emphasis on the writer, but the first production dogma from DR Fiction also underlines the importance of writers drawing on the expertise within the department, where producers are the ones who are steadily employed. When focusing on one vision it is thus relevant to take a closer look at how writers experience the concept of one vision and the nature of their collaboration with producers as well as with directors and actors. Some producers have discussed the DR framework as more of a 'twin vision' based on a close collaboration between a writer and a producer all the way through production (e.g. Clausen 2010). This interpretation of the vision or control behind a project mirrors the writer/producer role of the showrunner to a greater degree. The following analysis intends to get behind the official narrative of the one vision concept through exploring how it is implemented and interpreted before comparing it to the influential concept of the showrunner in US television.

Establishing the concept of one vision

As discussed in the previous chapter, brothers Stig and Peter Thorsboe were among the first educated screenwriters from the National Film School of Denmark (NFSD) to take an interest in television, and they have focused almost exclusively on television throughout their careers. Their highly popular series have had a major impact on changing the audience conception of Danish television drama. In combination with the high viewing figures for their series, their international awards have helped legitimize the existence of in-house production at DR, and now established head writers, like Adam Price and Søren Sveistrup, gained their early writing experiences as episode writers on their series.

After graduating from the NFSD, Stig and Peter Thorsboe were hired to be 'the playmates', as they both put it, of the legendary writer/director team Henning Bahs and Erik Balling at the production company Nordisk Film. Stig Thorsboe regards this experience as incredibly formative since they learned from the beginning to 'rewrite, rewrite and rewrite. The attitude was that one was not at all a world champion. It was just a matter of getting started and then of writing things over and over again' (Thorsboe 2012). In his opinion, many writers coming from a film school training lack this kind of industry attitude, and this caused problems in the first more organized attempt to create a system of using episode writers with him as the head writer. After creating the series *Landsbyen*/'The Village' (1991–1996) together with his brother for TV 2, the series was bought by DR and then continued as an in-house DR production. From episode 19, episode writers were introduced. Stig Thorsboe found that it took too much time to make the new writers find the right direction of the material, and that they were not used to rewriting or to having their material rewritten by others. He describes how they had a different 'culture' where it hurt to have their material changed, which he perfectly understands, but it did not work as a process with him in charge (Thorsboe 2012).

The description points to the fact that the two-year screenwriting education at the film school leaves little time for learning the process of rewriting. Screenwriter Rasmus Heisterberg is among the alumni who has criticized the length of the education, since he finds that students don't have the time to move beyond the joyful process of creating the first draft to the highly demanding process of reading it critically and tearing it all apart, 'where you keep going at it until you find the right solutions' (in Redvall 2010a, 93). Good writing has often been said to be rewriting, and Heisterberg argues that this also takes learning. Moreover, it takes a certain mentality to enter the vision of somebody else's work. The TV term has helped raise awareness about these kinds of processes among alumni in recent years, but it can still be a shock to move from a film school to an industry context.

According to Stig Thorsboe the idea of having a head writer was established with *Taxa* (1997–1999). The production was built around the concept of using episode writers, among them Adam Price and Søren Sveistrup, and the series ended up as 56 episodes. Thorsboe describes the series as character-driven but fundamentally case-based with a main conflict resolved in each episode, which he believes to be the best for delegating writing responsibility; it is harder to have several writers on series where minor psychological twists over time are as important as plot turns, as he finds it to be the case in the family series *Better Times*

(2004–2007) telling the personal stories of several characters through 25 years of history.

Thorsboe was not pleased with the head writer/episode writers structure of *Taxa*. He does not criticize the quality of the writers involved, but points to more structural elements like the clash of different work cultures with new writers not being used to the process. Several episode writers wanted to take the material in different directions, making the job of head writer a challenging task. His brother Peter Thorsboe and his co-writer Mai Brostrøm point to similar problems, when Peter Thorsboe was the head writer of the crime series *Unit One* (2000–2004), the next major series following *Taxa*. Brostrøm was attached as episode writer and describes how it is natural for a new writer on a series to arrive with an eagerness to make a difference. She finds the challenge of working with several writers to be that all creative people get a lot of good ideas; the complicated task is to make them go in the same direction. It takes time and skill for new episode writers to be able to catch the continuity and the characters of a series. In the first attempts of using this structure, there was little understanding of the specific demands of this process and how it takes time to 'learn the language' of a series. According to her, the lack of tradition for the new model led to exhausting, artistic fights (Brostrøm 2012).

Being a head writer calls for the ability to guide the other writers, and Stig and Peter Thorsboe do not exclude the possibility that they might not be the best people for that part of the job (Peter Thorsboe 2012; Stig Thorsboe 2012). Their descriptions of the challenges related to implementing a new framework for writing and producing series like *Taxa* and *Unit One* not only point to complications related to writers not being used to working with the others' material but also to complications related to the task of a writer suddenly having to take on the responsibility as work leader. These roles can be hard for all involved, and Stig and Peter Thorsboe's recollections of their early experiences illustrate how many elements in the collaborative framework had to find their form when new ideas of production were introduced.

Another challenge was to make directors understand that the writer was in charge. Stig Thorsboe is grateful for producer Sven Clausen taking responsibility for many of the demanding discussions with directors in this regard, thereby protecting him as the writer (Thorsboe 2012). For Peter Thorsboe, one of the virtues of the concept of one vision is that it clearly places the responsibility for a series with the writer. The introduction of the concept has thus been helpful in signalling to directors that the production processes at DR were different from those known from the film industry and that directors would have to be able to accept the fact that the writers were in charge (Thorsboe 2012).

After the experiences on *Taxa* and *Unit One* both Stig and Peter Thorsboe have written their subsequent series from their homes with their spouses Hanna Lundblad and Mai Brostrøm as co-writers. They have meetings at DR and after the shoot they spend time in the editing rooms to ensure that what can be regarded as the last rewriting of the material is still based on their vision in the final cut. Looking back at his work with the series *Unit One*, *The Eagle* (2004–2006) and *The Protectors* (2008–2010), Peter Thorsboe finds that it has been a continuous process marked by 'complete artistic freedom' (Thorsboe 2012). Mai Brostrøm describes how one vision is based on giving writers the freedom to go with their ideas and desires. However, this freedom comes with the big responsibility of being the one in charge (Brostrøm 2012).

To try to maintain a clear sense of direction, a substantial amount of time is normally invested in the development of series and the creation of a 'concept paper' with a clear premise and descriptions of the core of the series, similar to what is often called 'the bible' on American series. Stig and Peter Thorsboe have been continuously employed on freelance contracts since *Taxa* and *Unit One*, also to come up with new ideas in between the making of series. They can be regarded as what the DR Fiction production dogmas refer to as 'in-house screenwriters' even if they are normally not referred to in this way. However, as part of what can be regarded as the generational shift at DR in the 2010s, they are now developing series for other broadcasters.[1] The most productive and prolific writers of the DR framework in the 2000s have thus left the scene to new names, who have trained on their series and later created new productions with what has turned out to be not only a national but also an international appeal (Figure 5.2).

Training for the job in a one vision framework

Whereas Stig and Peter Thorsboe are the first examples of writers taking on the role of running productions with several writers attached, later DR head writers like Adam Price and Søren Sveistrup have grown up within this production model moving from episode writers to the role of head writers.

Adam Price is a self-taught screenwriter who was part of the first attempt to develop *Taxa* and later attached as episode writer. He came up with the idea for the series *Nikolaj and Julie* (2002–2003) before

Figure 5.2 After the success of *Rejseholdet/Unit One* (2000–2004), Peter Thorsboe and Mai Brostrøm created 'the crime odyssey' *Ørnen/The Eagle* (2004–2006) with the Icelandic policeman Ørnen (Jens Albinus) solving international crime. Photo by Ulla Voigt. Courtesy of DR

becoming head of TV 2 drama 2001–2005, where he later resigned to be the head writer of the TV 2 cop series *Anna Pihl* (2006–2008). Following this, he returned to DR where he developed his original idea for *Borgen*. In 2013, following the last season of *Borgen*, he was hired to develop a new series for DR with questions about religion at the core, while also working on a series with *House of Cards*-writer Michael Dobbs for the BBC.

Søren Sveistrup graduated from the screenwriting department of the NFSD in 1997. He was also an episode writer on *Taxa* and after writing episodes of *Hotellet/At the Faber* (2000–2002) for TV 2 he returned to DR as the head writer of *Nikolaj and Julie*, which won an Emmy in 2003. He then created *The Killing*. Following its third season in 2012, DR gave him a paid sabbatical to think about what he might like to make for television in the future. In 2013, Head of Drama Piv Bernth mentioned Sveistrup as the writer asked by DR to think about a series for a possible collaboration with HBO (Bernth in Thorsen 2013).

Adam Price works with a writers' room in the DR context and is generally regarded as a writer with a great openness to the input of others in the process. Price argues that the concept of one vision is crucial to keep series consistent and that the philosophy of putting one man in charge does lead to series mirroring the mindset of the head writer (Price 2012). However, he highlights continuous dialogue with several collaborators as the most important element in his work process. This dialogue is not only the one taking place in the writers' room but also the one with his regular producer Camilla Hammerich as well as the episode directors and actors on the series. Price is known to invite comments and argues that the artistic nerve of series like *Borgen* has to be shaped and refined through arguments and dialogue. He compares the process of having one vision to fencing. You have to hold on to your vision, but you have to allow for input and improvisation: 'If you hold too tight onto the foil you'll never be an accomplished fencer; your movements will be too stiff. It's the same as with dancing. You need a certain amount of structure but also the ability to improvise and follow the music' (Price 2012). As will be discussed Chapter 6 on the writers' room for *Borgen*, Price has given a lot of room – and credit – to his co-writers Jeppe Gjervig Gram and Tobias Lindholm, but no one challenges the fact that the series is based on his original idea and that he has been able to make the final choices for how to create an appealing drama, which might make people more interested in politics. When foreign journalists have asked Price about the reasons behind the recent success of DR series, he has stated that DR understands the necessity of artistic freedom (in Gilbert 2012) and thus supports the statements by Peter Thorsboe about writers having creative control of their vision for new series.

Søren Sveistrup has described how it took a while to get used to being the 'subcontractor' of a head writer when he was hired as episode writer for *Taxa* straight after film school. He didn't like having his material rewritten, but he appreciated how he got a lot of experience in a short time span (Sveistrup in Nordstrøm 2004, 98). Moreover, he discovered the relief in entering a work situation with the acceptance that someone else is in charge. Thorsboe was the one with 'the sleepless nights', and in Sveistrup's opinion starting as an episode writer seems like the right way to learn how to write for television rather than beginning a career with the full responsibility for a series (2004, 98). Sveistrup first worked as head writer on the series *At the Faber*, which – inspired by *Taxa* – was the first attempt to produce a long-running series for TV 2. He was part of developing the series, which was made by the production company Jarowskij. The production called for a remarkably different speed and price of production than at DR with 40 episodes written a year. According to Sveistrup this left little time for rewriting, and with a limited budget the strategy of production was more like a soap opera than a drama series with for instance few opportunities for shooting on location. Sveistrup has described the experience as frustrating and educational, stating that he learned how quality is expensive and also that one person needs to be in charge, which was not the case with *At the Faber* (2004, 99).

Sveistrup believes one vision to be the most attractive mode of production for writers since it offers the opportunity to write a scene at three stages in the process; in the script, on the set in collaboration with the director and the actors and, finally, in the editing. One vision is to be part of the whole process, not just the writing. After *Nikolaj and Julie*, which was co-written by several episode writers, Sveistrup wanted to refine his work process when developing a new series by only having two other writers involved. This was based on a feeling of being more sure of what he was aiming for and only wanting to work with writers with whom he could stand being in a room for the often long and stressful process of writing a series. He describes the making of *The Killing* as maybe taking the concept of one vision to the extreme, since he was involved in all decisions. This led to confrontations with both executives, actors and crew members, but he finds that one vision comes with the duty of taking full responsibility and being involved in all aspects of a series. In this regard, he defines the concept of one vision as a complete trust in the writer, when making decisions about things as different as the visual look, production design or sound (Sveistrup 2012). However, similar to Adam Price, he works with episode writers and is open to input from directors and actors. He regards the script as a working paper, which is open to changes up to the very last minute. As will be discussed in Chapter 7, this has occasionally put the production of *The Killing* under a lot of pressure, but in his opinion this needs to be the case when trying to create the best series possible.

Price and Sveistrup can be regarded as the second generation of head writers working in the production model established from the late 1990s with the use of what Chapter 4 described as relay production and episode writers for drama series, and with a more established notion of one vision to support the writers during the different stages of writing and production. Both writers have had a steady collaboration with a producer for several years, Camilla Hammerich and Piv Bernth respectively, whom they highlight as important to their work. Moreover, Sveistrup has had a regular collaborator in actress Sofie Gråbøl who played one of the leads in *Nikolaj and Julie* before becoming Sarah Lund in *The Killing*. The two writers created their series *Borgen* and *The Killing* for a domestic market, and the impact of their somewhat surprising international

success since the 2010s can be regarded as challenging the current production framework by having created a whole new set of expectations
for the succeeding head writers.

Working within an established framework

From a Screen Idea System perspective, it is remarkable how all head
writers behind new series at DR, with the exception of Adam Price, have
trained at the Film School and then risen through the ranks within DR
Fiction since the 2000s. The writers have intimate knowledge of the
mode of production as well as of the fundamental expectations to a
series with a public service mandate. One can argue that being at DR,
it is easier to get a sense of what kind of series executives are looking for and that the network for proposing ideas to the right people is
in place. However, the fundamental principle behind the commissioning of new series seems to be based on going with the desire of writers
rather than using their presence in the system to make them go in a certain direction or repeat existing formulas. *The Legacy* by upcoming head
writer Maya Ilsøe is based on her idea for a character-driven family series
with a complicated inheritance discord as the motor. The series has
questions about differences between parents and children, between the
youth rebellion of 1968 and modern family patterns, at its core. Jeppe
Gjervig Gram's idea for the new series *Follow the Money* takes on the
financial world – and financial crime – with *The Wire* (HBO 2002–2008)
and its combination of looking at conflicts through the lens of several
arenas as a source of inspiration. Whereas these series can be regarded
as the continuation on the focus of original family and crime/thriller
series, they mark a generational shift and are examples of series coming from writers who have almost exclusively worked for DR Fiction
since graduating from Film School. Ilsøe as the writer of the popular
family advent calendar series *Absalons hemmelighed*/'Absalon's Secret'
(2006) and *Pagten*/'The Pact' (2009) and Gram as an episode writer of
Sommer/Summer (2008–2009) and *Borgen*.

　　The writers have high ambitions, and they are also keenly aware that
writing a Sunday series for the first time is a great responsibility in the
way that one has the opportunity to 'speak to the nation'. As Maya Ilsøe
has commented on the writing process: 'Sometimes when writing I tell
myself: You now have the right to or the room for speaking to a million
people for an hour. Is this really what you want to say?' (Ilsøe 2012) As a
head writer there is a sense of having the possibility to make a statement
and express something personal in the series format, which is exciting

and intriguing but can also be nerve-racking if all material is contin-uously measured against justifying its essence in an imagined dialogue with the large audience. The fact that the series from DR have moved on to the international scene has added yet another imaginary audience for the writers, and based on the success of previous series *The Legacy* was pre-sold to several countries before any material was produced. There is thus a pressure on writers to produce series with an appeal to the national mainstream audience, but even before their Danish premiere they are on their way out into the world.

In terms of 'growing up within the system', Jeppe Gjervig Gram has described how he spent the last season of *Borgen* 'training' for the job of head writer (Gram 2012). He made an agreement with Price that the intention was to learn as much about the head writer responsibilities as possible before starting up his own writers' room for the new series after *Borgen*. This can be regarded as a clear example of a family collabora-tion where participants help each other make transitions and explicitly share their knowledge with each other (John-Steiner 2000). Gram is very appreciative of the nature of this process and has a lot of respect for the role of head writer, which in his opinion demands extensive experience. Not only about the processes of writing and producing but also in terms of story material. As he argues, head writers need a big bank of ideas, which can be combined in new ways or reused to be able to produce material at the intended speed and constantly keep the flow in the writ-ers' room going. Like other episode writers of *Borgen,* he describes the process of writing the series as a very good experience and a concern about setting up a new room is whether the *Borgen* 'chemistry' can be reproduced (Gram 2012).

Whereas head writers like Adam Price and Søren Sveistrup were able to develop their series without much publicity or pre-sale activity on the side, the situation is now dramatically different for head writers with the new focus on series from DR and the generally increased interest in series and their writers on both a national and international level. These changes in the domain are not necessarily conducive for the creative process of developing and writing, as will be discussed in Chapter 7 on *The Killing.*

Directors as collaborators

While there were complications in introducing the head writer/episode writers structure, this structure now seems integrated in the production framework and the writer is acknowledged as the person with one vision for the production. This also goes for the credits for series. *The Killing* is thus presented as a thriller by Søren Sveistrup as the opening titles state. The head writers are clearly given personal, authorial designation, but all head writers at DR emphasize the importance of the collaborative effort in bringing their ideas to the screen. They do enjoy their position, but they are very aware that it means nothing without the right people to make the material come alive.

Peter and Stig Thorsboe describe only good collaborations with directors even if the early attitude of many of the first episode directors was that they only did television while waiting to make their next feature film. They find this to have changed and that directors have also gained a greater understanding of the totality of production over the years. Stig Thorsboe mentions how he experienced directors taking the material in strange directions, when the producer was on vacation and didn't keep track of what was happening (Thorsboe 2012). Producer Sven Clausen remembers early examples of directors appreciating the art of improvisation and creating scenes that felt true to the material on set, but did not work in the larger storyline of what was planned (Clausen 2010). Today, all writers highlight directors as crucial collaborators and they are normally reading and commenting on later drafts of the script, which allows for their comments to influence the text.

The conceptualizing directors naturally take on a special position when creating the visual style of a series, but all this happens in a constant dialogue with the writers, and the hiring of conceptualizing directors is related to what the writers envision for a series. In most production set-ups at DR, directors shoot two episodes before another director takes over. As previously discussed this is generally regarded as a productive and dynamic mode of production, but the structure calls for a clear communication of the basic ideas of a series and for directors being open to entering an existing framework.

Søren Kragh-Jacobsen directed episodes of *The Eagle* and *The Protectors* and was the conceptualizing director of *Borgen*. In his opinion, the power of the writers at DR Fiction is absolute (Kragh-Jacobsen 2012, 6). Kragh-Jacobsen finds that there is a great difference between the role as episode director and conceptualizing director, comparing the latter to the role of the director in feature filmmaking – however, that is only the case until the launch of the series where he describes the strange feeling of no one being interested in the opinion of the director, since the writer is the star. At that point, the director loses the sense of ownership when the train moves on without him or her (2012, 9). Whereas conceptualizing directors have a substantial impact on defining the style of a series

and episode directors get to bring their expertise to part of the relay production, the writers are involved from the beginning to the end of the
process and the people perceived as the authors in the public realm.

Few viewers are aware of who has directed what on a series and can
tell episodes apart based on their directors. In-house this is different:
writers see differences in the final look of episodes from different directors, both in terms of the acting and the visuals. To Price, it was essential
to find directors who wanted to 'respond' to the material of *Borgen*, but
he describes how this has sometimes created some 'artistic, storytelling
movements' in the whole. However, these have been 'within the concept' and he finds that such movements add to the dynamics of a series
without confusing the audience. In his opinion, an important part of
one vision is to constantly keep an eye on the continuity and consistency in this regard (Price 2012). This demands that head writers are not
only writing, but seeing the material through to the very end. When
production is up and running this is a time consuming task, since the
head writer is then writing new episodes while simultaneously being in
pre-production, production and post-production with others.

Actors as collaborators

Since *Taxa*, DR has developed a system of moving into production with
one to three finished episodes and then having the writers producing
the following episodes of what is normally a ten-episode season during
the shooting. This allows for the production to feed back into the writing process, but this is also why directors sometimes complain about
scripts arriving late, with the third season of *The Killing* being the latest
example of a production with a delayed hand over of final drafts and
many last-minute changes. This will be further discussed in Chapter 7
as an example of one vision relating to not only a writer having a certain
vision for a project but also a certain work method for how to make this
vision come alive.

Writers Stig Thorsboe and Hanna Lundblad describe writing during
production as putting rails in front of a fast moving steam train, and
the exhaustion following their writing of *Better Times* was enormous
(Thorsboe 2012; Lundblad 2012). All writers agree that this kind of writing process is stressful, but they also agree on many strong advantages
in this mode of production. Some writers, like Søren Sveistrup, need the
deadline of production to move from the initial stages of mess-finding
and idea-finding to the solutions, saying that things only start falling
into place when the day of production approaches (Sveistrup 2012).

Mai Brostrøm finds that the speed needed creates a good work ethic and enjoys how the material 'starts to grow' during production (Brostrøm 2012). Peter Thorsboe highlights the energy coming from the production apparatus and how it adds colour to the text (Thorsboe 2012). There are many gifts coming from suddenly having a cast and locations to write for and seeing certain characters or relations develop in an unexpected way. Moreover, one can more easily deal with unexpected events, such as when main actor Jens Albinus broke his leg right before the shooting of *The Eagle* and the writers then had to deal with that (Thorsboe 2012; Brostrøm 2012).

All writers include the actors in their work process to some extent. Stig Thorsboe and Hanna Lundblad mostly invite comments in relation to the reading of the script for an individual episode where all actors are present. They describe how they are probably the writers at DR who keep their scripts the most to themselves. They listen to the opinion of the director and actors, but they rarely make major changes, since they have already been over the material many times and have settled on their perceptions of the best solutions. After a meeting with the director, they expect the text to be shot as it appears on the page, and actors are not supposed to come up with new lines on the set. If they want to say something differently, they have to call the writers (Thorsboe 2012; Lundblad 2012). This approach gives priority to the text on the page. Scripts are often discussed as more or less finished blueprints for production (e.g. Staiger 2012). In the work process of Thorsboe and Lundblad, the text appear to be regarded as a rather finished recipe for production with the conceptual stages of the script primarily situated in the work of the writers before production starts.

Other head writers appear to have a more open approach to the nature of the script, partly based on a desire to have actors read early drafts and comment, in some cases also during production. As an example, Søren Sveistrup allows actors to come up with last-minute changes. According to him, *The Killing* was marked by lead actress Sofie Gråbøl being able to suggest changes up until the shooting of scenes (Sveistrup 2012). Sveistrup describes himself as a great believer in what he calls the 'dialectics with actors' based on an understanding of the head writer as the conductor of a big orchestra. As he says: 'If I am to create the best series possible, then I have to continuously have actors who are attentive and awake. They need to come with their sense of mistakes to me, so that I can deal with them, otherwise I don't stand a chance. They have to pay attention to their field, so that I can focus on mine and bring their work into my work' (Sveistrup 2012). Sveistrup describes Gråbøl as having many good suggestions and also being a good dramaturge. He is highly appreciative of her input on *The Killing* and he wants actors to be critical and come up with new ideas. This does not mean that all their ideas come through, but the dialogue always leads to good discussions and a better sense of a character and what to look for. In his opinion, *The Killing* was a good process in this regard, even if it was maybe hard on some actors who were not used to this way of working and might have preferred to just get some lines (Sveistrup 2012).

The writing during production can create peculiar situations for the actors, as was the case with the third season of *The Killing* where the actor playing the killer had no idea that he was the perpetrator until the reading of the script giving that information away.[2] A challenge on the first season of *The Killing* was to have actors present in 20 episodes before there would be some sort of conclusion to their character, and Sveistrup describes how the first season had a number of angry meetings with people walking out. Whereas the head writer might decide to invite certain actors to collaborate, others can thus be kept in the dark regarding certain aspects of the story. This is the call of the head writer who in this way distributes his overall vision to a greater or lesser extent, depending on what he finds to be the right creative choices. To people who are not part of the circle of insiders, like the actor from the reading, this seems to sometimes create the feeling of being played rather than of being able to contribute, and important questions are thus who are invited to be part of the creative decisions influencing the text and who are regarded as merely executing the material from the writing process.

As observed during the writing process of *The Legacy* and *Borgen*, one vision also comes with the head writer having to deal with an enormous amount of decisions and communication. On *The Legacy*, first time Sunday series writer Maya Ilsøe thus describes how she gradually learned to protect herself more in the process and to create stricter rules for feedback, notes and meetings to not drown in the work load (Ilsøe 2012). Part of this protective strategy was to set up individual meetings with actors following the reading of each episode. This created a room for a thorough discussion of the actors' perceptions of scenes, dialogue or character motivations, but as Ilsøe explains the aim was also to limit the input to that particular space rather than receiving notes or comments at other times (Ilsøe 2012). Writing the series during production Ilsøe found great value in the feedback from actors, not only on the specific text but also through improvisations around the text. The conceptualizing director of *The Legacy*, Pernilla August, worked with 'leading in' to the shoot by improvising around the script. According to Ilsøe, this

Figure 5.3 The three siblings Frederik, Emil and Gro Grønnegaard (Carsten Bjørnlund, Mikkel Boe Følsgaard and Trine Dyrholm) in DR's new Sunday night drama series *Arvingerne/The Legacy* (forthcoming 2014) by Maya Ilsøe. Photo by Martin Lehmann. Courtesy of DR

resulted in several inspiring ideas, moments and lines for the future writing process. These kinds of improvisations can be regarded as a playful example of allowing others to imagine potential scenes, lines or developments for the inspiration of future material rather than always focusing on more analytical discussions of the explicit text (Figure 5.3).

Observations during the development and writing of *The Legacy* clearly pointed to writers having to think carefully about the degree of openness to their work process, since the concept of one vision in the DR Fiction framework seemed to be accompanied with the inherent danger of being overwhelmed by the opinions and input of others. While the third season of *Borgen* had an established structure for note meetings and feedback, both working with a new producer and establishing a writers' room for the first time on *The Legacy* led to numerous challenges for head writer Maya Ilsøe in terms of when to stop discussions around the material. Moreover, the hiring of famous and experienced talent, such as actor/director Pernilla August as the conceptualizing director and Trine Dyrholm as one of the main actors, led to Ilsøe having to struggle to hold on to her vision (Ilsøe 2012; Rank 2012). Maya Ilsøe and producer Christian Rank both point to part of the development stages being marked by their limited experience as to the production of a high-profile series, yet both agree that they managed to get things on track when they clarified how Ilsøe needed to be the person in creative control and how they had to trust each other even when others were maybe doubtful of their creative decisions; according to them, a lesson learned was that this kind of high-profile production is not possible without a complete trust between writer and producer (Ilsøe 2012; Rank 2012).

Peter Thorsboe and Mai Brostrøm argue that you have to listen to the opinion of the actors since they are in the front line. Being the face of a series for a long time is a hard job and they put themselves on the line. Over time a symbiosis between actor and role emerges, which can be inspiring for writers. Thorsboe and Brostrøm describe how this might not always be a face-to-face dialogue between writers and actors. It might also be that as writers they see something in the editing room, which brings a new element to a character that they hadn't thought about. They argue that one has to be very open to what can be learned in the collaboration with actors and describe the frustration of writing a new series for the German market where all material had to be finished before the shooting, leaving no possibility for having the direct or indirect input of actors influence the writing (Thorsboe 2012; Brostrøm 2012) .

In terms of *Borgen*, Adam Price argues that a close collaboration with actors can also allow for writing more edgy material, since you know the strengths of the actors and what they are capable of. He argues that the emotional spine of *Borgen* is in the eyes of Sidse Babett Knudsen, in the voice of Birgitte Hjort Sørensen and in the movements of Pilou Asbæk (Price 2012). Actors are at their best when they have the impression that their thoughts matter and when they feel that they can defend the actions of their characters. The dialogue with actors allows for creation of more risky scenes, and Price argues that the writing of *Borgen* gained a lot from the input from the actors, which helped getting a sense of where the material could be taken even further than what was put down on paper in the first place (Price 2012).

The examples in the above illustrate how the framework for writing and production at DR Fiction is built around letting the on-going production influence and improve the writing process. The two stages of conception and execution are thus partially blending together, leaving room for the production processes to feed back into not only future episodes but also the episodes at hand. This way of working calls for writers being able to deal with large amounts of input and demands a specific speed of production, sometimes making directors and the crew frustrated by the late delivery of scripts complicating their work. In spite of the stressful processes often related to this structure, most writers and producers regard this as the best way of producing series with the text as a blueprint for collaboration rather than a recipe, which should be meticulously executed. However, this way of working also calls for someone having a sense of the totality of not only the content of an individual episode, but of the back story and future of characters or the content of the entire season, pointing to the value of having a head writer with the overall vision in charge.

The elements of time and trust

Most writers agree that once production starts the high-speed process can work only if one has spent sufficient time developing a series in great detail before moving on to the actual writing of episodes. The series from DR are based on original ideas by writers, but – as with the early stages of most ideas – these are from the outset often based on a desire to explore a topic, a setting or a theme rather than a fully fleshed, pitch-perfect story, which just needs to be put down on paper. Several writers tell of being hired for more than a year trying to crystallize and improve these ideas, drawing on a number of people as collaborators. The writers place great emphasis on this way of being allowed to spend time in the initial stages of what in the language of Creative Problem Solving (CPS) would be called the mess-, data- and problem-finding, before settling on a problem statement, which can then be further developed in the idea finding stages (Isaksen and Treffinger 2004, 14). Thinking about screenwriting, one can see the research and development stages as the initial stages in the model of CPS, when different pitches and premises, characters, themes and arenas are tested, before deciding to pursue a certain direction, which can then be more explicitly described in outlines, treatments and drafts.

Most writers describe having spent substantial amounts of time on the pay roll at DR developing the conceptual basis for a series before moving on to the actual writing of drafts. Stig Thorsboe and Hanna Lundblad spent at least a year developing *Better Times* and *Happy Life* to the point where a first episode could be written. Once production started, they had six to eight weeks to write an episode (Thorsboe 2012; Lundblad 2012). Søren Sveistrup developed *The Killing* together with two writers for more than a year before the writing started. During development, an original idea can move through major changes. As described in Chapter 7, the idea for *The Killing* grew from a shorter series to the 20-episode drama and changed its setting from a small town province to a series having Copenhagen as the arena. The three writers researched several real life murder investigations before settling on what kind of case to have at the centre of the story and on the story as partly being about reconstructing the night of a teenage girl victim. The writers regard this time to thoroughly explore an idea and carefully consider its main premise and dramatic motor as crucial for later being able to write episodes at a certain speed.

All television series move through stages of researching and refining an idea, but there are huge differences in the amount of time allocated to this process – and in the amount of money invested in this. Most writers at DR seem to find that they are given the time needed to create a solid basis for a project before the writing starts, and the concept of giving writers sabbaticals while thinking about future ideas is, of course, much appreciated by the ones who have been given this opportunity to explore different strands of ideas (e.g. Peter Thorsboe 2012; Brostrøm 2012; Ilsøe 2012; Sveistrup 2012). Writing a television series is a long-term commitment and having highly motivated writers feeling that they are given the room to go where their desires take them does not seem like a bad investment. This does not imply that ideas are not challenged along the way. They are later analysed and discussed and have to meet the logistics and economics of production, but several writers describe being asked what they would like to do next time around following the run of a successful series. Series have thus been growing from the ground up following the problems of trying to make several writers work on the idea of an executive with *Taxa* (as described in Chapter 3).

Going with the interest of writers calls for a great amount of trust in their ability to come up with strong ideas and turn them into interesting television. Writing about how to facilitate creativity in organizations, Göran Ekvall has highlighted trust as one of the important elements in 'an organizational climate' (Ekvall 1996). Writers at DR all express a high degree of what I have elsewhere discussed as 'institutional trust' (Redvall 2012c). This trust is for instance exemplified by the DR producers and executives as the gatekeepers or experts in the field having an openness to long periods of mess-finding as well as for risk-taking rather than presenting a number of set criteria and deadlines for projects from the outset. Adam Price argues that the recent success of series from DR builds on the ability of DR Fiction to hand over the responsibility to the talent. He finds that the changing luck of other Danish broadcasters can possibly be explained by their not having the same faith in this sort of delegation of responsibility. In his opinion, one can't leave artistic decisions to focus groups and plenum discussions, since that blurs the dramatic core of a project (Price 2012).

In a similar vein, Søren Sveistrup states that he has been met with a 'limitless trust' by Head of Drama Ingolf Gabold. The attitude has been: 'If Søren believes in it, then I believe in it' (Sveistrup 2012). Developing *The Killing*, there were not '25 people on his shoulders' wanting to read or comment. Sveistrup describes this kind of trust as crucial and regards his time at DR Fiction as a period of talented executives with a trust in the writers, which is otherwise rare in the Danish film and television industry. He insists that DR Fiction deserves a lot of credit for adopting a wait-and-see attitude rather than letting the general nervousness related to expensive production mark projects at early stages in their development. According to Sveistrup, one of the things achieved by this strategy is that it creates a great sense of responsibility in writers wanting to prove worthy of the trust; something 'fantastic' happens when you have the sense of 'a freedom that comes with responsibility' (Sveistrup 2012). However, Sveistrup stresses that only more experienced talent with a certain track record is given this kind of trust, and even with more established names there is still a great element of risk. In the Screen Idea System framework for production, the training and track record of talent is of great importance, but so is the interplay of certain managerial ideas fitting the work processes of the talent. Sveistrup says that *The Killing* would never have happened if a number of people – among them his producer Piv Bernth and Ingolf Gabold – had not been willing to risk a lot by putting their faith in him (Sveistrup 2012).

Whereas the institutional trust in writers is regarded as important, trust is also needed between writers and producers in production. As discussed, most writer-producer collaborations at DR Fiction have lasted for a number of years, and the writers cherish these steady collaborations. As mentioned in relation to *The Legacy*, there can be many challenges in new writer-producer relationships as well as in many people on the same production taking on a specific professional role for the first time. New collaborations more easily lead to doubts about each other's competencies, which it is important to resolve before the production machine starts rolling at full speed.

The producer as part of a 'twin vision'?

All writers find that their producers are crucial to their work. For some, it is more about setting up the framework for production than about having them as part of the writing process. Stig Thorboe praises his producer Sven Clausen for his production skills, but he prefers not to have a producer involved in the writing process (Thorsboe 2012). Maya Ilsøe had her producer Christian Rank as a close collaborator in the development process on *The Legacy*, calling him when game-changing ideas emerged in screenwriting meetings and having him comment along the way. Adam Price and Søren Sveistrup both have their regular producer read drafts as they evolve from the early stages.

Most writers find that there is a clear division of roles between writers and producers. As Peter Thorsboe puts it: 'The producer is central to the process, but he doesn't write and the writers aren't producers' (Thorsboe 2012). While writing and production is closely linked, writers and producers have different responsibilities in the process. As an example, showrunners in the US production framework are not always present in the writers' room but rather make selections from the material emerging from the room. In the Danish framework, head writers working with a room will be present and part of the entire process, while producers are in charge of other aspects around production. However, several writers are open to including the producers in the overall vision for a project. Maya Ilsøe argues that the most important thing in a collaboration between a writer and a producer is a fundamental desire to work together on a specific story. The story builds on an original idea of the writer, but the producer needs to feel strongly for that idea to be able to protect it as it meets the many challenges of production. As a writer she needs to be certain that the producer is completely behind the core of the project (Ilsøe 2012).

Søren Sveistrup describes his collaboration with former producer and now Head of Drama Piv Bernth as vital to his work. He argues that writers need skilled producers to get projects off the ground, and these are not easy to come by. Sveistrup stresses the importance of finding a producer with a desire to tell his kind of stories and of feeling trusted. When making new series there will always be periods of doubt, and this is where the trust of the producer can be the safety net, which makes things hold together rather than fall apart (Sveistrup 2012). Stig Thorsboe and Hanna Lundblad also place great emphasis on the role of the producer, to the extent that they have proposed a series for another broadcaster after their former DR producer on *Happy Life*, Katrine Vogelsang, became Head of Drama at TV 2 in 2011. They argue that the collaborations on a project are crucial, and when you have found a good work relationship it is worthwhile pursuing even if it might be in a different production framework (Thorsboe 2012; Lundblad 2012).

Producer Sven Clausen suggests that the mode of production at DR might be better described as a 'twin vision' rather than a 'one vision' framework with the inclusion of the producer in the vision for a project (Clausen 2010). As previously discussed, television has traditionally been regarded as a producer's medium and the concept of one vision shifts the emphasis away from the producer. However, most producers are attached from the very idea for a series and are crucial for its development and survival in the system. All writers seem happy to give their producers a lot of credit, but the ideas for series come from writers and they are the ones regarded as making the creative choices. The vision of a project is thus grounded in the writer, but as discussed in the above there are many important collaborators in making that vision come alive, and projects would never see the light of day without in-house producers and a managerial set-up with the willingness to support and trust their vision.

Sven Clausen was part of introducing the concept of one vision, and one can argue that it might be hazardous to expand the now established concept to also include the producer, thereby challenging the basic notion of having projects with one clear voice behind them, which seems to be regarded as crucial in the DR framework. Outside DR Fiction, other executives are, however, similarly arguing for an expansion of the one vision-concept, like Co-Production Executive at SVT Drama Stefan Baron describing the 2013 strategy of the Swedish public service broadcaster in this way:

> We all think of the "one vision" but I would call it 'two visions'. The Scandinavian concept is to have a strong producer together with a strong writer or a couple of writers and then we bring in directors.
>
> (in Pham 2013)

Baron goes on to explain that the structures of having big teams around showrunners and the budgets of US series are hard to match, but that SVT works in similar ways to the US industry, just with much less money. SVT has undergone major changes in the 2010s, to a wide extent trying to mirror the production model and the emphasis on one-hour ten-episode drama series by DR (Bondebjerg and Redvall 2011, 104). One vision appears to be an integrated concept in the new structure, but as the quote shows, producers are officially presented as part of the vision in a comparison with the role of the showrunner.

The idea of a 'twin vision' or 'two visions' does in many ways mirror the role of the showrunner from the US television industry, but as outlined in the above there is a rather clear division of roles between the head writer and producer in the DR context and a general agreement that the writer is the one with the vision for the project at hand. Rumle Hammerich has argued that no one in the Danish industry has the extensive experience as both writer and producer to earn him- or herself the title of showrunner as known from the US context. However, one can to some extent think of the role as the showrunner as divided into the very stable writer-producer collaborations like Peter Thorsboe/Mai Brostrøm and Sven Clausen, Adam Price and Camilla Hammerich or Søren Sveistrup and Piv Bernth. In collaboration, they are the 'chief custodians' in terms of content and character as well as of a well-functioning mode of production. One can argue that the writer holds the creative vision, while the producer holds the production vision, which is necessary if the vision of the writer is to make it to the screen.

The production framework at DR when writing during production and working with a head writer/episode writers set-up shares many similarities with the US showrunner system, but the term 'showrunner' is not used to describe the role of the head writer at DR. Søren Sveistrup is the only writer interviewed for this study who mentions that the term might be the most appropriate for his work. Partly because he likes how the word 'showrunner' contains activity, while one vision sounds passive; someone sits around with a vision instead of being 'a one visioner'. The word 'showrunner' appeals with its sound of action (Sveistrup 2012).

Sveistrup is also the only writer talking about his series *The Killing* as 'a brand' where everything is interconnected, mirroring aspects of Denise Mann's thoughts on US showrunners as brand managers (Mann 2009). Recent writings on the auteur theory have discussed how the concept of the auteur can be instrumental in presenting directors as brands (Grainge 2007) and how to think of 'industrial auteur theory' in relation to television production (Caldwell 2008). In the DR context, the television writers cannot be regarded as star brands themselves, even if some writers – like Søren Sveistrup and Adam Price – are now famous among audiences, and new series from their hands will automatically receive a special interest in the national domain. However, while they might not be brand names in the auteur line of thinking, their series have become recognized brands, and somewhat curiously – as remarked in the review of *Borgen* from *The New York Times* quoted in the introduction for this book (Stanley 2012) – it is rather DR as the broadcaster than the creators of the series, which seems to have obtained a certain brand identity among international audiences as a provider of a special kind of quality drama series.

The analysis of the development of one vision within the DR framework points to the creation of series from DR sharing similarities in
terms of all writers experiencing a privileged position at the centre of
the process and a great degree of institutional trust. The structure of a
head writer working with episode writers is now firmly established and
writers decide the extent to which they want to involve a variety of
collaborators along the way. In terms of sufficient control, the processes
involve numerous people, but they are marked by the talent of contributors feeding into the overall vision of the writer. To audiences, the series
are presented as 'by' the head writer, and studying the processes these
writers do seem to be in control of the different contributions when
following the development of the text all the way to the editing room.
The next chapter explores one example of such a process through a case
study of the writers' room for *Borgen*.

6
The Workings of a Writers' Room: *Borgen*

Introduction

There is a limited tradition of working with writers' rooms on high-profile drama series in the European television industry. European writers are sometimes described as going from 'from shell to shell' (Redvall 2012a, 17), whereas the US system is built around rooms of several writers developing material together under the supervision of a showrunner. Part of the explanation for the structural differences is the fundamental need to have several writers attached in the US system where vast amounts of material has to be produced in a short period of time, when pilots for new shows are normally ordered in January and delivered at the end of April or beginning of May after which shows for the summer or autumn are ordered. By June a writers' room for a new show should be in place to start submitting storylines to the broadcaster and get notes. While there is no standardized season for pitching or production in most European contexts, US showrunner Frank Spotnitz has described the US system as moving 'pretty fast and orderly' (in Redvall 2012a, 30). At the European TV Drama Series Lab, Spotnitz addressed the challenges of establishing a writers' room when moving to the UK to develop the series *Hunted* for the BBC (2012–). According to him, the process was marked by the meeting of two very different production cultures: At the level of management, executives wanted a US showrunner without really knowing what this might imply, and at the level of writers, there were challenges in the UK writers not being used to working in a writers' room (in Redvall 2013, 12).

Some European countries use writers' rooms for long-running soaps or telenovelas, which call for a daily or weekly production of new material. DR does not produce series in these genres, but as described in the previous chapters, DR Fiction has been experimenting with different forms of the head writer/episode writers structure for drama series for a number of years.[1] The writers' rooms for these series have always been rather small. Whereas there are normally five to eight writers in US writers' rooms for major network or cable series (Redvall 2012a, 17; Phalen and Osselame 2012, 6), the structure for series like *Forbrydelsen/ The Killing* (2007–2012) or *Borgen* (2010–2013) is to have one head writer working in close collaboration with two episode writers. Several writers describe 'three as the magic number' in terms of getting the right synergy. Critical voices might object that a constellation of only three people is rather a writing team than a writers' room, when comparing with the size of rooms in US television, but this way of working is understood as a writers' room, or 'the storyline room', at DR Fiction and will be discussed as such in this context.

This chapter explores the workings of the *Borgen* writers' room when writing episode 25 for the series' third season during 2011–2012. The case study is based on observations in the writers' room during the two weeks of storylining in December 2011 and during later note meetings, until the reading of the script in the week before the shooting in June 2012.[2] The chapter offers a detailed analysis of the casting, the structure and the work process of the room and of the nature of the collaboration between the series' creator Adam Price and writers Jeppe Gjervig Gram and Maja Jul Larsen. The chapter discusses what can be regarded as the different roles in the room and how to understand the process as collaborative writing with one vision before proposing to think of writers' rooms as different forms of thought communities.

Researching writers' rooms

In the US, the tradition of working with team writing or writers' rooms goes back to the early years of broadcasting, particularly for sitcoms (Henderson 2011, 1; Caldwell 2008, 211). The collaborative writing process is sometimes called 'writing by committee' (Caldwell 2008, 211), and John Thornton Caldwell has discussed how this process is often regarded more as an industrial rather than an artistic process (2008, 201). He quotes one showrunner for comparing the writing of television to going into a museum and calling for some random paintings to be put on the blank walls, describing television as a space 'trying to be filled' rather than a space calling for artistic expression (2008, 202).

Caldwell's analysis of US writers' rooms points to the complicated nature of discussing authorship in relation to the collaborative processes, and his study does not paint a pretty picture of the state of US writers' rooms. He describes the early writing teams for sitcoms such as *The Dick van Dyke Show* (CBS 1961–1966) as populated by 'collegial, good-humored turn-takers', while the function of the writers' rooms of today are 'intense, strategic pressure points in the development of a television program' (2008, 211). Among his critical points on labour issues is how having no copyright to the material produced makes 'the actual writing of a film or a television show, at least in the legal sense, little more than work-for-hire day labor' (2008, 209). He explains how writers are expected to work 80-hour weeks and late nights if needed (2008, 215), and how some depictions of writers' rooms sound more like 'nonunion digital sweatshops of below-the-line workers' than upbeat above-the-line descriptions of the work conditions in the network era (2008, 214). Notes on the work coming out of the rooms are interpreted as ' "orders" from ostensible superiors to clients in the production chain' based on some 'implicit theory of the audience' (2008, 221). While there is some discussion of the potential creative benefits of brainstorming and developing ideas together, the overall impression of writers' rooms is a rather grim portrayal of a space marked by stress, anxiety and 'professional one-upmanship' (2008, 216). Other studies focusing particularly on the work of writers in Hollywood and on writers' rooms point to the potential dangers related to the casting and politics of the rooms, when analysing issues of gender, race or age (Bielby and Bielby 2001, 2002; Henderson 2011; Phalen and Osselame 2012).

As often highlighted by writers, the writers' room is a place where you cannot go unless you are invited. This is not only the case for researchers; the creator of *Dexter* (Showtime 2006–2013) James Manos Jr. stresses that writers' rooms are 'sacrosanct' and off limits to actors and executives (in Redvall 2012a, 14). The exclusivity of writers' rooms helps create an aura of mystery around them and few researchers have gotten access to actually studying the work in the room. Felicia Henderson describes her study of the work 'behind the closed doors' in writers' rooms as autoethnography with her in the role of a 'boundary-crosser' using her experience as an industry professional in her research (2011, 1). Several media industry or screenwriting scholars have a background of working in the industry and draw on their own experiences in their research. Practice-based research can offer many interesting perspectives, and industry knowledge and networking is useful for researchers in terms of getting access to the often well-guarded sites of production. However, there are still surprisingly few studies based on experiences or observations of the work processes in writers' rooms rather than on interviews.

One recent exception is Patricia Phalen and Julia Osselame's study of what they call 'rooms with a point of view' drawing on both a six-week observational study and interviews with television writers (2012). Opting for an exploratory approach to the work in the room, the study addresses several critical points raised by the writers related to, for instance, the hierarchical structure of the room or examples of sexual harassment, but it also has the writers characterize 'the good room', which is defined as being about having the right chemistry and a feeling of safety ensuring that people do not hold back ideas out of fear (2012, 10–11).

Other publications like Tom Stempel's *Storytellers to the Nation* (1996) have previously offered an 'insider's history' on the work of US television writers through numerous interviews, and more recently Lawrence Meyers (2010) has gathered established writers for roundtable conversations about various aspects of working in writers' rooms with the promise of providing practical advice for succeeding, but without further comments on the points emerging from the talks. Much can be learned from writers talking about their work, but the writers asked are normally the successful above-the-line stars rather than below-the-line writers who might have more sweatshop-like experiences as described in the work of Caldwell. Accordingly, when US showrunners described the work in writers' rooms at the European TV Drama Series Lab, they mostly focused on the many positive sides of their successful rooms, like the fun of developing ideas together, of being surprised by the ideas of others or of how there can be a constructive side to wanting to out-do others' ideas if this happens in a collaborative rather than competitive spirit (Redvall 2012a). However, they did not pretend that the hours are not long or that there are no conflicts between writers.

In her study of gender and race in US writers' rooms, Henderson stresses how her work in the industry has been marked by no experience ever being like any other, since 'every show's culture is unique' (Henderson 2011, 1). Similarly, showrunners often remark that all rooms are different and that all showrunners work in different ways (e.g. Spotnitz in Redvall 2012a, 17). It is worthwhile trying to understand the unique culture of a particular series, while also trying to synthesize and discuss more general points from the findings. This case study thus aims at a detailed description of one example of a collaborative writing process in the DR production framework, which is regarded as current best practice by both the writers involved and several people outside the room. The case study has been driven by questions related to under-standing how writers work together when developing and writing new episodes for a successful series; of how to understand the concept of one vision in relation to this; and of how the process relates to the practice of working with showrunners and writers' rooms in the US mode of production. The first part of the case study deals with the specific process of developing a concrete episode, while the second part analyses this process in relation to questions of the different roles in the room and to issues of achieving a process of collaborative writing with one vision.

Borgen backstory

Borgen is a series about political power play, dealing with the personal costs and consequences of the struggles of people at the centre of the political world in Denmark and of the media covering it. The first season, which was shown in Denmark in 2010, follows the rise to power of female politician Birgitte Nyborg (Sidse Babett Knudsen). The second season (2011) is about Nyborg's challenges as the first female prime minister of Denmark, while the third season (2013) is about her starting a new political party two and a half years after the election in which she failed to win the required number of seats to maintain the existing government.

Borgen was created by Adam Price, who had previously worked as episode writer for both TV 2 and DR. Coming off the police series *Anna Pihl* (2006–2008) for TV 2, he wanted to write material, which was driven by a tight plot without being a crime series. He was also interested in working with more challenging material, and as a fan of *The West Wing* (NBC 1999–2006) and a person with a keen interest in politics he came up with an idea for a series with politicians and the legislative work behind a democracy as the main arena (Price 2010). A successful series in the international domain was thus a major source of inspiration, and during talks in the writers' room and interviews people have continuously referred to international shows rather than other national or European series. These comparisons can be more fan-like comments, but also take on a more analytical form as illustrated by writer Jeppe Gjervig Gram comparing the number of beats in an episode of *The West Wing* with an episode of *Borgen* in order to explore the basic storytelling structures of the series (Gram 2012).[3] The focus on international series was not based on an ambition to create a worldwide success, but it is a sign of how the writers are inspired by quality product from abroad and want to bring aspects from their favourite series into the national domain.

The commissioning of *Borgen* points to the importance of 'double storytelling' within the DR production framework. When Price first suggested a series on the political life of Denmark to DR, this was regarded as a too elitist topic to gain the interest of the 1.3 million viewers, who are now expected for a successful Sunday night series. However, he stuck with the idea, and after having developed it further together with writers Jeppe Gjervig Gram and Tobias Lindholmd, he pitched it as a series with a female politician in charge and the premise 'Can you hold on to the power and still hold on to yourself?' in the spring of 2007. This take on the topic made DR decide to see whether a political series could maybe work (Gabold 2010). At the European TV Drama Series Lab, producer Sven Clausen highlighted *Borgen* as an example of series where commissioners took a chance on the material when being overwhelmed by the passion of the writer (in Redvall 2012a, 21). An effective verbal pitch to busy executives is given great importance in the US industry (Redvall 2012a), where some showrunners even argue that pitching is 'an art form' (James Manos Jr. in Redvall 2012a, 31). In the DR framework the verbal pitch to the broadcaster is also part of getting a greenlight (Figure 6.1).

Pitching skills are necessary for all creators of new series in the Scandinavian context, particularly since there is no system of agents pitching the projects of client writers to people of interest. Writers have to do this initial work, from informal 'elevator pitches' to pitches in regular meetings, on their own or in collaboration with their producer, which calls for the ability to clearly present an idea and its value in the right way. Some ideas will always be more easily pitched than others, but in the DR framework the broadcasting decision-makers will already have heard about projects from the in-house production unit DR Fiction, and DR Fiction can be regarded as the first gatekeeper in the process. Before pitching to the commissioning executives, a writer has to convince DR Fiction to support the early development of an idea.

In this case, Head of Drama Ingolf Gabold found that Price's particular approach to the material was interesting. Gabold describes how DR Fiction had previously considered making a political series, but regarded that the general 'dislike of politicians' among the population was too big for such a series to work (Gabold 2010). However, the *Borgen* angle convinced them that a series dealing with politics was possible, since the series was not aiming at 'pointing fingers at politicians or at political parties', but about making a series 'about the state of our democracy and

Figure 6.1 Jeppe Gjervig Gram and Adam Price storylining in the writers' room of *Borgen* in DR Byen. Photo by Peter Mydske. Courtesy of Polfoto

of its importance' (Gabold in Redvall 2010c). Gabold highlights *Borgen* as an obvious example of double storytelling with all the immediately exciting plots and conflicts that grow out of the political scene, allowing for both identification with the people fighting for their ideas and for a sense of fascination by getting to peek into the 'political workshop'; concurrently, the series has ethical and social connotations through discerning fundamental aspects of a democracy or of the Scandinavian welfare state, while also addressing the demanding job of being a professional politician and the sacrifices that have to be made in terms of family and privacy. Gabold finds that the series also contains 'a good, old-fashioned, healthy discourse of gender politics' by focusing on a female politician trying to combine having a husband and two children with a demanding career (in Redvall 2010c). DR Fiction thus found the idea for *Borgen* to be a good example of public service double storytelling, and the series has been accompanied by a number of web-based initiatives related to its more topical or educational aspects.[4]

However, the series has also stirred controversy by mirroring real life politics. Price has described his intention with *Borgen* as wanting to create an entertaining experience for people at home in their couches, but also to hopefully create content that might make people want to leave their comfortable couches and actively engage in the democratic processes of the public sphere (Price 2010). Even before airing, the series caused controversy since some politicians were convinced that the series would be a left-wing-biased portrait of the political life of Denmark (Redvall 2010d). Aspects of the series have continuously been debated in the public realm, not the least during the third season where episode 24 and 25 led to media debates about the episodes' depictions of the nature of pig breeding and whether to legalize or not to legalize prostitution, respectively. A social democratic politician filed an official complaint to DR about the 'glorifying' portrayal of prostitution in episode 25, and both episodes ignited discussions about the relationship between fiction and reality in the series and of whether the public service obligation of DR demands that fictional series offer nuanced portrayals of the topics covered.[5]

Borgen has thus played a part in the public realm as more than 'just' entertainment, but according to a survey done by researchers from the Copenhagen Business School, the series has not moved any votes (Jessen 2013). Whereas the impact on the national sphere was expected, the content of the series was considered to be too national to interest foreign audiences at the time of its 2010 premiere (Gabold 2010; Price 2010). This has proven not to be the case with the widespread acclaim for the series in, for instance, the UK and the US (e.g. Stanley 2012; Romano 2012).

The casting of the room

Borgen was developed in a close collaboration between Adam Price, producer Camilla Hammerich and writers Jeppe Gjervig Gram and Tobias Lindholm. Price and Hammerich had previously worked together for many years at TV 2, where he was Head of Drama, before leaving the position to Hammerich to become the head writer of *Anna Pihl*. Hammerich was later hired by DR to produce the series *Sommer/Summer* (2008) with the promise of subsequently getting to produce a new series of her own (Hammerich 2012). She wanted this to be a series by Price and found the idea for *Borgen* to be excellent for a new DR drama series. Hammerich describes *Borgen* as 'school TV in a dramatic form' with public service and quality as the first words that come to mind.

On *Summer*, Hammerich had worked with Gram and Lindholm, who had been hired straight after graduating from the National Film School of Denmark. They had also been promised the opportunity to develop a series of their own after finishing the second season of *Summer*, but when Hammerich asked them to be part of developing *Borgen*, they found the political and media arena so intriguing that they decided to take part. Gram describes how they made 'a musketeer oath' ('one for all, and all for one') with Price from the very beginning of the process defining that Price was the creator and head writer of the series, but that the writers' room needed to be 'democratic' in the way that all writers would have to agree on ideas before moving on. According to Gram, this has marked the work in the writers' room all the way, and at DR Fiction Lindholm and Gram are acknowledged as crucial to the making of *Borgen*.[6] The writing of *Borgen* has been based on a writers' room consisting of Price, Lindholm and Gram for the first two seasons. The writing of the third season was marked by Lindholm stepping out of the room to write and direct feature films, creating an opening for the writers Jannik Tai Mosholt, Maren Louise Käehne and Maja Jul Larsen, the writer of episode 25.

Casting a writers' room is often described as a complicated affair. When discussing the contribution of writers in relation to quality television series, Máire Messenger Davies has highlighted how an executive producer of a hit series explains that in spite of having access to top writers, it was a hard task to find the right voices for the material and only 1 in 20 writers would work in this regard (2007, 173). *Borgen* was marked by a steady collaboration during the first two seasons and is described as a good process by the three writers involved. Having to find new writers for the third season was thus related to some anxiety, particularly since all writers, similar to the points brought up by Phalen and Osselame (2012), comment that not only the right skills are needed for the job; finding the right writer is very much a question of getting the right 'chemistry' in the room. Vacancies in writers' rooms are not advertised. You have to know that they are there or be asked to apply. Larsen explains how she got the job by approaching Price through personal contacts before submitting episodes written by her for other series as examples of her work. Following a meeting she was hired to take part in the last weeks of talking about the major arcs for the season in the spring, before the storylining and writing of individual episodes started after the summer.[7] She found that her first writing on the series, of the second episode, was very much a test, but after that she was part of the team, and she was surprised how quickly she felt like an integrated part of the room.

Gram describes worries about whether the 'energy' of the room would change with the coming of new writers, but found that the new writers entered 'an existing factory'. The atmosphere changed slightly, but the existing sense of 'flow' continued and the new writers seemed to take ownership of the material in a positive way. Gram knew all the new writers hired for the third season in advance, since they were fellow alumni from the Film School, and the process of hiring seemed marked by drawing on personal networks. As Angela McRobbie has concluded when analysing work in the UK cultural economy, most work is marked by freelance contracts and what she terms 'portfolio careers' (2002, 111). Addressing the work of screenwriters in the UK industry specifically, Bridget Conor has stressed that the structure of the industry calls for much more than mere screenwriting skills. As she states, 'skills required to network, take meetings and pitch ideas have become central to everyday screenwriting careers' (2010, 32). At DR this also seems to be the case with not only a specific track record but also the network from the Screenwriting Department of the Film School as an important part of one's portfolio.

Since the general impression among writers is that you use your personality and real life experiences a lot in the room, you not only need qualified writers, but writers with a personality that fits in, and this is of course easier to assess if you know the person in advance. In this specific case, there were also considerations of the value of getting female writers in the room, since *Borgen* is perceived as a 'very female series' (Hammerich 2012). Hammerich finds that it was good to get women in the room, not the least for writing material such as episode 25 with discussions about prostitution at the core. However, observing the room there was surprisingly little talk of gender or comments related to the sex of individual writers, but all writers did comment at some point that it would probably be good for the reception of episode 25 that the episode writer was female and episodes were switched around to ensure this. The issue of gender seemed to be more about anticipating the public debate about a potentially controversial episode, which the producer and writers thought would, perhaps, be criticized for its depiction of the topic if written by a man, rather than an issue during the conversations in the room.

The time for writing

Borgen is perceived as having a well-structured plan for the writing process, which has more or less been the same since the first season. The structure grew out of the work on *Summer*, where Gram and Lindholm found that more time was needed for mutual discussions about the material before writing. Gram describes how they felt that if they were to throw their 'desires and passion' into the writing of *Borgen* it had to be a process marked by a feeling of coming up with things together and working on an equal footing. The musketeer oath was a crucial part of this, but so was having more time for storylining together in the room. Not the least since writing about politics is complicated and calls for extensive research (Gram 2012). It was thus decided to have two weeks for storylining each episode with Price, Gram and Lindholm all present in the room.

The work on the third season started during the spring of 2011, when Price, Gram and Lindholm met to discuss where to take the third season as a whole. The third season had been commissioned rather late in the process of writing the second season, leaving no time to really incorporate a cliffhanger for the future story. According to Gram, they were left with two choices; either to prolong Birgitte Nyborg's time as prime minister to also last for the entire next season or to let her resign at the end of the second season as planned and come up with an entirely new set-up for the third season. Price opted for what Gram describes as 'the brave choice' by ending the season as originally envisioned, thereby forcing the series to reinvent itself when starting again. The late commissioning was thus partly responsible for the changing of the focus in the third season, which ended up having the premise 'Can you achieve power and remain yourself?' rather than asking about the consequences of holding on to power.

Price came up with the pitch for the third season, which became to show how party politics works. This was a part of the political life, which the writers found that the previous seasons had not portrayed in detail. Inspired by Christoffer Guldbrandsen's documentary *Dagbog fra midten/*'Diary from the Middle' (2009) about the rise and fall of the political party Ny Alliance ('New Alliance'), they would like to explore the process of establishing a new party in spite of this changing the basic arena for the series dramatically. Gram describes how writing *Borgen* has been a process of going where they wanted to go with the material, also when people started watching abroad. During the observations in December 2011, there was great excitement among the writers about the positive UK response to the series and the launch of *Borgen* on the French/German channel Arte, and sometimes during development they would laugh about how something might be interpreted by international audiences. However, choices did not seem to be influenced by the increased awareness that foreign audiences were now also watching.

Moving into the third season it was clear from the outset that Lindholm was not to write, but he spent some days discussing possible developments of the third season and handing 'his baby' over (Gram 2012). After two weeks of brainstorming in May, Maja Jul Larsen was invited to join the conversations for another two weeks. The work resulted in an overall plan for the ten episodes and a general sense of the major character arcs. There was a more detailed sense of the first and last episodes of the season, while some of the mid-season episodes were to be more procedural rather than moving the stories of individual characters forward. *Borgen* has an, in many ways, rewarding storytelling structure of having the on-going personal drama of the characters at the core, but also being able to have closed political cases in episodes, mirroring the structure of more classical procedural material like cop series or medical series.

Episode 25 was to be one of the case-driven episodes, and the storylining of the episode basically started from scratch with the writers only knowing that this was to be an episode on the controversial question of whether or not to legalize prostitution. The writers spent two weeks storylining, putting all major beats up on whiteboards in the room before weaving them all together during the last days of the second week. On the last day of storylining, Larsen presented the detailed storyline notes as a verbal pitch to the producer and the researcher, who thus met the material for the first time as an oral presentation. At this point the storyline is normally too long, and the pitch often lasts for an hour and a half. This way of presenting the material is perceived as unique to *Borgen* and apparently grew out of Price using this method for pitching the very first episode of the series, after which it was established as a useful approach.

Gram explains that since Price is excellent at presenting material verbally, pitching in this way was natural for him, but Gram and Larsen describe the long pitch as an intimidating and demanding discipline calling for a challenging overview of material, which has just been put down on paper, as well as the skills to present the beginning, middle and end of a scene in a clear manner while basically reading through the storyline notes. However, both Gram and Larsen state that they have come to appreciate the method, and Hammerich finds that listening to the story is an excellent tool for getting a sense of where one might be bored as a viewer. According to her the writers have asked her not to think too much in terms of production at this stage, but rather to experience the story as a member of the audience. However, the verbal pitch of episode 25 was marked by comments on a number of logistical concerns, with Hammerich and researcher Kofoed addressing issues about the length of the story, the number of exterior vs interior locations, the number of locations shifts, the number of scenes with main actress Sidse Babett Knudsen (who had restrictions on her number of shooting days for the third season), the inclusion of established actors coming in for scenes with no lines and other practical matters. The writers had reflected on issues like these while developing the episode, but the pitch at the end of the two weeks of storylining is where the demands of production meet the text, and a number of changes were discussed during the two-hour meeting following the presentation of the episode.

Following the pitch meeting, the episode writer has a week to produce a treatment, followed by another note meeting, and then two weeks to produce a first draft, after which there is yet another note meeting, again with all writers, the producer and the researcher. Based on the notes, there are two weeks for the episode writer to produce a second draft, and then Price does all later rewrites. According to Hammerich, there would normally be seven drafts during the first two seasons, but there were five drafts during the last. The later drafts are based on written notes from the producer and the Head of Drama as well as input from the main actors and the episode director, but the broadcaster, ordering the series from the in-house drama department, is not involved. From the moment of the greenlight, DR Fiction is running the show, unlike many production processes in the US where network representatives will typically be involved along the way (Redvall 2012a).

All the actors of an episode and the crew get to meet the text at a reading where the episode writers are also taking part, even though they have not seen the text since handing it over after the second draft. The reading of episode 25 took place on 6 June – almost half a year after the storylining – before the shooting of the episode started on 18 June. The final episode aired on 3 February 2013. It thus takes remarkably longer to move through the process of making a season in the DR framework than in most US contexts, but it is also a writing process, which seems far from the depictions of US writers' rooms. During the storylining the writers would normally come in around 9 am and leave around 3–4 pm. The writers find that it does not make sense to go on for longer, since the work in the room is exhausting and much energy is expended. Larsen argues that the *Borgen* episodes are not born 'out of stress' and that it is 'invaluable' to be able to go home once exhaustion sets in and then reflect on things and get some sleep before continuing. According to her, this is why the episodes are often quite finished after the two-week process of storylining.

The work being exhausting would sometimes be commented on in the room, when writers could feel 'the lactic acid running to the muscles' in the afternoon. Moreover, life outside of the room also has demands, such as children that need to be picked up from day care. This is respected in the *Borgen* production framework, and according to Hammerich the schedule for production has been more or less on track since the first season. According to Larsen, things did get more intense at the end of writing the third season, when there were some delays and Price was busy with other things around production than the work in the room. She describes this as 'no fun' and states that the stressed schedule made it clear to her that two weeks for storylining are, in fact, needed.

Observing the storylining in the room, things did get remarkably more busy at the end of the second week where the storyline had to come together before the pitch, but the days did not become longer and even though there was more stress in the room, this did not influence the tone among the writers or the fundamental nature of the work. There was less small talk and the researcher brought lunch, so that the writers would not have to leave the room, but there were no major deadline dramas. In the DR framework, it takes more than a year to write a season, meaning that seasons are often quite far apart. If this were to change it would have implications for the number of writers needed, the length of the workdays or the overall timeline for production. There does not seem to be an inclination to move in this direction, and production-wise *Borgen* seemed to be regarded, by both the writers and the producer, as an example of best practice when it comes to organizing a writing process.

The room for writing

The writers' room of *Borgen* is located at DR Byen where the production of the series is housed, and where around 80 per cent of the series is shot in studios with sets of the political hallways of the parliament Christiansborg, of the apartments of the characters Birgitte Nyborg and Katrine Fønsmark and of the in-house television production facilities dressed to be the fictional TV1 broadcaster in the story. As Hammerich comments, it would be expensive to produce *Borgen* outside of DR, since the series benefits greatly from being able to draw on the in-house newsrooms, equipment and studios for the media storylines. The writers' room is in the midst of the production with the producer, line producer, researcher, production designer and other crew right outside. The room has glass walls, and people can thus observe the work both from the production hallway and from the other glass-wall offices around the indoor hallway on the other side. Whereas there can thus literally be said to be transparency as to when the writers are there and what they seem to be doing, the room is a space for the writers only. The producer would occasionally come in and quietly make a coffee on the fancy espresso machine in the room – a sharp contrast to the regular coffee offered to all other people on production – but otherwise people would rarely disturb the writers.

Among the people in the hallway, one could occasionally overhear comments about the writers coming in later than planned or not having to get their own lunch when under deadline pressure, but there was no sense of a star-like attitude among the writers. In spite of some complaints about the special status of the writers in terms of working hours or assistance, there seemed to be a great respect for what was happening in the room, since, as several people commented, the series is nothing without the writers (Kofoed 2012; Sutherland 2012), and production events would be scheduled around the writing process. At one point when the production designer would like to show the writers the sets being built in order to facilitate the writing for specific rooms, the writers were in the middle of an important discussion, and this had to be postponed according to their work flow (Figure 6.2).

All people in production place great emphasis on the fact that the writers are physically present at DR. Hammerich describes this 'closeness' as crucial to the communication around production. The *Borgen* production can be regarded as an example of a 'production hotel' (as discussed in Chapter 3) with the different professions present in the

Figure 6.2   Images from the 'production hotel' of *Borgen* with some of the many awards for the series just outside the entrance to the writers' room. Photos by Eva Novrup Redvall

same space and short paths of communication. The writers would often benefit from being able to ask the researcher to check up on the back-story and specific political matters or to find a person to interview, just as there would be daily conversations with many people in the hallway about small or large matters surrounding production.

People outside of the room would have a sense of the topics dealt with inside the room a long time before they ever got to read the text, and there was often a sense of shared excitement as to how this would end up on the page. Rather than being secretive about the material, there was a sense of involving others that sometimes led to personal anecdotes on the topic or someone having a connection that might be of interest. The final scripts have an introductory page or two, written by the researcher, explaining aspects of the topic treated and the reasoning behind major decisions surrounding the episode. This kind of sharing ideas and work in progress can be regarded as an asset, creating the opportunity for others to contribute and a sense of taking part in the process. Showrunner James Manos Jr. has argued that collaboration and collectiveness is the most important thing when dealing with a series, and that one should always take the time to talk to people on production about the script, since you want people to have a personal relation to the material, which will hopefully encourage them to do the best job possible (in Redvall 2012a, 13). Having production hotels facilitates this kind of sharing and communication long before the reading of the final draft.

A few people are invited into the writers' room during the storylining for research reasons. The *Borgen* room had a tradition of always pitching an episode to the DR in-house political editor Ask Rostrup in order to test whether their take on the political and media stories seemed plausible, as well as to get further input. This is regarded as important for keeping the series real. Moreover, other people can be consulted as research issues emerge. In episode 25, a representative for the Danish Sex Workers' Organization (Sexarbejdernes Interesseorganisation, SIO) was asked to provide her perspective on the best way to legislate about prostitution. The researcher and writers always do substantial topical research, but in this case the writers found that it was helpful to meet someone with personal knowledge and experience from the world of prostitution, not only to get first-hand information but also to get a sense of the way in which this representative spoke about the topic and to get inspiration for physical appearance, age or gestures of potential characters.

Hammerich underlines how not the least advantage of having a writers' room in the production hallway is that it facilitates involving the head writer in all decisions. It is easier to solve problems when the writers are present, and it is great to have the writers be aware of the large apparatus surrounding them. When asked about the strengths of writers' rooms compared to writers working from their homes, Hammerich replied in surprise: 'Isn't there always a writers' room?' To her the writers' room is an obvious and fundamental part of making a quality drama series and of ensuring the existence of one vision.

The process of writing

The idea of doing an episode on prostitution had been around for a long time. The starting point for discussions was to define where the main characters would position themselves in discussions about legislation. Who would argue in favour of what and how would that create conflict? The arguments for characters were often based on discussions from the real political scene and on research from newspapers and reports. Gram describes how the episode was unusual in the sense that the writers wanted to include a lot of facts, but they also had to be careful of not writing something that 'only wanted one thing politically'. He finds that it was a 'good and interesting' process. Larsen and Hammerich characterize the episode as hard to write because of the topic, but how the structure of the process was typical.

A challenge of the episode turned out to be that the complex topic called for a lot of explaining, leading to too many scenes and too much dialogue. There is often too much material and it is always a challenge to write a first draft of no more than 60 pages. The rewriting is marked by trying to tell things more efficiently, but most storylines and events generally stay. In episode 25, the overall structure of the final episode was basically in the storyline after two weeks, but scenes were merged or omitted along the way. Larsen describes one of the pleasures of writing for *Borgen* as actually getting to see your writing on screen. She finds that the time allocated for thorough discussions leads to a solid first draft, which is not substantially changed later in the process. Both Gram and Larsen find that the political plots normally stay more or less the same, while the relational plots are more likely to be amended.[8] In episode 25, there was an intention to have the side plots on the personal lives of the characters mirror the topic of prostitution by having discussions of sex playing a part in all of them.[9]

In the writers' room, the beats of each character storyline were put up on individual boards, before weaving them around the political plot. Price would do most of the writing on the boards, while the writer who was to write the episode (Larsen) put everything down on paper, once they started writing down the storyline during the second week. The process of storylining seemed very collaborative, with all three writers contributing major points and being active in the discussions of where to take the material. Showrunner Simon Mirren (e.g. *Criminal Minds*, CBS 2005–) has stated that writers' rooms are marked by a complicated ping-pong of 'outdoing each other': 'You are always trying to do outdo the other, but at the same time you would always try to help him outdo you and he would help you outdo him' (in Redvall 2012a, 51). In this case, there was not an atmosphere of trying to outdo each other, but more of refining the material through constant discussion.

Price finds that the basic principle of the room has been to 'cherish the principle that it is through dialogue, in an argument- and dialogue-based room, that the artistic nerve of the series is constantly found and sharpened' (Price 2012). Showrunner Frank Spotnitz has argued that what he loves about writers' rooms is the fact that being in a room with other talented writers 'you have to argue and defend your idea. That makes you get to the bottom of things much faster. You figure all the beats before you get to the script' (in Redvall 2012a, 17). Spotnitz finds that there is always competition in US rooms due to the fact that writers want their ideas to be better than those of other writers, but that this is only an advantage, since it raises everybody's game (2012a, 17). Stephen Gallagher, creator of *Eleventh Hour* (ITV 2006; CBS 2008–2009) and *Crusoe* (NBC 2008–2009), has argued that, in spite of this, one has to create a room with the sense of being a team and not competitors, and several showrunners underline that even while trying to come up with the best idea, one has to be 'egoless' (in Redvall 2012a, 17, 21). As Spotnitz states, one has to listen if others have better ideas, since you have to think of what is best for the show; 'If good things come to the show, good things come to all' (in Redvall 2012a, 17).

As analysed in Chapter 5, there were initially problems when DR Fiction tried to implement the head writer/episode writers structure. Some of these problems have been explained by the head writers of the time not being used to taking on the role as work leader. Gram and Lindholm both appreciate the way in which Price runs the room. They characterize one of his head writer qualities as appearing to be truly appreciative of their input and the dialogue in the room. Larsen describes how some head writers always talk of 'I' rather than 'we', and how you often get the sense that instead of being open to difficult discussions about challenges in a text they just plan to change things to their liking in later drafts. She finds that Price has a talent for giving others a sense of ownership, and when asked to describe the *Borgen* writers' room she defines it as 'dynamic', 'generous' and 'egoless' as well as marked by a sense of 'confidence' and of feeling 'safe'. There was room for bad ideas and disagreement, and Larsen calls the approach of Price 'collective'. She regards the *Borgen* room as different to other rooms she has previously been in, because there was a sense of a structured method in the way in which the storyline was developed in great detail together. In her opinion, the political material calls for precision. Accordingly, she argues that 'you need to be three brains to nail it'.

Gram explains how Price is 'no dictator', but on the other hand very 'giving' and 'generous'. When he has told other writers about the musketeer oath of the room, he explains how they have often responded by labelling it as crazy, since there is a general conviction that several people having to agree could not possibly work. Gram argues that the concept has been to allow the best idea to win rather than to settle on compromises. This has only worked since Price was willing to let go of ideas. According to Gram, this has not been a problem since Price does not get scared by being challenged, which he believes to be a major strength for a head writer.

Contrary to the depictions of US writers' rooms in the work of scholars such as Caldwell, the *Borgen* room thus has two highly satisfied episode writers who describe a good working process and even seem content with their pay and the working hours. Again, it has to be stressed that there are of course major differences between the DR public service framework in a small nation context and the commercial US production culture behind most major series, but it is worthwhile noting that it does seem possible to create rooms, where writers actually have a positive experience while producing quality, high-profile content.

Collaborative writing with one vision

When discussing the process in the room, there seems to be a conviction at DR that there should be three people, no more, no less, in a writers' room. Hammerich describes three as 'the magic number': 'It is probably because the three people then have different roles and then they all get speaking time in some way. Two is too few and four are too many.' Larsen describes the room as very 'sensitive', and when they were four people during the writing of the last episode, she felt that the room went 'off balance': 'One can feel the dynamics decreasing when there are four people – then there are too many. When you are three people you have the sense that you can always get the word when you feel like it, and you can also be quiet, since the two others are speaking. But something bad happened, when we were four...' Being four in the room was partly because there were two new writers present at the end of the season, but Larsen finds that it was not a question of experience. When the experienced writer Gram stepped out of the room to start developing his own series, the room would 'level' again.

During the storylining of episode 25, there did seem to be a good balance between leading or listening, and no major conflicts were observed. The episode writers would be outspoken about when they did not see an idea as working, and there was a sense of the material continuously moving forward. Gram has described the room as 'unusual' with so few conflicts over the years. He left *Borgen* at the end of the third season to set up a new writers' room for developing his own idea for a series, and commented that a concern of his was whether the *Borgen* 'chemistry' could be reproduced. Price characterizes the work as 'an extremely happy collaboration' marked by 'an incredibly creative room'. He highlights never having left the room without feeling that the story had moved forward during the day's work. He prefers a room with 'lots of talk and life'. It has to be a fun process, since the room is 'the distiller for the drama' where you arrive at 'good images with clear colours and good contrasts'. This is the process in which he believes, but he also stresses that this is the process, which suits him the best. As discussed in Chapter 3, not all writers enjoy the role of leading a room or of rewriting the material of others.

Observing the room there was a sense of the writers having time to diverge and go off in different directions, before converging when moving through what the model of Creative Problem Solving (CPS) would describe as the stages of mess-finding, data-finding, and problem-finding towards idea-finding, solution-finding and acceptance-finding (Isaksen and Treffinger 2004, 14). One can regard all the stages as happening in the room, when working with individual ideas within an episode that are gradually developed and explored, before final choices are made during the last days of storylining. However, the CPS outline of the stages can also be regarded as a model for the process in its entirety where the initial mess-finding took place during the early talks of the season as a whole in the spring, whereas the work in the room was more about fact-finding, problem-finding and idea-finding. The treatment can be regarded as the first 'problem statement', where the ideas of the episode are externalized and can thus meet the comments of others. Following this, the process moves into the stages of solution- and acceptance-finding during note meetings and the rewriting of drafts. Thinking of the process in this way, clarifies how television production is marked by the input of numerous people from the early stages in the process – contrary to many other artistic processes where creators can produce finished works without ever having to communicate with others – but the mess-finding, fact-finding and problem-finding happens behind the closed doors of the writers' room before opening the process to the input of others. This ensures that there is a certain foundation and shared agreement between the writers about the content and nature of the problem statement, before this meets the many opinions and concerns of people outside the room.

In episode 25, the text left the room after the pitch. The further idea- and solution-finding was based on comments on the first draft from the producer, the researcher and the episode director (Louise Friedberg), while still having all writers attached. Based on the second draft by Larsen, Price wrote the later drafts in which the final solutions for the episode were found. While there is thus a process of diverging and invit- ing a number of people to comment along the way, the different drafts can be seen as a continuous move towards making the text converge, and the final choices in this process are made by the head writer.

In the notes on episode 25, Hammerich commented on logistics, such as locations or having to take out one actor, since he would not be available. However, she would also comment on character motivations, dramaturgical concerns and specific lines as well as on what might be the general interpretation of the episode as a whole. Episode director Friedberg mostly commented on details that seemed unclear to her in the storytelling. After Friedberg's comments on the second draft she had a meeting with Price, and then later gave written notes on the third draft.[10] Having the episode director read early drafts ensures that the head writer and director have a mutual understanding of the material before the reading, where the actors and the rest of the crew meet the text and get to voice their questions and comments.

Head of Drama Piv Bernth read the third draft and only had a few comments in a brief email where she warned about a tendency to have too much explanatory dialogue and encouraged the writers to consider whether Birgitte Nyborg's illness (which develops during the third sea- son) should maybe get more attention in this midseason episode.[11] Her notes opened by stating that the episode deals with 'an exciting debate', which will 'most definitely stir things up'. At the end of the notes, she underlined that no matter what the writers decided to do as to the dialogue or the disease, it would definitely be 'an interesting episode'. Hammerich had voiced her concerns about the controversial nature of the content since the pitch meeting, but there was never a sense that she was asking the writers to change things or modify the content to avoid debate. There was more a sense of raising certain points and questioning certain choices in order to make sure that the writers were conscious about how others might react to the material or perceive things that might be clear to the writers, but not to others.

The episode did in fact cause a stir in the press and led to debates about whether *Borgen* was an attempt to promote certain political views and if so, whether this was compatible with the public service obligation of DR.[12] The process of note giving showed that Bernth was aware that there might be controversy, but this was apparently acceptable. Concerns about the potential international audiences were never mentioned in any notes, and there was never the sense that notes were 'orders' as described by Caldwell (2008, 221). The head writer seemed free to make the final choices as he pleased.

Hammerich describes the process as everyone supporting the vision of Price, but also continuously challenging it. She regards the making of *Borgen* as a definite example of one vision, but it is a vision where several contributors 'carry wood to the fire', particularly the other writers and her as the producer. During the editing of the episode, Hammerich said that she still was not sure how the episode would be perceived, and that she was nervous about some people maybe interpreting the content as 'glorifying' prostitution. In her opinion, the episode tells about 'a grey area' that stays a grey area in the story, but maybe viewers would obtain a more enlightened approach to the complicated topic through watching the episode. There can thus be said to be a notion of 'educating' the audience, but all through the process a major part of the writers' work was to try to balance the different viewpoints before the end of the story, where nothing ends up being done and the topic of prostitution thus continues to be a grey area.

The roles in the room

Regarding the hierarchy or the roles in the room, Gram and Larsen both acknowledge that Price is naturally the one making all final choices when taking over the text after the second draft. They also stress that he is the one with the responsibility. When episode 25 was debated in the press, he was thus the one answering questions from journalists. In terms of allocating authorship, *Borgen* is perceived as a series by Price in the press, even when Gram and Lindholm got credits as co-writers rather than episode writers on the first seasons and in spite of them

Figure 6.3 Birgitte Nyborg (Sidse Babett Knudsen) and her bike in *Borgen*. A politician biking to work is not a spectacular event in the eyes of Danish audiences, but this seems to have had a more exotic flavour in the foreign gaze. However, the international interest in the series did not seem to influence the choices around production during the making of episode 25. Framegrab. Cinematography by Lasse Frank. Courtesy of DR

attending press events where Price has explicitly acknowledged their contributions (Figure 6.3).

As for issues of authorship in the room, there was no sense of specific ideas originating from one person, who would then defend them for personal feelings. The room seemed very non-hierarchical, but there was a sense of the writers having different roles with Price continuously coming up with new ideas, which would then be discussed. Hammerich finds that the writers have different functions and describes Price as 'a fast guy' who is always somewhat in a hurry. She regards the other writers as responsible for ensuring that things will be properly discussed before moving on, which is helpful in terms of giving the material more depth. Gram and Larsen agree that their function is often to be 'the devil's advocate'. Gram finds that the most defining characteristic of Price may be his ability to be 'an idea machine'. He is also 'a man of the scene' and likes to keep things rolling by jumping to the next scene, which can then quickly be followed by suggestions for a number of other scenes. Gram describes this 'idea richness' as a trait of 'experienced showrunners' and finds that one of the reasons why it is hard for younger writers to become head writers is that you need to have a big back catalogue of stories to be able to keep on generating new material for a series.

While Price is thus continuously 'giving birth' to a lot of material, as Larsen puts it, an important part of the role of the other writers is to sort and challenge it. Challenging the material might arise from not finding the suggestion believable in terms of the story universe or in terms of the real-life context, sometimes referring to the material in the research. During the first two seasons, Gram finds that Lindholm was 'the reality guy', while he himself has a tendency to start thinking about a structure at an early stage. Whereas Price would keep inventing story moments, Gram says that he and Lindholm would take on the role of thinking more of the story as a whole. He loves how Price creates energy in the room, but sometimes the episode writers have to slow down the process, since there can quickly be too many beats at a point when they are only two-thirds through the episode.

Larsen agrees that the role of the other writers is often to challenge the ideas before moving on, but she also finds that the roles change during a day; there is a shift between generating ideas and challenging them before making choices. In the words of CPS, one can argue that the writers take turns diverging and converging, and some writers might have a tendency to do one thing more than the other. As discussed in Chapter 1, group collaborations are often characterized by consisting of people complementing each other and having differentiated roles, but integrated norms. Writers can complement each other in terms of professional skills, where some writers might for instance be regarded as particularly strong on characters, plot or dialogue. Head writers might also look for particular skills when casting a room. Frank Spotnitz has explained how it was crucial for him to have a writers' room when developing his first UK series, since he needed assistance on national topics like class and racism when dealing with a show consisting of 90 per cent British characters (in Redvall 2012a, 18). Spotnitz insists that having other voices in a room will always make the material better (in 2012a, 33). Similarly, Stephen Gallagher has argued that having different personalities in the room is what keeps the approach to storytelling fresh, since there will always be someone else's joke or view on things (in 2012a, 24). James Manos Jr. has argued that the collaborative process is what makes the writing fun, and highlighted how it should be 'like family' (in 2012a, 33).

Caldwell has analysed how many writers compare the writers' room to a family, a comparison, which he regards as 'overly optimistic' (2008, 213). As Phalen and Osselame comment, their study points more in the direction of a dysfunctional family or as one of writer puts it 'a functional dysfunctional family' (2012, 12). None of the writers at DR interviewed for this book have brought up a family comparison for the collaborative writing process, but they all emphasize the importance of having a fundamental respect for each other and of enjoying being in a room together. In the *Borgen* room there is a sense of having complementary skills with Price constantly driving the process forward and the other writers questioning the many ideas before they settle on a decision, which all writers are in favour of. The three writers all have a positive perception of the process, and they all feel a strong sense of ownership. Larsen defines the process as marked by the concept of one vision, but stresses how Price has a talent for making others feel as co-creators, leaving you with the sense that a particular episode could never have been made without your specific input.

Gram similarly appreciates the generosity of Price in this regard, and explains how the third season was special for him, since he asked to be as involved in the work of the head writer as possible. He knew that he would be establishing his own room for a new series straight after *Borgen* and would like the third season to work as 'an apprenticeship'. Price agreed to teach the tricks of the trade, and while no one talks of the room as a 'family', this sort of collaboration can be regarded as what Vera John-Steiner terms 'a family collaboration' where roles can change over time like when participants in a collaboration assist each other in moving from being a novice to taking on a role of more expertise (2000, 201). There were no talks of 'mentoring' in the process, but as discussed by Phalen and Osselame having a mentor is often important in launching successful writing careers, and more than half of their respondents described having mentors (2012, 16). As analysed in Chapter 5, there has been a history of writers growing up within the DR system in the recent past and gradually making the move from episode writer to head writer, among them Adam Price and creator of *The Killing* Søren Sveistrup. The *Borgen* room is an example of actually having an agreement between writers about the one 'training' the other to take on the role of head writer. Afterwards, Gram moved on to set up his own room as planned, whereas Larsen was hired to write *Arvingerne/The Legacy* (forthcoming 2014). The lessons learned while writing *Borgen*, considered to be an example of best practice, thus stayed within the production framework for the benefit of future series.

Writers' rooms as thought communities

As discussed at the beginning of this book, it is of course easier to get access to studying creative work, when there is a mutual sense among the practitioners involved that they enjoy a good working process and are producing a quality product. The observations and interviews around *Borgen* point to a writers' room marked by a sense of openness, generosity and trust. Other case studies at DR could have been more critical cases dealing with, for instance, the deadlines being remarkably pushed during the making of the third season of *The Killing*, putting the people in production under pressure, or with the challenges of establishing a writers' room as first time head writer, still in the mess-finding process of the material, as observed during the initial stages of developing *The Legacy*. As stated earlier in this chapter, writers often emphasize that no two rooms are alike, since they are so dependent on the chemistry among writers, as well as a number of other parameters surrounding the process, such as the time allowed for developing material in the room. *Borgen* is one particular example of a writing process at DR, but it relates to many of the dogmas and discussions described in previous chapters in the way in which the process is regarded as a clear example of a series based on double storytelling and one vision, while also being regarded as an example of an exemplary collaborative writing process by the writers in the room.

Theories of group dynamics often highlight that a shared goal and trust are among the important aspects of group interaction (e.g. Johnson and Johnson 2006). Good writers' rooms are highly dependent on these aspects, and one fruitful way to think about these rooms is to apply John-Steiner's concept of 'thought communities' from her study of how 'generative ideas emerge from joint thinking, from significant conversations, and from sustained, shared struggles to achieve new insights by partners in thought' (2000, 3). Thought communities are based on longitudinal collaborations where members take emotional and intellectual risk (2000, 196). Based on John-Steiner's definitions of different forms of collaborations, the *Borgen* writers' room can be seen as an example of a family collaboration where participants help each other in changing roles, in this case not during the course of making a series, but in terms of preparing to move on to the next. Not all rooms are an example of this kind of collaboration, but thinking about writers' rooms as different forms of thought communities is a constructive way of emphasizing what goes on during the collective process of trying to transform existing knowledge and patterns into new visions. What kind of collaboration seems to be happening in the room? Do writers feel a sense of ownership, of being an important part of the dialogue and of being included in a shared vision for what is produced? The writers and the producer of *Borgen* describe the series as being grounded in Price's vision, but they all feel as cherished co-creators.

As stressed in most definitions of creativity, the emergence of creative products is marked by a proposed variation being original, of high quality and appropriate in the sense that it meets the restraints for the task at hand. The work in all writers' rooms most likely aims for this to happen. The writing of *Borgen* can be regarded as a process leading to a product, which is generally regarded as living up to those demands. The backstory of new, acclaimed series are definitely not always based on good work processes, and it is worthwhile looking into the making of successful as well as less successful series to try to discern what can be learned from studying the particularity of the specific production process, and what might potentially be the larger lessons learned from analysing those.

Thinking about the *Borgen* writers' room from a Screen Idea System approach, it is remarkable that all episode writers involved during the three seasons have the same educational background, and that the original trio of writers all had previous work experiences within the DR framework. There has been a sense of a shared mission statement from the outset as well as a musketeer oath about the nature of the collaboration. Drawing on what the writers perceived as the best series in the international domain, they aimed at bringing something new to the domain of Danish drama series, where there had previously been no high-profile drama series dealing with the political arena. The original idea was met with initial scepticism from the gatekeepers within DR. However, since the greenlight for the series, the executives at DR seem to have been supportive of letting the writers take the material where they wanted, even when topics were conceived as controversial, and the experts in the field of reception have acknowledged the series as an interesting contribution.

The process of the *Borgen* room is remarkably different from US writers' rooms in terms of the size of the room and the timeframe for the work. Yet many of the fundamental issues related to the nature of the room and to what marks good processes reflect the findings of other studies (e.g. Phalen and Osselame 2012). At a time when the European television industry is considering how to implement a structure of working with showrunners and writers' rooms to a larger extent, there are good reasons for looking into the current modes of writing and producing in different television cultures to grasp some of the complexities. As stated by Gram, nothing upsets him more than when people think that there is an easy recipe, and even after having spent numerous years working on *Borgen* he is still worried about whether he will be able to replicate the chemistry of the room. The workings of a writers' room is a complicated affair and it is worthwhile trying to demystify the process behind the closed doors. This chapter has offered an analysis of one example of a framework for collaborative writing with one vision in the DR production framework, suggesting thinking of it as an example of a family collaboration along the lines of thought communities. The next chapter analyses the writing and production story of *The Killing*, pointing to how all head writers find their own way of structuring their work processes within the same system. The overall managerial ideas for production are the same, but these can be interpreted and implemented in very different ways.

7
Prime-time Public Service Crime: *Forbrydelsen/The Killing*

Introduction

Søren Sveistrup's crime thriller *Forbrydelsen/The Killing* (2007–2012) is the best-known example of a DR series, which has made it onto the international scene. The press coverage during the UK airing seemed unprecedented for a subtitled series with articles discussing how the portrayal of a modern welfare society mirrored the state of affairs in Britain, or gender issues related to the portrait of the series' detective Sarah Lund. On a less serious scale, there were attempts at doing semiotic analysis of Lund's iconic sweater and encouragement to readers to send pictures of their own similar knitting designs. Camilla, the Duchess of Cornwall, announced that she was an 'addict' of the show, and when visiting Denmark in the spring of 2012, she got a special tour of the set of *The Killing III* and a copy of the sweater as a souvenir.[1] The series won the international BAFTA award in 2011, beating series like *Mad Men* (AMC 2007–) and *Boardwalk Empire* (HBO 2010), and it has been remade as *The Killing* (2011–) for the US cable channel AMC (Figure 7.1).[2]

The series aired in the UK in 2011 – four years after its original premiere in Denmark – and from a Danish perspective the international reception was followed with both great pride and some surprise. The international coverage generated numerous national articles on how the series is perceived abroad, since some of the elements that seem to fascinate international audiences are those regarded as the everyday realism of the series from a domestic point of view. The interplay of fascination and identification takes on a different dynamic when content is moved out of the national realm and interpreted with a foreign gaze, not the least when a series like *The Killing* is suddenly exclusive and exotic programming on a niche channel rather than the major prime-time series

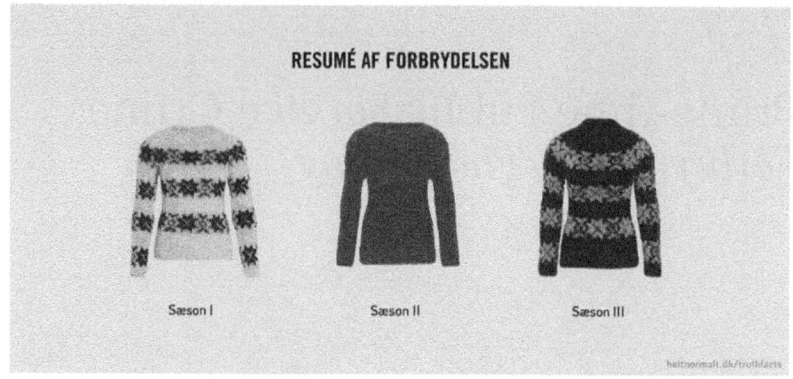

Figure 7.1 When the third season of *The Killing* premiered on Danish screens, some found that the seasons could be summed up by the different sweater designs. Courtesy of Mikael Wulff and heltnormalt.dk

for the large mainstream audiences in the domestic market (Redvall 2012d). Accordingly, the widespread interest in *The Killing* has led to writings on how the series raises issues of European social imaginaries across borders (Bondebjerg and Redvall forthcoming 2014) as well as books on how to be Danish 'from Lego to Lund', discussing the sudden UK interest in a range of different products and trends from Scandinavia (Kingsley 2012).

Whereas there are many interesting questions regarding distribution or reception of European products to investigate in relation to the international success of series from DR like *The Killing* or *Borgen*, this chapter focuses on *The Killing* as a result of a writing and production process with central elements from the DR dogmas at the centre even if these have not necessarily been articulated during the making of the series. As the creator Søren Sveistrup states, it would be damaging for his creative process if someone told him to create a series based on an idea of double storytelling, and as soon as someone mentions anything that sounds like a recipe he intuitively wants to challenge it (Sveistrup 2012). However, he acknowledges that a series like *The Killing* could only come about since he found a producer and a broadcaster investing a great amount of trust and time in him and since he found people willing to run the risk of trying out something new. The case study illustrates how ideas from the production dogmas about one vision, double storytelling and crossover fitted his approach of deliberately trying to reinvent what a TV series can be even if the concepts from the dogmas were not explicitly discussed.

The Killing can thus be regarded as an example of allowing the creator Søren Sveistrup to develop a series based on his one vision in spite of the original scepticism of whether it would be possible to have an extended murder mystery as the structure for 20 episodes. The three-layer structure of all three seasons – dealing with the police investigation, the political intrigues and the private lives of the victims of the different crimes – mirrors the idea of double storytelling with larger ethical and social connotations as an important part of the overall thriller set-up. Moreover, the idea of crossover between the film and television industry is present, not only in the choices of the people making the series come alive on screen but also in the initial ambitions of making cinematic drama for the small screen.

From a Screen Idea System perspective, the production story of *The Killing* illustrates how the emergence of new quality series is a result of an intricate interplay between individual talents, the domain and the field. The chapter focuses on the writing and production of the series. However, before moving into this analysis the scene is set for how to understand the series in terms of 'Scandi-Crime' or 'Nordic Noir' as a new trend and brand for a certain kind of Nordic television drama. Part of this discussion is how changes in the scheduling strategies of a broadcaster like BBC4 have been influential for its international success. The chapter then moves on to analyse the development of the series, focusing on the choices of content, structure and style as reflections of the ideas of quality hailed in the DR production dogmas. The case study is interpreted as an example of a series where a practitioner with the outside recognition and the in-house track record to have earned the trust of the broadcaster is given the opportunity to propose a new kind of product based on deliberate intentions to reinvent the traditional approaches, drawing on what is considered to be state of the art in the international domain.[3]

Scandi-Crime and Nordic Noir

As discussed in Chapter 2, there is a tradition of crime and police series in Danish television even though the crime genre has sometimes been regarded as problematic in terms of its public service value (Agger 2005a, 365). The first police series dates back to *En by i provinsen/*'A Town in the Provinces' (1977–1980) by head writer Leif Panduro. *En by i provinsen* is often discussed as a Danish take on *McCloud* (NBC 1970–1977), and since then there have been several DR variations on the crime genre – often compared to US or UK counterparts – such as the private eye parody *Anthonsen* (1984–1985), the action-filled six-episode mini-series *Een gang strømer...*/'Once a Cop...' (1987) or the *Hill Street Blues*-inspired police series *Station 13* (1988–1989). TV 2 had their largest TV drama success ever with *Strisser på Samsø/Island Cop* (1996–1998), finding an audience of around two million viewers to the story of a big city cop making the move to the small island of Samsø. Three out of DR's four Emmys for best international drama series have been for crime dramas with the series *Rejseholdet/Unit One* (2000–2004) in 2002, *Ørnen/The Eagle* (2004–2006) in 2005 and *Livvagterne/The Protectors* (2008–2010) in 2009 by Peter Thorsboe and Mai Brostrøm. Whereas the crime genre as known from the US often deals with a big city setting, many Danish crime series have traditionally been set in the provinces. Television scholar Anne Marit Waade has discussed the use of site-specific realism and rural landscapes as a signifier of many Scandinavian crime series (2010), but in recent years series from DR like *The Eagle* and *The Protectors* seem to have largely moved away from the regional cases around the country by focusing more on international crime.[4]

The series from DR, based on original ideas written for the screen, have been the only Scandinavian high-profile series winning international Emmys in the 2000s, but a number of adaptations of popular bestsellers from Sweden have in fact been the driving force of what has become known as Scandi-Crime or Nordic Noir in film and television. As discussed by several scholars, there is a long tradition of crime literature with what Gunhild Agger has termed 'a social conscience' in the Scandinavian countries since the ten successful novels by Swedish husband-and-wife writing duo Maj Sjöwall and Per Wahlöö, collectively titled *The Story of a Crime*, of the 1960s and 1970s (2010). This social conscience is linked to 'dissecting the men of power and their often criminal actions' (Agger and Waade 2010a, 13) based on 'a concern for the developments of the welfare state' (Agger 2010, 20). Characters from popular crime novels like Sjöwall and Wahlöö's police detective Martin Beck and Henning Mankell's Kurt Wallander have successfully made the move from page to screen in many different versions, like the work of Henning Mankell existing in the form of the Swedish Wallander film/television franchises with first Rolf Lassgård (1994–2007) and later Krister Henriksson in the title role (2005–2006 and 2009–2010) as well as in a UK version with an English-speaking Kenneth Branagh solving crimes in Wallander's hometown of Ystad (BBC 2008–).

The literary crime books have attracted extensive academic attention for a number of years (see Forshaw 2012). More recently, film and television studies have also turned to detailed discussions of what is now a substantial amount of Scandinavian television crime series with audiences in many countries (Agger and Waade 2010b; Nestingen 2008; Nestingen and Arvas 2011).[5] Not the least the film/television versions of Stieg Larsson's Millennium Trilogy (2009–2010) led to a new interest in the appeal and characteristics of Scandinavian crime fiction from best-sellers to blockbusters (King and Smith 2012; Peacock 2012) and to new talks of a special brand of 'Nordic Noir' (Forshaw 2013).[6]

When travelling, *The Killing* has been discussed in relation to the many previous literary, film and television works of Scandinavian crime fiction, which have created an audience interest for 'death in a cold cli-mate' as the crime fiction expert Barry Forshaw calls it (2012). These chilly crime stories are traditionally case-based detective fiction, taking the form of 'a stalwart, methodological practicality' and focusing on 'the often monotonous, day-to-day details of police work' (Miller 2010). The noir element derives from the murky nature of the material focusing on the darker sides of society and on the existential malaise of most charac-ters. In the material's visual form the noir element is also linked to the imagery and style as exemplified in the often dark images in *The Killing* and the quite grim portrayal of a rainy Copenhagen in November, the time of year for all three seasons of the series.

Whereas the success of *The Killing* should be understood as part of this taste for a particular popular product, the transnational success of the series also relates to certain European broadcasters having created successful slots for programming foreign fare, gradually making audi-ences accustomed to shows from other countries. In Germany, ZDF has pioneered a special slot for Nordic crime series (Redvall 2013, 58), and *The Killing I* scored an average rating of 2.79 million viewers and a 15.1 per cent market share when being shown as *Komissarin Lund – Das Versprechen.*[7] In the UK, the digital television station BBC4 has played an important part in what Elke Weissmann has described as 'redirect-ing the nation's interest in television drama to non-American nations' (2012, 189). *The Killing* aired on BBC4, which between 2008 and 2010 found what Steven Peacock has called 'a winning formula' of screening double episodes of Swedish detective series like both the *Wallander* series (2012, 5).

The Killing aired as double-bills on Saturday evenings, attracting an average of 500,000 viewers for the first season (Frost 2011a) and scoring impressive audience appreciation figures of 94 per cent (Midgley 2011). The second and third season found a larger audience of around one million viewers. The success of *The Killing* has been described as putting a torchlight on subtitled content (Frost 2011b), but the way had been paved by the good audience response for previous Scandi-Crime as well as for the French police series *Engrenages/Spiral* (2005–), which led to the BBC looking at other 'Euro crime drama' such as *The Killing* (Frost 2011a). Weissmann argues that an important part of the attraction of *The Killing* is 'exactly its difference from other UK television' and how Scandinavian productions 'present new structures and forms to UK audiences who find that neither the US nor the UK nor their co-productions can offer quite such innovation' (2012, 190).

Whereas contextual elements such as the trends and tastes in the domain and the emergence of successful scheduling strategies for European series chosen by experts in the field are of great importance to the international distribution and reception of *The Killing*, the series would of course not have encountered the enthusiastic response without having qualities in its own right. These qualities have previously particularly been discussed in terms of the series' approach to issues of genre and gender (e.g. Agger 2011; McCabe 2012) with, for instance, Gunhild Agger arguing that the series represents 'a reversal of masculine and feminine stereotypes and the invalidation of family life in the process' (2011, 111). *The Killing* contains many interesting elements for further textual and stylistic analysis, but the following traces the writing and production of the series, which according to creator Søren Sveistrup was never discussed in terms of Nordic Noir-elements, but has naturally been interpreted in a certain light when premiering in what he calls 'the slipstream of Stieg Larsson' (Sveistrup 2012).

Backstory: The original idea

Søren Sveistrup has an educational background at The National Film School of Denmark (NFSD), where he graduated from the Screenwriting Department in 1997. As discussed in Chapter 4, he was thus among the first classes of students to encounter any teaching on television writing, but Sveistrup argues that it does not make sense to separate different kinds of dramatic storytelling. To him, writing is about creating the best stories for whatever medium and one should not try to think of specific strategies for specific media, but rather always think in terms of the best stories. It was never his plan to write for television, but he started appreciating working for DR after having experienced the challenges of trying to get his ideas through as a writer in the film industry. He worked as an episode writer on *Taxa/Taxi* for DR (1997–1999) and then on *Hotellet/At the Faber* (2000–2002) for TV 2, before returning to DR as the head writer of *Nikolaj og Julie/Nikolaj and Julie* (2002–2003), which had been created by Adam Price. The series on the romantic hardships of the couple Nikolaj and Julie (starring Peter Mygind and Sofie Gråbøl) found large domestic audiences and won an Emmy as best international drama series in 2003. Following this success, Sveistrup was hired to come up with a new series for DR, based on the notion within DR Fiction that series have to build on original ideas of writers with one vision for a project. As the producer of *The Killing* and now Head of Drama at DR Piv Bernth has put it, the idea is to start with 'who' and then move on to 'what' (Bernth 2012a). She had produced *Nikolaj and Julie* and went on to produce all three seasons of *The Killing*.

Sveistrup describes the process of developing *The Killing* as marked by a clear intention to break away from what he perceived as character-izing series from DR at the time. He wanted to create something very different from *Nikolaj and Julie* and was bored with the one arena of many series putting a certain location or space at the centre of atten-tion. Moreover, he was tired of the case-based structure of having one case for one episode, which he found to be old school. The ambition from the very beginning was to be incredibly ambitious and aim for creating a worldclass series. Sveistrup felt that he was at a point in his career where he had learned important lessons and had the experience to develop something original. Having won an Emmy, he also had the trust of the broadcaster. Sveistrup argues that whenever you want to create something exciting you have to push the existing limits, and 'the belief that the audience is intelligent has to be present; if I am bored looking at arena-based stories, then other people are definitely also bored' (Sveistrup 2012). There was thus a deliberate ambition to create a new and original variation for the domain inspired by what Sveistrup perceived to be the most interesting examples of best prac-tice in international television production rather than focusing on the domestic output. He compared himself with 'the global scene' and not with the local production (Sveistrup 2012).

In the beginning of the 2000s, *24* (Fox 2001–2010) had pioneered a new way of storytelling with its structure of having each season take place within a 24-hour period. Sveistrup found this to be an interest-ing new approach. He had always been fascinated by the long-running mystery of *Twin Peaks* (ABC 1990–1991), but regretted that the series ended up as comedy rather than being interested in actually provid-ing an intriguing answer to the question of who killed Laura Palmer. He would like to create a long-running mystery where the story was taken seriously, and he looked to series like *Murder One* (ABC 1995–1997) where the first season revolves around a defense attorney working with a single high-profile criminal case, while other smaller cases are also handled and usually wrapped up within each episode. Furthermore, he found that the portrayal of power plays in a political series like *The West Wing* (NBC 1999–2006) was interesting with the backstabbing going on behind the scenes.

The first concrete idea was to create a mini-series in eight episodes dealing with the murder of a young girl. Sveistrup pitched the idea to then Head of Drama Ingolf Gabold, who wasn't keen on producing more crime stories. DR Fiction was producing *Unit One* and developing *The Eagle*, and Gabold asked Sveistrup to rethink the idea of doing a crime story. Moreover, DR was focusing on producing longer series and looking for material for seasons of ten one-hour episodes, and the initial suggestion did not fit into the slots envisioned (Gabold 2011). In spite of the original scepticism, Sveistrup describes how 'there was enough goodwill' to ask him to develop his idea further and see where this might take it (Sveistrup 2012).

Sveistrup returned with a pitch where the story was now about what the murder of a young girl does to a number of people around the crime, interweaving their destinies. Gabold explains that Sveistrup used the chaos theory metaphor of the butterfly effect where the flapping of butterfly wings in one place can set off a snowstorm somewhere else and found it to be a 'tale of destinies' similar to the ones by Danish author Karen Blixen (1885–1962) (Gabold in Nielsen 2012c). DR producer Sven Clausen has described the series as based on 'a theory of interdependence' and has stressed how Danish crime series should be perceived as 'a mirror on reality' with *The Killing* as a good example of how one incident has an impact on many different layers of people in society from a whole school to the career of one politician (in Gemzøe 2010, 202). The new take on the story was thus perceived by experts in the field to be an interesting variation on the existing crime series in the domain with its wider societal and ethical implications beyond the fundamental crime plot. As will be discussed further in the following, the series has later been highlighted by executives from DR Fiction as an obvious example of double storytelling.

Research and development

With the interest in this kind of crime series among experts in the field, the series moved into what models from Creative Problem Solving (CPS) calls the the stages of data-finding, idea-finding and problem-finding

(Isaksen and Treffinger 2004), while Sveistrup tried to figure out how to go about creating this kind of series with an appropriate form and profile for DR. Sveistrup describes how he is often inspired by biblical allegories. A foundation for *The Killing* became the story of Oedipus from the Greek mythology. Oedipus has to learn the dark truths of his life; Until he does and drives away the Sphinx, nothing can grow in the city of Thebes. In a similar vein, this was to be a thriller where no one could breathe until the mystery had been solved (Sveistrup 2012).

Confronting the demands of the DR time slots, Sveistrup argued that one could keep the one case of who killed the girl going for 20 episodes. The basic structure of the series thus grew out of the institutional demands calling for a series of a certain length for the Sunday night slot. Sveistrup finds the all-important aspect of creating a new series to be making the expectations of the broadcaster constructively meet one's own artistic expectations. He believes that the best ideas often emerge when the original ideas are challenged. In this case the scheduling demands of the broadcaster were part of creating the rather unique structure of keeping a whodunnit murder mystery going for 20 episodes. Commenting on the commissioning process, Sveistrup regards himself as lucky to have found a producer with 'the hubris courage' to try out this idea (Sveistrup 2012) and a broadcaster who also supported the attempt to do something different in spite of 'everyone saying that they were crazy', according to current Head of DR Fiction Nadia Kløvedal Reich (Reich 2012).

Sveistrup spent around a year researching together with two episode writers before moving on to any actual writing. The original idea was to set the series – with the working title 'The Story of a Murder' – in the provinces, and the writers did extensive research into real life murders of young girls around the country. Sveistrup describes the process as hard and frustrating, since he is not good at making choices at the early stages in the process when everything is possible. According to Sveistrup, things only really started happening when the writers decided to change the location of the story to Copenhagen, making the sense of a thriller clearer and creating a better backdrop for the political ideas of the story, which tended to be too small-scale outside of the capital. Sveistrup was afraid of losing the open landscapes if moving the story to the city, but found that there are plenty of locations just outside of Copenhagen, which would allow for opening up the images. He argues that if one should talk about having one arena for the series, the city of Copenhagen would be this rather big arena.

Piv Bernth argues that rather than thinking about *The Killing* as having three arenas because of its combination of a police investigation, political intrigues and the personal realm of characters, it is an example of having a three-plot structure. The intention was to break out of the work place arena for crime series to instead think more in terms of having stories and characters as the elements, which brings the series together. In terms of space, the concrete locations have become still more 'atomized' during the three seasons with still more location shooting rather than set-building in studios (Bernth in Berg and Diesen 2012). Sveistrup prefers to think of the series as marked by 'the unity of action' rather than a unity of place (Sveistrup 2012). All three seasons have had the structure of three story strands interweaving with police detective Sarah Lund and her investigations as the element gradually bringing the different storylines together.

Sofie Gråbøl's Sarah Lund is of course crucial to the series, which was a continutation of a good collaboration between Sveistrup and Gråbøl on *Nikolaj and Julie*. According to Bernth a mantra for the series was that the sun was never allowed to shine and Sofie was never allowed to smile (Bernth in Nielsen 2012b). While most characters change between the seasons, Lund and her journey are the central elements, which bring the three seasons together in spite of being years apart. The series was originally conceived as a trilogy (Bernth in Nielsen 2012b), but the seasons were commissioned one at a time, and they thus ended up being years apart.

One vision – For a product and a process

As discussed in the above *The Killing* is a case of DR asking a specific writer to suggest a personal idea for a new series based on his successful track record and a good working relationship. Sveistrup finds that the process of making *The Killing* has been marked by 'limitless trust' with his producer and the DR executives being open to his ideas (Sveistrup 2012). This does not mean that his ideas have not been challenged along the way, but Sveistrup argues that criticism was raised in a clever manner leaving time to reflect on the critical points. As an example, he originally planned for the murdered girl to be a child, which Gabold did not perceive as a good idea for the prime-time audience. Gabold voiced his concern, and Sveistrup eventually changed this aspect but according to him for whole other reasons; he gradually found that he needed a teenage girl with a life of her own to make the story also be about putting together the night of her killing. Everyone was thus happy with this decision, and the example points to how disagreements around a screen idea can possibly find a natural solution without anyone dictating demands, if there is actually time to explore and reflect on the reasons behind the different choices.

Everyone around *The Killing* finds that the series is a clear example of one vision. Bernth states how everything builds on 'the originality' of Sveistrup (Bernth in Berg and Diesen 2012). One of the two steady episode writers for all three seasons, Michael W. Horsten, stresses that it is Sveistrup's series, which others have supported him in creating (2013). The writing of *The Killing* has been based on a tight-knit writing team consisting of Sveistrup and the episode writers Horsten and Torleif Hoppe, who have taken turns producing drafts for episodes.[8] Contrary to the writing room of *Borgen* with head writer Adam Price and two episode writers all present when outlining episodes during production (as described in the previous chapter), Sveistrup – according to plan – spends two–three weeks outlining each episode with the individual writer of that episode who then produces a first draft in two weeks. Based on notes from Sveistrup and Bernth on the first draft, the episode writer has a week to write a second draft, which is followed by further notes and a week for the episode writer to produce a third draft before the reading with the actors.[9] Following the comments from the reading, Sveistrup only has a couple of days to produce the final draft before the shoot. It is rather remarkable how Sveistrup does not do any actual writing until the last draft, and the process can be regarded as mirroring the US structure of the showrunner overseeing the writing process rather than writing even if there is no writers' room as such.

Some actors get to influence the text during the writing of different drafts. Lead actress Sofie Gråbøl comments on the script before the reading with all actors and the crew, after which there are also meetings with the actors of each of the three story strands. Sveistrup describes his method as emphasizing the value of 'the dialectics with the actors' and as a way of trying to keep the text open for as long as possible (Sveistrup 2012). Changes can happen up to the very last minute, meaning that there are many so-called 'pink pages' with the alterations from the white pages of the final draft. Bernth describes the process as 'flexible', 'stressful', 'energetic' and 'exciting', but also sometimes 'too exciting' (Bernth 2012b). On the last season, only one episode had been written when production started. According to Bernth, delays once the shoot started led to only having ten days for storylining an episode, five days for writing a first draft, three days for writing the second draft, three days for writing the third draft and then 48 hours for a final draft (in Berg and Diesen 2012).

Sveistrup finds that he might have taken the concept of one vision to a new level in the DR framework, by insisting on being involved in all decisions around production. Based on his experience from *Nikolaj and Julie,* he moved on to *The Killing* with the ambition to be a part of all major decisions surrounding the project and to leave nothing to chance. This has been a time-consuming and demanding process, which has often led to conflicts because of his opinions on everything during the creation of the universe for the story. However, once production starts he is rarely on the set. Bernth is 'the bridge' between the production and the writers, since Sveistrup finds that the director needs to be 'the king on the set' and thus he shouldn't go there to 'undermine his or her role' (Sveistrup 2012). Moreover, once production starts he is more than busy with keeping the writing on track. In the DR framework, writing during production is generally regarded as an asset, since it allows for the production to influence the text. In the case of the last season of *The Killing*, however, Bernth describes how there were too many last minute rescues, since the schedule became too tight (in Berg and Diesen 2012).

Sveistrup and Bernth seem to agree that the making of *The Killing III* has been much too stressful, with the late delivery of scripts complicating the task of others to do the best job possible. The process can be regarded as a consequence of organizing production according to the work process of Sveistrup, who in his own words can only really start making choices once he feels the production breathing down his neck. Based on the understanding of creative processes from the field of CPS, one can argue that he finds the process of converging hard, and as the producer Bernth allows for late solution-finding and acceptance-finding (Isaksen and Treffinger 2004). Bernth regards Sveistrup as 'one of the best writers in the world just now' and has a great trust in him (in Berg and Diesen 2012), even though his work process makes the job of many other people in the crew very hard indeed. Bernth acknowledges that Sveistrup has:

> a work process where things only start happening in his head once the machine is up and running. When he knows that there is a production coming at him like a thundering express train, then he writes. If he has too much time and there is no pressure, he keeps going 'no, let's move in another direction. Let's try one more time...' which is his great strength, but at the same time also a problem.
>
> (Bernth in Berg and Diesen 2012)

Sveistrup is well aware that he is pushing the limits of production, but he also knows that he has the trust of the producer, which allows him to stretch the deadlines. In his words, no one thanks you for handing in a script on time, and if the final material is good then people forget the stressful process (Sveistrup 2012).

According to both Sveistrup and Bernth, the making of *The Killing III* was marked by a problematic performance anxiety and self-awareness caused by the sudden international success of the series. They find that this has not been conducive for the work, and episode writer Horsten adds that even though there are obvious benefits from knowing your main character and the story world of a series very well, writing a later season can actually be harder than writing the first seasons since there is a constant fear of repeating oneself. Bernth explains that after winning the BAFTA and the production of an American remake there was a feeling that the whole world was watching, and they started looking at their process too much from the outside instead of just continuing to do their own thing. She finds that this slowed the process down remarkably (in Berg and Diesen 2012). Horsten describes how script decisions got harder to make when continuously thinking about the high expectations for the series (Horsten 2013) (Figure 7.2).

Besides being influenced by the work process of Sveistrup, the stages of writing and production was thus further delayed by the pressure felt by the writers as to the high demands of the series. As an example of a one vision process within DR Fiction, the production story points to how the concept of one vision is not only related to focusing on the original idea of a writer and allowing him or her to see it through but also to his or her work process with the way one specific writer works having a number of implications for production. As discussed in Chapter 5 on one vision and in the chapter on the *Borgen* writers' room, the same overall institutional dogmas guide the approach to production, but the actual work takes on many different forms depending on the people involved and the context for a series.

Double storytelling with three layers

The opening credits of *The Killing* present the series as a thriller by Søren Sveistrup. The genre contract with the audience is thus explicitly communicated from the very beginning, and the series works extensively with thriller elements like suspense and cliffhangers. However, the series can be regarded as mixing elements from several genres with the political and personal dramas running parallel to the crime

Figure 7.2   Sofie Gråbøl, creator Søren Sveistrup, producer Piv Bernth and director Birger Larsen with BAFTA awards for *The Killing* in 2011. Photo by DR. Courtesy of DR

investigation at the core. Gunhild Agger has discussed the series as drawing heavily on conventions from the melodrama when analysing the depiction of emotions in the storylines of the families affected by the crimes (2011). From an industry perspective, German co-producer Peter Nadermann has highlighted a quality of the DR series as being 'emotional in their structure' yet at the same time 'formally ambitious' (in Redvall 2013, 58). As presented in the above, the ambition with *The Killing* was to use a crime as the inciting incident for interweaving a number of characters whose lives were otherwise not linked. When talking about his approach to writing, Sveistrup insists on always having emotion at the core. He aims to create something, which he is emotionally drawn to, believing that others will feel the same (Sveistrup 2012).

All three seasons of *The Killing* have a three-plot structure with a crime plot, a political plot and a family plot. In the first season, the story followed the murder investigation and its implication on the political life of Troels Hartmann and on the grieving family of the murdered girl. The second season took the crime plot to another level by linking it to

Denmark's role as a warring nation. According to Horsten, the writers felt that the more emotional story of the family suffered somewhat in this season, since the father was in prison, making it hard to create good family scenes (Horsten 2013). An intention of the third season was to again have a stronger family storyline, but this time the emotions surrounding the parents of the abducted girl at the centre of the story also relates to the political plot with the father of the family being the head of the multinational shipping corporation Zeeland.

The three-plot structure grew out of the ambition to rethink traditional crime stories and to have politics and private lives of characters as an important part of the story. This structure naturally provides many opportunities of dealing with various ethical and social issues as called for in the dogma defining the DR Fiction concept of double storytelling. Sveistrup describes how the approach has been to frame the story as a crime story, centred on solving a specific case, but the crime is primarily to be interpreted as a motor for storytelling. As he states, 'it is just an excuse for telling a lot of other stories' (Sveistrup 2012). From a public service perspective, *The Killing* being more than 'just' a crime story makes the production of genre fare easier to legitimize, and DR Fiction executives have continuously stressed how the series is 'not just about finding the murderer' (e.g. Bernth in Jane 2012). The three-plot structure offers opportunities to explore a range of storylines, and the series is also perceived as having larger societal issues at the core. Head of DR Fiction Nadia Kløvedal Reich thus argues that the second season is not a crime story, but a story about the killing of civilians in Afghanistan, about how far to bend a democracy in the attempt to defend it and about what it means to be a nation at war, while the third season is perceived as taking on larger issues of the financial crisis (Reich 2012). Audiences might primarily think of *The Killing* as an entertaining crime series or a new Nordic Noir, but in the corporate storytelling of DR Fiction it is a series with several other layers beneath the crime investigation, legitimizing it as a public service television product.

The three-plot structure of *The Killing* leads to a large cast headed by Sarah Lund, whose journey is at the heart of the three seasons. The writing of episodes begins with outlining her process of investigating as well as her private scenes before moving on to the political and private storylines of other characters. Sarah Lund's plot normally takes up around 30 scenes or half an episode. According to episode writer Horsten, the key to what makes *The Killing* work is how the different stories intersect and influence each other. They all have to 'colour' and 'push' each other to create a complex entity. Horsten finds that the hardest part of the writing has always been to naturally integrate the political plot, which he defines as 'the ambitious gene of the series' with themes about 'politics, society and the present' taking on a different form than in most other crime stories (Horsten 2013). Horsten thus also finds that the larger themes is what sets *The Killing* apart from other series in the domain, and these themes are apparently the hardest to fit into the whole.

Having three plots to cover in each episode calls for a lot of 'scene weaving', but rather than constantly cutting between the plotlines Sveistrup has deliberately tried to create longer sequences of several scenes from each plot. In his opinion, longer scenes or sequences create a more cinematic feeling and they were also regarded as important for getting an epic element into the story of a number of characters, whose lives are suddenly all part of the same 'drama of destinies' (Sveistrup 2012).[10] The weaving of the lives of the many characters is also evident in the end montage of each episode, which shows the main characters accompanied by the music. According to Sveistrup this montage was a must. He had already used that kind of montage in *Nikolaj and Julie*, and the montage was a central part of the writing from the beginning and always part of the scripts. It was a way to remind audiences that all characters are part of the same story, but the montage was much debated since *24* used a similar kind of ending and there were concerns about looking alike (Sveistrup in Nielsen 2012a).[11]

Choosing to work with three different plots creates a number of logistical challenges. In terms of production, there are obvious reasons why working with one arena or one 'precinct' as it is sometimes also called (Redvall 2013, 36) is preferable. Having several plots in different spheres not only calls for many actors but also for many locations. The first season had three major studio sets; the town hall, the home of the Birk Larsen family with the moving company and the police station. The expensive sets called for two-thirds of each episode to be shot in the studio and only one-third on location (Bernth in Berg and Diesen 2012). The second season only had two studio sets – the police station and the justice department – while the third season had the police station as the only studio set and shot other important places as the Zeeland headquarters on location. Bernth explains that a major reason for this was that writers get bored writing for the same sets. They want to write for new places and accordingly it was decided to be much more on location in the last season. In this way, the rethinking of existing story formulas not only has implications for the work of the writers, but naturally also has numerous consequences in later stages of production.

In a similar vein, the process of working with the long-running episodic structure also created a special work environment for the actors. The writers deliberately kept the identity of the perpetrator a secret to the very end, and actors would thus have to deal with not knowing where the story was going. For the third season, DR made an event out of the actor Stig Hoffmeyer (playing Zeeland executive Niels Reinhardt) only learning that he was the murderer during the reading of the script for the last episode by posting the revelatory moment on the series' website. The actor commented that it would have been nice to know so that 'he could have played it'. The example points to how the writer enjoying the one vision privilege in the process is a powerful figure deciding how to distribute knowledge to certain collaborators and not others. Some are invited to collaborate during early stages with the possibility of influencing the text and of calibrating their performance to what they know will be the future developments of the story. Others are expected to execute what is on the page and to keep their performances open to a range of possible developments. In the case of *The Killing* there was a need for secrecy around the plot, but it was also a decision by Sveistrup to have actors not knowing the outcome for their characters based on a belief that this would keep an ambiguity in their acting. Whereas the late delivery of scripts creates a particular work environment for others, this conviction of the head writer similarly leads to a particular approach to production, which might suit some actors better than others (Figure 7.3).

As for the lead character Sarah Lund, a main intention was to make her stay mysterious throughout. Bernth has stated that while some other characters have a backstory, there is no biography of Sarah Lund; Sveistrup has one potential backstory, Gråbøl and Bernth have others. They share several elements, but they also differ (in Nielsen 2012b). Bernth finds that the US remake lost a crucial element from the original when starting to explain Lund's background in more detail, and the reception of the original series does point to the pleasures of being able to individually fill in the gaps of the taciturn Lund allowing for a wide range of interpretations.

In terms of *The Killing* as an example of double storytelling, the series can be regarded as based on more than 'just' an entertaining story. However, the concept of double storytelling does not seem to be used by the writers of the series, who prefer to discuss its nature in terms of its three storytelling layers. When asked about the concept of double storytelling in the interview for this book, Sveistrup

Figure 7.3   Sarah Lund (Sofie Gråbøl) and Mathias Borch (Nikolaj Lie Kaas) inter-rogating Zeeland executive Niels Reinhardt (Stig Hoffmeyer) with their boss Lennart Brix (Morten Suurballe) in the background in episode nine of the third season of *The Killing*. Hoffmeyer did not know that his character was the murderer until the reading of the last script. Photo by Tine Harden. Courtesy of DR

describes instinctively wanting to rebel against executives presenting any kinds of concept for series such as certain ideas of public service storytelling. However, he respects how DR executives try to explain and frame the series produced and how specific conceptions of qual-ity drama on the management level naturally influence the choices of content and can also retrospectively be used to interpret the series in the public realm (Sveistrup 2012). His statement points to the com-plicated nature of putting guiding principles for production down on paper without them being perceived as constraints by practitioners. Even without explicitly formulated dogmas and concepts, there are always complex negotiations between talent proposing new series and the experts in the field having certain ideas of quality and demands of appropriateness for what is to be produced. Certain dogmas or concepts can create a shared language and a sense of direction, but these might be better suited as an externalization of a certain managerial outlook, rather than a recipe for practitioners of how to approach the making of new series to make them fit into certain categories. The original screen ideas of writers have to fit into the ideas of the experts in the field in order to move into production, but when aiming for going with the desires of writers, it does seem like part of the intention of starting with 'the who' rather than 'the what' is to not overemphasize a concept like double storytelling, which might be interpreted as constraining by writers.

Crossover and cinematic crime

Whereas the idea of 'crossover' between the worlds of film and television is also part of the dogmas, this appears to be more of an analytical category in a similar vein to the concept of double storytelling. It is not a concept that is used and discussed during production. No one states a need to have crossover. However, *The Killing* can be regarded as marked by a meeting of elements from the world of film and television, both in terms of the people attached to the production based on the notion of producer's choice and in terms of visual and storytelling ideas of cinematic elements informing the world of the small screen.

Since the developing of the first season, an ambition with *The Killing* was to create a cinematic look for the series. Sveistrup argues that we all watch films on the television screen, and he could not see why TV series could not also be told using the visual language known from the world of film. As a fan of spaghetti westerns, he would like to see more visual storytelling and move away from television being talking heads. A number of elements for what Sveistrup calls the visual storytelling were integrated in the script from the beginning, like the idea of long sequences. Related to this was an intention to work with longer takes, and Sveistrup was also keen on working with filming the actors from behind so that audiences can't see their faces. This can prompt a desire for a reaction shot before satisfying this desire, and he finds that this leads to an atmosphere of having to discover something rather than of getting everything served up. Sveistrup argues that this strategy is not the least helpful for series where you spend a lot of time with the same characters and do not want to constantly 'decode' them in close ups with the risk of viewers maybe losing interest, because they have already seen it all (in Nielsen 2012a). This approach was one of the attempts to make the genre part of the way in which a scene was shot and edited, and early in the process there were other discussions of how to marry the genre, the story and the visuals with the conceptualizing director Birger Larsen and production designer Niels Sejer leading to the series' use of light and colour with, for instance, the street lights reflecting the rainy streets of Copenhagen.

All series work with finding their own visual identity and mode of expression, but Ingolf Gabold believes that series from DR are characterized by extensive work in this regard (Gabold 2010). Bernth agrees that a lot of time is spent talking about the visuals, explaining that the conceptualizing director is attached almost from the beginning of the process when the script and characters are still being developed (in Berg and Diesen 2012). The director chooses his director of photography, but Bernth and Sveistrup have to approve. The director also suggests an editor, but Bernth and Sveistrup are also part of this choice, since they are often the ones who spend most time in the editing room in the end. Bernth explains that it thus has to be an accomplished editor, but also someone with the right chemistry for all the conversations in the room (in Berg and Diesen 2012). As discussed in the previous chapter, chemistry is all-important to become a part of the writers' room, but it is also a decisive element in many other aspects of production where the head writer is part of hiring the people to become part of his vision. The principal casting is done in collaboration between the director, Sveistrup and Bernth, while the episode casting is done by the episode director in collaboration with Bernth. When in doubt, Sveistrup is asked.

The Killing is a good example of how DR Fiction – in spite of being an in-house production unit at DR – is working with producer's choice and crossover, hiring skilled freelancers from the film and television industry rather than working with an in-house crew. According to Bernth, the only DR employed personnel besides her on *The Killing* were the line producer, a scripter, a grip and the head of post-production. All others were work for hire, including Sveistrup (Bernth in Berg and Diesen 2012). The people brought in had experience in both film and television. As an example, Niels Sejer won the annual Danish film award Bodil for his production design on Nikolaj Arcel's Oscar-nominated historical drama *En kongelig affære/A Royal Affair* (2012) only some months after *The Killing III* being shown on Danish television.

The opening of *The Killing III* at a worn down ship exemplifies how the series draws on the imagery and sound design of film to create a suspenseful atmosphere. The third season was shot 80 per cent on location using sites like junk yards as back drops for the theme of a world marked by the financial crisis (Bernth in Berg and Diesen 2012). According to Bernth, it takes around 15 days, or three weeks, to shoot an episode, and then there are six weeks of editing, four weeks of sound design and a week for colour grading.[12] An important aspect in the post-production is the use of music, which has also been a crucial element for Sveistrup from the very beginning where he absolutely did not want music with singing. He had many talks with the composer Frans Bak about how to use repetition as an element in the music and how to aim for a hard and cynical sound while also having sequences with a more emotional core. Sveistrup describes the music of the end montage as marked by the ideas of repetition, giving you a sense of standing still and holding your breath. According to Sveistrup it took almost a year to develop the right music after trying out a lot of different things, but everyone was pleased with the end result, which has also been used in the US remake after an audition with ten other film and TV composers (Sveistrup in Nielsen 2012a).

The work on the music is an example of how Sveistrup has been closely involved in most aspects of making the series and how many of the distinctive traits of the series have been a long time in the making. Several defining stylistic features have been present since the early stages of writing, but they have then been developed further in a close collaboration with several key people invited to take part in conceptualizing the series rather than merely being asked to execute the ideas on the page or to add to the work once the material was shot. However, entering a strong existing vision can be quite a task, and as stated by the director of the first episode in the third season, Mikkel Serup, his main concern was 'not to fuck things up' (Serup in Bjørnkjær 2012). Whereas directors, directors of photography, editors and actors have changed between seasons, Søren Sveistrup and his episode writers, Piv Bernth and Sofie Gråbøl have been the steady people behind the production trying to ensure consistency in content, character and quality. The concept of producer's choice and the hiring of crossover talent with experience in film as well as television have been important for the look and feel of the series. However, the ambition to have a cinematic mode of expression was to a large degree grounded in the intention by the creator to make a series with a different visual style and with a marriage between suspense and mystery in the storytelling on the page and the storytelling on the screen.

Beyond the national mainstream

The production of *The Killing* was marked by high ambitions of creating a series, which could compete with what was perceived as the best series in the international domain even if the series – as all series from DR Fiction – was primarily targeted at national audiences. From a co-production perspective, Peter Nadermann has commented that with the limited competition and the popular Sunday night slot DR could

easily settle for less and still get good audience numbers. He finds a signifier of the series from DR to be how the talent behind series as well as
the executives of DR Fiction still insist on 'going a little bit over the
top' (Nadermann in Redvall 2013, 62). On a similar note, the crime
fiction expert Forshaw makes the claim that even 'the least ambitious
Nordic fiction is often prepared to take some audacious steps into the
unknown, producing fiction which can function as both popular product and personal statement from the author' (2012, 3). Scandinavian
crime works within well-known genre patterns and targets the mass
audiences, but in spite of this there is often the sense of a personal voice
behind the product and some attempt to reinvent certain established
aspects of the genre. From a Screen Idea System perspective, this can
be interpreted as a process of both talent and experts in the field being
inspired by what they regard as the best products in the international
domain, but grounding new variations of these in a one vision approach
to production focusing on the original idea of a writer and insisting on
the importance of 'the who' behind a series.

Most creators of series naturally aim high from the outset, and then
different types of constraints often lead to changes and compromises
along the way as the original screen idea moves through the many stages
of development and production. The process of making *The Killing* illustrates how a producer and a production framework is in dialogue with
a creator about an idea from the very beginning and how people go a
long way to encourage and facilitate his vision and work process. The
series is the result of a rather long development process with several
people involved. Sveistrup has argued that one of the reasons why Scandinavian product is currently of international interest is that people are
really making an effort to create something different within the genre
of crime fiction (Sveistrup 2012). There are many adaptations in the
current Scandi-crime/Nordic Noir wave. *The Killing* is an example of a
series trying to rethink the more traditional arena- and case-based crime
story with a number of stylistic features also being developed from the
ground up with the head writer at the centre all the way through the
process.

Whereas the dream of many US broadcasters is to have long-running
hits or series moving into syndication, there is officially no ambition
to continue *The Killing* in spite of the overwhelming response and the
somewhat open ending of the third season with Sarah Lund heading for
doom or new adventures. Sveistrup argues that he has to stop out of fear
of repeating himself after having made 40 episodes. The ambition was to
create something original, and he doesn't want to become an example

of having a precise recipe, which was exactly what he tried to oppose from the outset. Moreover, he argues that audiences also lose interest in new inventions after a while (Sveistrup 2012). Rather than repeating a successful recipe in the domain, it is time to once again think of a new variation. Apparently, DR Fiction shares this point of view with Bernth, now being Head of Drama, telling upcoming head writer Jeppe Gjervig Gram that it is now his duty to 'destroy' *The Killing* by taking a few good things from it and then throwing out the rest (Bernth in Nielsen 2012b). Bernth finds that it is important to not satisfy the audience desire for more of the same thing, but to rather have a rotation where they are offered something new instead.

The analysis of the development, writing and production of *The Killing* in this chapter points to how the originality of the series is in many ways based on an interplay between the domain, the talent and the field in the Screen Idea System. The creator Søren Sveistrup wanted to break with certain traditions in the national domain as well as with specific ideas of best practice for television crime series. He was inspired by new trends in the international domain and coming off an award-winning, highly popular series he was given substantial time and trust to develop a new idea for a potential series. However, his initial idea had to be appropriate in terms of the demands of executives with a public service mandate looking for more than 'just' crime series as well as series of a certain length. The original idea was thus shaped by meeting these demands and the further development of the series was marked by extensive time for research and for inviting a number of people to contribute at an early stage in the process. The production was organized to facilitate the work process of the writer, even if this put great pressure on the rest of production. According to Sveistrup it has been a process marked by a high degree of trust, allowing him to be in charge based on the notion of one vision (Sveistrup 2012). Producer Piv Bernth and episode writer Michael W. Horsten support the series being based on Sveistrup's vision from beginning to end, but with numerous people contributing important parts to the finished series.

The case study is one example of what the highly collaborative process of making a television series can be like when working within the DR Fiction framework based on official production dogmas calling for one vision, double storytelling and crossover. As exemplified in the previous chapter, the writing of *Borgen* had a different structure, but was similarly organized as a process with the head writer at the centre and a clear sense of who was in creative control. A series will always be marked by the coming together of many different talents, of a number of more or less deliberate choices, of lucky as well as unlucky hazards and of certain constraints, which can be regarded as productive or unproductive to the work at hand. As remarked by art historian Ernst H. Gombrich, 'works of art are not the result of some mysterious activity, but objects made by human beings for human beings' (1950/2006, 28). The same goes for writing and producing television. The Screen Idea System helps clarify the way in which most processes are a complex interplay of several components. In the case of *The Killing*, this interplay led to a result, which has been hailed as a creative new variation in both the national and international domain.

8
Conclusions and Cliffhangers

This book has explored the approach to writing and producing television drama in one specific, national production culture by offering analyses of some of the many complexities related to creating new screen ideas. The book has offered insights into the mode of production at DR Fiction and into the creative work of practitioners working within this public service production unit. As pointed to in the different chapters, the mode of production of DR Fiction has changed dramatically since the 1990s, and the current success of series like *Borgen* (2010–2013) and *The Killing* (2007–2012) should be seen as linked not only to the talented people involved in the making of the series – ranging from writers, producers, directors, actors, production designers, directors of photography, composers and others – but also to the mandate or the managerial ideas of DR Fiction as well as to changes in the domain of television drama.

John Thornton Caldwell argues that 'research on creativity and constraints should consider legal, economic, unionist, historical, and institutional factors – not just organizational structures or interpersonal interactions – in order fully to understand a specific culture or subculture of production' (2013, 3). This book shares the belief that contextual elements must inform studies of production cultures and creative work, but one naturally has to choose a main focus of investigation in specific studies, while trying to include as many important aspects surrounding a core problem statement as possible. The focus of this book has been on the work of practitioners, proposing the Screen Idea System as a fruitful framework for understanding the processes of developing, writing and producing new screen ideas as an interplay between many elements.

Whereas there is great value in studying the aspects outlined by Caldwell as well as the impact of the ever influential technological changes in terms of film and media production, this book has stressed the value of also thinking about writing and production as based on different ideas of originality, quality and appropriateness among practitioners and commissioners, and in approaching work processes as different kinds of collaborations. Creativity researchers often define the emergence of what is regarded as creative products as based on a mix of being of high quality and original as well as appropriate to the task at hand. The question of appropriateness is ever present in terms of television production, and the nature of the negotiations between talent and experts in the field about what to produce for the future domain is highly relevant and should be explored.

As analysed in this book, the first production dogma of DR Fiction is to put the writer at the centre of developing new series based on the concept of one vision. One of the intentions of the book has been to create a nuanced understanding of what this implies for experts and talent alike and what a 'one vision framework' for production can look like. The case studies have pointed to how the same kind of institutional structures can encompass very different interpersonal interactions and work methods, and how implementing a concept such as one vision takes time as well as trust. The macro level context is important, but so is the detailed study of how different individuals find their own ways of navigating and collaborating within the same framework. Using the Screen Idea System as the basic understanding for the processes at hand, the chapters have highlighted how the past years have seen remarkable changes in terms of the talent behind new series as well as the nature of the field and domain of television drama. This chapter sums up the main conclusions of the book and point to challenges and cliffhangers for the future landscape of Danish television drama writing and production.

Talent targeting quality television

In terms of the individuals behind new series from DR Fiction, the book has analysed how the background of the talent writing new series has changed remarkably with the emergence of writers focusing particularly on television writing since the 1990s. Moreover, the structures for learning the craft have seen great changes with The National Film School of Denmark (NFSD) beginning to take television seriously as an artistic medium and gradually including the teaching of television writing in the curriculum. DR Fiction was actively engaged in this development during the 1990s when experiencing a lack of talent for making the kind of flagship series, which executives at DR Fiction perceived to be the best way to brand DR and to legitimize the existence of an in-house unit.

The Film School has been influential in establishing certain ideas of best practice among writers through the TV term collaboration with DR and in focusing on the different roles and collaborations of writers and producers in the process of developing new series. As discussed in Chapter 4, the teaching of television writing is not only a question of understanding storytelling structures or the best beats in a scene. It is also about learning 'the rules of the game' when pitching to a specific broadcaster and about gaining an understanding of the collaborative processes of television production. The institutional collaboration between DR and the Film School seems unique for a European production culture, but it has been copied in the 2010s by the film schools in both Norway and Sweden. Moreover, the European television industry has taken an interest in what Head of Drama Piv Bernth has described as one of the secrets of the recent success of series from DR (in Pham 2012). It seems only natural if other broadcasters in the national television landscape might also start to focus more on this kind of talent training in the years to come. It is remarkable how almost all writers presently working for DR Fiction are alumni from the Film School, who have had the opportunity to present themselves to DR during the TV term.

International inspirations for the national ambitions

Whereas a whole new structure for educating television writers emerged during the 2000s, the outlook of writers also appears to have been still more marked by ambitions to draw on trends and tastes in the international domain of television drama rather than the established, national traditions. Following *Taxa/Taxi* (1997–1999), the crime series *Rejseholdet/Unit One* (2000–2004), *Ørnen/The Eagle* (2004–2006) and *Livvagterne/The Protectors* (2008–2010) proved to national audiences that domestic product could compete in this genre-territory. Together with the family series *Nikolaj og Julie/Nikolaj and Julie* (2002–2003), *Krøniken/Better Times* (2004–2007) and *Sommer/Summer* (2008), these have been crucial in building the impressive audience figures that series from DR have continuously enjoyed in the past decade. However, the series which have found a wider international interest in the 2010s are those, which have reinvented the well-known arena or case-based structure of much genre fare by working with several arenas simultaneously, playing with the serial format and introducing content, which was not initially considered to be the obvious choice for high-profile drama series. *Borgen* thus pioneered a political series on Danish grounds, and *The Killing* took a new approach to the murder mystery by keeping the name of the killer dangling for 20 episodes.

As described in the case studies of these series, the ambitions of their makers have been high from the outset, as has the desire to reinvent what a series in the national domain could be like. As noted by Søren Sveistrup in relation to *The Killing*, his ambition for the series was all about creating something new: 'I wasn't interested in creating something, which looked like anything I had previously done. In fact, I wasn't really interested in making television, which looked like anything I had ever seen before' (Sveistrup 2012). Adam Price similarly proposed a political series in spite of there being no tradition for this kind of content in the domain and a general perception that scripted drama on politics would not interest wider audiences. International quality television has been a major source of inspiration for several creators of new series, but they always have to keep in mind that series from DR target the large, mainstream audiences. As recently stressed by a media observer in the Danish press, US cable series such as *The Wire* (HBO 2002–2008), *Mad Men* (AMC 2007–), *Californication* (Showtime 2007–) or *Breaking Bad* (AMC 2008–2013) may be the series that national trendsetters in the press adore, but only around 20,000 viewers found their way to *Mad Men* on TV 3 (Jensen 2013). In contrast, DR series continuously enjoy large audiences. Several US cable series have found a transnational niche in the past years, but the vast majority of Danish viewers still prefer series in the Danish language with a broad appeal.

First who, then what: Time and trust

The writing process and negotiations of how to turn the original ideas of writers into series considered to be of high quality as well as appropriate for the public service audiences point to structures where a great amount of trust is granted to writers who have already proven their worth within the system. In Chapter 7 on *The Killing*, Head of Drama Piv Bernth stressed that the process is to first focus on 'the who' behind a series and then 'the what' in terms of content. Head of DR Fiction Nadia Kløvedal Reich has coined this as a 'first who, then what-principle' for production (in Nielsen 2012d). The principle is based on the belief that stories should emerge from writers with a personal desire to tell something specific, and according to Reich trust is a crucial element in this regard. She argues that developing and producing television drama builds on trust rather than control, which is also what the eighth production dogma of

DR Fiction tries to capture by stating that executives should be in charge of, but not in control of the processes (in Nielsen 2012d).

This description of the decision-making of experts in the field to focus on the creator of series and their desires prior to discussions about specific content is linked to the concept of one vision. This implies listening to the ideas of writers and allowing time for development, even if their ideas might initially seem inappropriate in comparison to other products in the domain or to the mandate for what is to be produced. The development and writing processes of *Borgen* and *The Killing* illustrate how there was originally scepticism towards the ideas for both series. Despite this, the writers were given time to develop their ideas further based on the trust in their talent earned by a successful track record.

Whereas the drama production of, for instance, Norway and Sweden has seen many adaptations of popular novels, the strategy of DR Fiction has been to go with original ideas of writers. This strategy seems to establish a strong sense of ownership for an idea with the particular writer, but the strategy also calls for substantial time to develop an arena for a series – or in the case of *Borgen* and *The Killing* several arenas – when creating everything from the ground up. These processes necessitate a willingness to finance long periods of research and development, while the idea of the writer gradually finds its right shape.

Not many writers are given the opportunity to develop series in this way within the DR Fiction framework. The series from DR in the 2000s have been written by only a few writers making a strong imprint. Established and experienced head writers Stig and Peter Thorsboe were head writers on the majority of family and crime series of the decade, and with the international success of the three seasons of *The Killing* and *Borgen*, Søren Sveistrup and Adam Price have been the main head writers of DR Fiction in the 2010s. The consistency in writers and producers behind the series has been remarkable, but the recent developments in DR Fiction indicates that there seems to be a generational change going on, with writers who have 'grown up' within the system making the move to head writers of high-profile series. Being used to the head writer/episode writers structure of series, these writers, such as Maya Ilsøe and Jeppe Gjervig Gram, want to work with writers' rooms and they take the concept of one vision for granted.

As analysed in Chapter 5 on the concept of one vision, it took time to establish the head writer/episode writers structure within the DR framework. However, this framework has been an important part of training future writers after their time at Film School. All writers agree that it takes time to acquire the skills needed to take on the challenging role of head writer in the one vision framework. The emerging head writers appreciate having had the opportunity to train for this task through what can be regarded as 'peer to peer'-training within DR Fiction.

Writing teams as thought communities

Rather than merely being examples of a distributed collaboration with writers performing different tasks, some of the writing collaborations studied for this book point to writers working as what Vera John-Steiner has described as family collaborations or integrative collaborations (2000). The work in some writers' rooms can be regarded as examples of what John-Steiner has outlined as the longitudinal work processes of thought communities, where ideas emerge from joint thinking and significant conversations based on participants having a shared sense of personal investment and risk-taking (2000). The writers of *Borgen* making a musketeer oath about the nature of the collaboration at hand is one example of establishing a sense of shared responsibility and mutuality in the writing process. Head writer Adam Price agreeing to teach upcoming head writer Jeppe Gjervig Gram as much about the head writer job as possible similarly points to a close collaboration and an outspoken agreement of passing on knowledge within the system.

In principle, the writers are not only collaborators but also potentially competing in terms of the writing of future series. However, there has been surprisingly little sense of competition in the work processes observed or in comments from writers about the nature of their work. This might partly be explained by the small size of the writing teams and writers' rooms. Compared to US rooms, the Danish writing teams are small and there is no detailed hierarchy ranging from, for instance, baby writer over junior writer to senior writer. With normally only three people in the room and the titles of head writer and episode writers as the only official job descriptions there is less need to position oneself once access has been granted. The focus is then on the work rather than navigating in a large group of highly ambitious writers all fighting to outdo each other.

The initial hardships of establishing a head writer/episode writers structure within DR Fiction was related to writers having to learn how this called for head writers to take on the role of work leaders and episode writers accepting that they are co-writers on a project with another writer in charge and will have their texts rewritten. This structure now seems to be firmly established with writers referring to the well-functioning structure of *Borgen* as 'a factory' (Gram 2012). However, the structure takes on a different form from series to series, with for instance head writer Maya Ilsøe spending many months trying to figure out how to best create a room that facilitated her work process.

In terms of collaboration, all writers and producers continuously stress the importance of having the right 'chemistry' for the process. As analysed in the case study of *Borgen*, this is partly referred to as having different skills in the process, with for instance head writer Adam Price being 'an idea-generating machine' and the episode writers taking on the role of questioning and sorting the many ideas. However, the notion of chemistry also refers to a more intangible sense of feeling safe and trusted, which some writers worry about being able to recreate when leaving what is perceived as a good room.

European takes on writers and showrunners

The focus on collaboration in this book stresses the need to take these complicated interpersonal and intangible aspects into consideration when studying production. It would be fruitful for further studies of screenwriting collaborations and writers' rooms from different production cultures to learn more about the nature of other Screen Idea Systems and of the collaborative nature of television writing in different contexts. The majority of explorations on topics such as these have focused on the US television industries, but recent research also centres on a comparative perspective when addressing issues about transnational television drama (Weissmann 2012) or how to understand the emerging concept of the showrunner in a European context (Cornea 2009).

Several influential ideas in the framework of DR Fiction are interpreted as deliberate attempts to copy work methods from the US industry, such as the establishment of relay production, working with a head writer/episode writers structure and writing series during their production. Not the least, the influential concept of one vision is interpreted as a DR Fiction take on what was perceived as US quality television series having a personal authorial signature in the 1990s. As analysed in Chapter 5, the concept of one vision shares some similarities with the notion of the showrunner, but the writer with one vision in the DR Fiction framework is normally much more of a head writer than an executive producer. As an example, when Adam Price works with a writers' room for *Borgen*, he not only oversees the work of the room, but he is continuously an active part of the writing process, while his producer deals with the many logistical and budgetary aspects of production. The successful series from DR have been based on long-term writer-producer constellations, which are granted great importance by all writers and perceived as a form of 'twin vision' by some producers.

There are, of course, major differences when comparing a small, national television industry with the structures of major US studios, such as the small size of the writers' rooms or the differences in the speed of production. Critical voices might argue that the limited number of writers in the rooms at DR Fiction makes it a case of team writing rather than of writers' rooms as known from US drama series. However, this writing process is understood as working with a writers' room in the DR Fiction framework and considered to be an example of best practice when implementing a one vision line of thought. Compared to what US scholars have described as the often harsh working conditions of US rooms (Caldwell 2008; Henderson 2011; Phalen and Osselame 2012) and industry debates about the 'broken' nature of the US mode of television production (Redvall 2012a), it makes sense to investigate the strategies of other production cultures with competing ideas of how to facilitate the emergence of quality product and how to think of creativity and control, constraints and collaboration.

Collaborative writing with one vision

Even though the definition of one vision in the DR framework carries the sound of a potential creative dictatorship, the processes observed seemed highly collaborative. Head writers have continuously been challenged and they have had to explain and defend their ideas while numerous people have contributed with input along the way. The processes are marked by extensive time for the initial stages of mess-, data- and problem-finding with a continuous dialogue about an idea between several writers and other collaborators. Moreover, the processes offer directors, actors and other crew members the opportunity of voicing their opinions during stages in production, where their thoughts can become part of the conception of the text. In this way, other professions involved in production who are traditionally regarded as primarily part of the execution of a text have the possibility of providing constructive feedback to the writers. As analysed in Chapter 5, some writers encourage this, while others are more protective of the text. Explorations of these kinds of processes offer productive perspectives on how to think of the script as a blueprint for production (Staiger 2012) or how to consider scriptwriting as different processes of 'scripting' (Maras 2009).

One of the main challenges of this strategy seems to be not to drown head writers in cascades of input, while they are involved in most major decisions around production along the way and listen to the ideas and concerns of several collaborators and experts in the field. An important part of working with the concept of one vision thus seems to be establishing routines around note-giving and feedback. Observing the third season of *Borgen*, there were steady structures for these processes, while the observations of the work of a new head writer pointed to the challenges of finding one's way in a one vision framework for the first time. As argued by several writers, the concept of one vision not only comes with a sense of artistic freedom but also with great responsibility, and particularly the collaboration with producers seems crucial for writers with a need for supportive structures in periods of stress or doubt.

In the DR Fiction framework, the head writer does appear to be the one with the overall vision for a project and they are the ones presented as the authors of series after their completion. However, it is a process of what Chapter 5 discussed as 'sufficient control', building on incorporating the competencies and creative contributions of many people along the way. From the outset, an important part of this study was to further understanding of the concept of one vision by exploring practitioners' perceptions of its connotations and the extent to which they found the concept to be an integrated part of their work. One vision does not seem to be only a fancy term in an in-house mission statement, but a concept which influences the approach to production, and which is regarded as crucial for DR Fiction among creative practitioners as well as experts in the field.

Production dogmas as a shared language

As highlighted across chapters, the production dogmas should not be regarded as explicit rules, which creators of new series are told to adhere to when developing new ideas. Several writers interviewed for this book thus testified to not having ever seen the dogmas or of not having heard of a concept like double storytelling. However, they all had their own descriptions of a two-layer public service approach to storytelling, and they were all aware of the concept of one vision and 'producer's choice'. A writer like Sveistrup expressed an appreciation of executives trying to condense the virtues of a certain mode of production on paper, but emphasized that the dogmas are an example of concepts growing out of production rather than being introduced from the executive level. Moreover, he described how he as a writer would instinctively want to rebel against anything sounding like a given recipe, such as being told to come up with a series based on the concept of double storytelling (Sveistrup 2012).

Several practitioners have similarly stressed how the dogmas are reflections and crystallizations on the nature of a certain mode of production, which had already evolved. Among writers, the dogmas were not conceived as an example of a top-down process of establishing a specific recipe for production, but rather as a managerial attempt to capture what was perceived as well-functioning practices. Studying the emergence of concepts like one vision and double storytelling, one can argue that the dogmas can, however, be regarded as an example of the intricate interplay of the Screen Idea System, where the different elements are linked and naturally influence each other. Several of the ideas in the dogmas seem to be based on managerial ambitions to rethink the approach to drama production in the 1990s and to copy work methods for what was perceived as quality product in the domain. However, these ideas were only put down on paper in 2003 and not circulated as part of the corporate storytelling around the recent success of series from DR until much later (Redvall 2011; Hartmann 2012).

The dogmas have not had the function of being a recipe presented to all practitioners, but they have had the function of explicating guiding principles for production among particularly the experts in the field. Certain concepts, such as the idea of one vision, have been widely used, and have created a useful, shared language about the fundamental nature of series from DR. Writers thus describe how the concept was useful in establishing the role of the head writer in relation to directors coming from the more director-driven film industry by clearly singling out the writer as the creator of series in the television industry.

Corporate storytelling of success

Whereas certain dogmas have thus been important as an analytical framework within DR Fiction for several years, they have only recently been presented as a more official framework explaining the international interest in series from DR. As argued by many media industry scholars, all media industries work actively with branding themselves and creating specific kinds of corporate storytelling in the public sphere. This is also the case for institutions with a public service mandate. When the drama output of DR was heavily criticized in the 1990s, new executives at DR Fiction decided to change the approach to production radically. Something had to happen to justify and ensure the continued existence of an in-house production unit.

Head writer Stig Thorsboe tells of writers continuously being told that series have to succeed to keep the in-house production alive, and how he has personally been exhausted by the constant rhetoric of executives about being world champions and winning Emmys. He understands the need for this kind of constant positioning and praising of the series from DR, but argues that a greater sense of humility seems like a better strategy from the point of view of writers; they know how hard the work is, they have the sleepless nights and they would rather discuss the nature of the stories than the level of their success (Thorsboe 2012).

While the success story around DR Fiction has been quite strong in the past years, the press coverage of the third season of *Borgen* and *The Killing* shows how the content of series is constantly debated and challenged in the public sphere, but also how stories of success can backfire when critics and audiences suddenly expect a continuous flow of episodes for Sunday nights, which can compete with the best series in the international domain. With the premiere of *House of Cards* (Netflix 2013–), *Borgen* suddenly had to stand up to this new political series in national reviews. The extensive writings on the foreign reception of *The Killing* in Danish newspapers seemed to have the level of national coverage of new series taking on new proportions and perspectives. Series like *Borgen* and *The Killing* are no longer only compared to the traditions in the national domain of television drama, but are now measured against the latest trends and tastes in the international domain.

Critical cases and failure studies

On several levels, this study has been marked by being conducted at a time of perceived success and of studying examples of what is considered to be best practice. People are naturally more inclined to grant a researcher access to what is perceived as productive work methods and more keen on discussing stories of success rather than failure. As in any production unit for high-profile television drama, there are also critical cases and cancelled series in the DR Fiction framework. Writers Peter Thorsboe and Mai Brostrøm would have liked to write a third season of *The Protectors*, but did not get the chance (Thorsboe 2012; Brostrøm 2012). Some ideas are developed and never move into production, but it does seem that rather than being a production culture marked by many projects competing for financing and attention, the strategy is to focus all resources on trying to ensure that the series that move into production will be successful. This might imply shooting a completely new first episode, as was the case with *Unit One* when focus group tests pointed to audiences not being as enthusiastic as expected.

The production story of *Summer* seems to be the most turbulent in this regard with changes in both writers and directors during production. Despite these troubles, the series ended up as one of the most popular family drama series of the 2000s.

There are good arguments in favour of doing 'failure studies' instead of always writing about stories of success (Hills 2013). As mentioned in the introduction it is, however, much harder to get data on projects, which are perceived as problematic, since people are normally less eager to discuss these in retrospect. Observational studies of on-going processes are valuable in this regard, when one can observe processes with the possibility of going in different directions and the negotiations of conflicts as they happen. As discussed in the different chapters, observing the writing of and meetings around a series such as *Borgen* there have been surprisingly few conflicts, and the research for this book is marked by the rooms and people to which I have had access and by the special point in time for Danish drama series. This book has thus primarily offered insights on what is considered to be best practice at a time of national and international success, but there are many other interesting aspects to explore in terms of the complicated interplay between individuals, the domain and the field during the making of television series (Figure 8.1).

Sites of synergy and scripting

From the outset, the main research questions for this book centred on aspects of creativity and collaboration, but several other areas of interest emerged along the way. One aspect, which seemed of particular interest, was the significance granted to the spaces in which the creative work takes places. As discussed in Chapter 3, the spaces of production at DR Fiction have changed in several ways since the 1990s. The building of new studios for television drama production created the possibility to plan the in-house production based on the needs of DR Fiction instead of being the guest in the studios of others. The notion of having production hotels is still regarded as crucial for facilitating informal conversations between people working on the same screen idea by gathering people of different professions in the same space. Writers' rooms within these production hotels are examples of spaces where even a fragile screen idea gets a physical life of its own.

Production studies are often challenged not only by the difficulties of getting access to the normally off-limits sites of production but also by the fact that production is often spread out between many locations

Figure 8.1 Livvagterne/The Protectors (2009–2010) followed the work and lives of Rasmus Poulsen (Søren Vejby), Jasmina El-Murad (Cecilie Stenspil) and Jonas Goldschmidt (André Babikian) for two seasons. Writers Peter Thorsboe and Mai Brostrøm would have liked to continue their storylines for another season, but did not get the chance. Photo by Mike Kollöffel. Courtesy of DR

over long periods of time. In journalism, newsroom studies have been an important source of information for studying the constant negotiations of the newsworthiness of events and the hierarchies between different roles in journalistic production. In newsrooms, there are actions to observe and opinions are voiced. In a similar vein, writers' rooms, note meetings, readings and other events behind the scenes before the actual shooting of series in studios or locations are a valuable source of learning more, not only about the sites of production but also about the negotiations of quality, originality and appropriateness constantly at play. From a screenwriting research perspective, the collaborative writing process in these physical spaces offers constant conversations about how to best develop new screen ideas, providing an opportunity to listen in on notions of best practice as a text evolves, rather than trying to reconstruct the process at a later stage.

This study has proposed thinking of production hotels as what Mette Hjort has called 'sites of synergy' (2005), offering the possibility of facilitating communication and collaboration. Film and television production is marked by a rather strict division of labour. Creating a mutual space for screen idea work groups around an idea furthers the possibility of different professions sharing viewpoints and opinions during early stages of development and of opening for the input of others at a stage where their contributions can still influence the text on the page. Drawing on the work of Steven Maras (2009), one could call these 'sites of scripting', involving not only the writers in the process but also other professions around the screen idea. Having a writers' room in the midst of a production hotel seems to increase the possibility of actors, directors of photography or production designers contributing with thoughts and suggestions, not only in the scheduled meetings around production but also during random meetings in the hallway or over lunch. *Borgen*-producer Camilla Hammerich thus finds that the physical presence of the writers in a room close to the rest of the people on a production is crucial for a dynamic exchange of ideas about a series (Hammerich 2012), and there seems to be interesting perspectives for screenwriting research in taking closer looks at different sites of scripting in various production cultures.

The many 'M's of media industries: Mandate, management and money

The Screen Idea System stresses how the experts in a field have to be considered crucial to the emergence of certain types of series at a certain point in time. Creativity scholars argue that one always has to consider the many different 'P's related to creativity by addressing the Person, the Product, the Process as well as the Press in discussions of creative work. In a similar vein, one can argue that when doing studies of film and media production one always has to address the many 'M's of media industries, referring to the mandate, management and money of particular institutions and industries.

Series from DR are marked by their production in a public service television framework spending all resources on only a few high-profile series annually. This book has argued that the current output of series from DR has to be interpreted in relation to the managerial ideas, which has changed the mode of production within DR Fiction since the 1990s, and that the in-house dogmas for productions create a particular understanding among experts as to what characterizes a series from DR. New screen ideas have to find acceptance among the experts with the power to greenlight their production, and upon their completion they depend upon schedulers and critics to get the right exposure and reception to be included as a new variation of high quality in the domain. The executives of DR Fiction in the last decade seem to be generally held in high regard among the writers, who find that they have experienced what one can term 'institutional trust' to go with their original ideas and desires.

However, the observations during the development of the new series *Arvingerne/The Legacy* (forthcoming 2014) pointed to how generational shifts and new developments within DR Fiction are currently creating some insecurity among practitioners. As an example, there were long periods of insecurity as to the envisioned length of episodes, the planned time slot for the series (as a more everyday series or a high-profile, Sunday night product) and – related to this – the budget for production. These insecurities made it hard for the writer to conclude what to focus on and how to embrace the original idea. Constraints such as these naturally influence the writing process, and new ambitions of DR Fiction, such as an intention to venture into production of less expensive weeknight drama while continuing the 'flagship productions', seemed to create confusion as to the expectations of certain series in development.

When constraints are in flux, they are hard to confront in a creative way. In the members' survey of The Danish Writers Guild from 2011, one of the points raised by screenwriters in their criticism of the work conditions at TV 2 was how the demands for series seemed to change during the course of their making (Danske Dramatikere 2012). Screenwriter Nikolaj Scherfig has described how screenwriters and directors working for TV 2 over the years have experienced work processes marked by the broadcaster constantly worrying and giving countermands, leading to end results which have often been 'a strange compromise which is neither bird nor fish' (Scherfig 2012). Confronted with the criticism from the Writers' Guild survey, Head of Drama at TV 2, Katrine Vogelsang, agreed to some extent, commenting that because of the commercial mandate of TV 2 numerous other aspects than 'quality' are part of the assessment of projects (in Danske Dramatikere 2012, 39). She pointed to how DR is obliged to produce a certain amount of television drama annually, whereas TV 2 might suddenly decide to prioritize other products than the series in development (2012, 39). Within DR Fiction, the managerial ideas of what to produce as a public service broadcaster seem to have been rather consistent during the 2000s, but it will be interesting to see the further development of the 2010s with new people in charge and new intentions of moving into different formats and maybe even into major co-productions with international players like HBO.

New players and new competition

As analysed in Chapter 2, the 2010s have seen increased competition from other broadcasters in the domestic realm of television drama with particularly TV 2 trying to compete in the crime territory through series such as *Dicte* (2013–). Moreover, the 2010s have seen the emergence of series that are independently produced, meaning that they are not primarily financed by one of the Nordic public service broadcasters. In 2011, DR aired the series *Bron/The Bridge* (2011–) with Danish Kim Bodnia and Swedish Sofia Helin solving cross-border crimes. The series was a co-production by Swedish production company Filmlance International and Danish Nimbus Film and ended up airing on Wednesday nights in both Denmark and Sweden, trying to ensure that the suspense of the story would not be spoiled by audiences having the possibility of catching episodes earlier in the one country rather than the other.[1] DR was a co-financer of the series, but not involved in its making. However, the series was generally perceived as a DR series, both among national audiences in focus groups tests at DR (as observed at DR in 2011) and in the international realm. One of the writers of *The Bridge*, Nikolaj Scherfig, has stated that it is good to have public service broadcasters such as DR and Swedish SVT involved as 'a brand' for a series, but he believes that the coming years will bring more series financed in the style of feature film production with no main financing from a broadcaster (Scherfig 2012).

The Bridge is an example of how Danish production companies that have traditionally been working with film are looking still more into also producing high-profile television drama, and how DR Fiction will most probably have to face increased competition from external production companies in the years to come. As discussed in Chapter 3, the public service scheme now provides funding for series from competing broadcasters, and companies like Miso Film, SF Film and Eyeworks have series in the pipeline. Miso Film produces the expensive historical drama *1864* (forthcoming 2014) for DR, but the production of new Sunday night series is otherwise still an in-house matter (Figure 8.2).

Talks of introducing what in Denmark is debated as 'the BBC-model' of a public service broadcaster ordering a substantial amount of the drama production from external companies is perceived by Head of DR Fiction Nadia Kløvedal Reich as a fatal strategy to pursue. When the Danish Producers Association called for a reorganization of commissioning in this regard, she argued that the BBC-model would cause 'irreparable damage' to Danish television drama (Reich 2013). One of the main

Figure 8.2 Swedish Sofia Helin (as Saga Norén) and Danish Kim Bodnia (as Martin Rohde) who have to collaborate when a body is found on the bridge between Denmark and Sweden in *Bron/The Bridge* (2011–). Photo by Ola Kjelbye. Courtesy of DR

arguments was that a certain in-house volume of production is needed to be a vibrant place of talent development and expertise. According to Reich, the BBC can order series from external production companies and still maintain a substantial in-house production, which ensures the existence of in-house competencies for developing new series as well as for assessing the quality of product proposed from the outside. In her opinion these two elements are closely intertwined (Reich 2013). Discussions of in-house productions are likely to be more fierce with the coming of more competition, and the continuous success of series from DR will be crucial to legitimize the existence of an in-house production unit to politicians, the industry and the licence fee-paying audiences.

New platforms and new audiences

Whereas new national players are thus changing the amount and nature of the output in the domain, new platforms are also putting the role of the traditional broadcasters, commercial as well as non-commercial, under pressure. With the coming of international content providers such as Netflix and HBO Nordic, Danish audiences now have access to a wide variety of series at a time of their liking. The competition for the attention of viewers seems to be constantly increasing, but so far drama series from DR are still the most viewed content on television week after week. Audience figures for the Sunday night airings have not declined, and the series are thus still regarded as 'appointment viewing' by the vast majority of viewers. There are no official viewing figures for series on the DR online platform, which is free of charge and has episodes available for several weeks after their original premiere. It seems like there is not a great urge to measure this, since the mass audiences still appear quite content with turning on the television for traditional broadcast TV. One concern in terms of audiences at DR, however, is how the drama series are not attracting younger viewers to the same degree as the older segments of the audience. A priority of DR in the years to come is thus to also try to catch the interest of younger audiences, who might tend to think that the future is in other digital media and on other platforms (Figure 8.3).

The strategy primarily seems to be to aim for developing traditional series, which might also have a younger appeal in their style and

Figure 8.3　Ole Bornedal's historical drama series *1864* (forthcoming 2014) is commissioned by DR, but produced by the production company Miso Film for Danish television with a huge production budget of DKK 173m (EUR 23m). Photo by Per Arnesen. Courtesy of DR

content. So far, DR has not ventured into transmedia drama experiments. Interactive storytelling universes such as *Conspiracy for Good* (2010) by creator of *Heroes* (NBC 2006–2010) Tim Kring show how there are many interesting possibilities in this regard, not the least in linking drama and real life participation as what Kring has called 'social benefit storytelling'.[2] However, one of the few, large-scale European attempts in this regard, the co-production *The Spiral* (2012) combing a TV series and a social online game, point to the numerous challenges in trying to make stories unfold on several platforms and of bringing together many sources of financing for ambitious transmedia projects (Redvall 2012a).[3] Presently, DR does not seem to have an inclination to move in this direction in order to attract younger audiences, but things might change in this regard.

In terms of new audiences, some journalists are enthusiastic about the 2010s maybe being a new era for subtitled drama (e.g. Frost 2011b). Scholars focusing on transnational television drama are, however, doubtful about whether the current 're-orientation' of the US and UK marketplaces suggest that 'counter-flows' are gaining in importance (Weissmann 2012, 191) or whether these new flows will rather be incorporated in, for instance, the US production cultures through an attempt to 'increasingly incorporate the transnational to sustain its dominance in the global market' (2012, 192). Weissmann speaks of the 'occasional boost in power for the smaller nation', but also of how 'such increased power fluctuates and wanes and is often dependent on national policies to sustain it' (2012, 192). Whether the foreign interest in Danish series continues remains yet to be seen.

That depends very much on the continued production of quality series, but also on general trends and tastes in the domain. From a Danish perspective one does wonder how long the apparent thrill of listening to the Danish language can capture UK audiences. In 2011, a special Christmas episode of the British sitcom *Absolutely Fabulous* (BBC 1992–2012) had Sofie Gråbøl appearing as a guest star to highlight how the star of the show, Jennifer Saunders as the self-absorbed Edina, is suddenly watching subtitled series as yet another 'accessory' to endorse her with cultural capital. From the perspective of a small, national television industry it would be an enormous advantage if the international interest in non-English speaking series turns out to be more than a fling. Netflix investing in a second season of the Norwegian series *Lilyhammer* (NRK1 2012–) could point in this direction, and the possibility of finding larger European or international audiences could be a 'gamechanger' for many European production cultures.

Think big – And foresee the future

All practitioners and executives at DR Fiction seem to agree that these are times of change, but few are eager to predict the nature of the future television drama production from DR Fiction. There are new series on their way, such as *The Legacy* (for 2014) by Maya Ilsøe, *Follow the Money* (for 2015) by Jeppe Gjervig Gram and a new series on religion by Adam Price (with the working title *Herrens veje*/'The Ways of the Lord'). Besides these concrete plans, there are the many discussions of what might be of interest to Danish public service audiences in the near future. Nadia Kløvedal Reich argues that part of developing and writing television drama is trying to think big and foresee the future. When *Borgen* went into production there had never been a female prime minster in Denmark, but shortly before the airing of the second season this was suddenly the case. The work of most writers is to ask intriguing questions of 'what if...' and invite audiences to go along with their imagination. Reich finds that for a public service broadcaster these questions about future stories are closely related to what one perceives will be on the public agenda in the years to come. There is a lot of luck involved when coming up with series that are considered timely at the moment of their premiere, but it is also a question of actively making an effort to ask questions about relevant topics in society through scripted fiction and of spending substantial time thinking about how these topics might manifest themselves some years down the road (Reich 2012).

Cultural Director of DR Morten Hesseldahl has also addressed the aspect of luck in relation to creating successful series. Answering questions about the success of series from DR he has explained that: 'You cannot plan yourself to a success [...] Only try to be in the place when the timing is right and then you can look back and tell the story which explains everything. There is a lot of luck involved in what happens' (in Gilbert 2012). From a Screen Idea System perspective, there can definitely be said to be an important element of luck in how the interplay of the domain, the field and individuals works at a certain point in time, but there does seem to be ways to improve the chances of success. Based on the research in this book, focusing on talent development and facilitating collaboration seems to be one way. Focusing on extensive time and dialogue for development and writing seems to be another as does creating structures where practitioners feel trusted and take great responsibility. As easy as it may sound, the case studies point to how each process is different and how this work is always complex.

As the historical perspective on the DR mode of production in Chapter 3 illustrated, things do not change over night. Much has happened from *The Kingdom* (1994) to *The Killing*. It takes time to implement new ideas or to challenge established traditions in a domain. Both executives and practitioners seem to think that the past years have been marked by successful strategies for production, but they also all point to how these now need to be challenged if series from DR Fiction are to stay ahead of the game. Søren Sveistrup calls for a change in paradigms, based on the conviction that just like he wanted to rebel against certain series, others now need to rebel against *The Killing* (Sveistrup 2012). There are thus many interesting cliffhangers, but people working within DR Fiction seem to agree that one thing in the mode of production needs to stay the same to achieve an interesting drama production. That is making series based on the concept of one vision and focusing on the original ideas of writers. As Head of Drama Piv Bernth has stated, 'writers are where it all starts' (in Pham 2012). This strategy has been central in the approach to television drama by DR Fiction analysed in this book, and it is still regarded as the defining factor in producing future quality series.

Appendix: Manual for a Concept for a TV series

The concept paper, sometimes referred to as 'The TV Dummy Paper', from the TV term at The National Film School of Denmark. Courtesy of Lars Detlefsen and The National Film School of Denmark.

On the Cover of the Concept

Title.
Tagline.
Genre.
Date.
Give the names of the people involved. And their functions: Producer, writer, designer and so on.

Table of Contents

Table of contents of the concept.

Intro

Introduction to your TV series. What is it about and why do you want to make it.

Idea and Genre

1. Describe your idea. You can refer to other TV series, movies, books, plays etc.
2. Genre, style and mood.
3. What is new and unique about your series?
4. What is the 'identification' and the 'fascination' of your TV series?

Theme and Premise

Premise, theme and subject of the series. How does it show in the series?

The Main Characters

Describe the main characters, the protagonists.
Give their goals, secrets, passions and ideals and so on.
Describe their looks, homes, clothes, things, pets, cars, and so on.
And describe their important relationships.

Supporting Characters

Describe the supporting characters and their relationships.

Antagonist

Describe the main antagonist of the series.

5 Questions

It is interesting to hear your characters speak. Ask them the same five questions, so we can hear how different their views are. The questions should be about the subject, dilemma and theme of your TV series.

Arenas, Locations and Time

Describe the main locations of the TV series: The city, the homes, the workplaces, the bars, etc.
Give the time of year where the TV series takes place. And how you will use it in the series.
Give the time span of the series. And how time is used as a dramatic factor in the series.

Style and Mood

Give the colors, the style and the mood of the series. How should it be filmed and edited and so on.

Title Sequence

Describe the title sequence of the TV series.

Sound and Music

Describe the sound and music of the series.
Describe the title song (if any). What is it about?

The Arc of the First Season

Write a synopsis for the whole first season. Describe the main conflict, how it develops and how it ends.
Give the motivation for the characters.
Give the structure of the episodes. And give the storytelling elements of the series, like flashback, voiceover, suspense and so on.
Give how many episodes there are in the first season.

Story Lines

Write pitches for all the episodes of the first season.

Script

Write the script for the first episode of the season.

The Second Season

Make up a cliffhanger for the end of the first season. And write a short synopsis for the second season.

Cast & Crew

Make a list of the actors.
Make a list of the crew.

Production

Describe how the TV series could be made: Budget, finance, plans, strategies, studios, filming schedule and so on.

The TV Slot and the Audience

Give when and where the TV series should air. And who your target audience is.

PR and Merchandise Ideas

How will you make people aware of this new TV series?

Credits

Give the names and contact info of all the people who have been involved in creating the TV series concept.

Notes

Introduction

1. A brief note on terminology. This book uses the term 'script' and not 'screen-play' for the text written as an episode for a series; script is also widely used in this sense in 'how-to books' on television writing (e.g. Goldberg and Rabkin 2003; Douglas 2007; Sandler 2007; Del Valle 2008; Smethurst 2009).
2. A list of interviews is in the references. In the following chapters these are referred to by the last name of the respondent and the year of the interview. The interviews have been supplemented with e-mail correspondences, which are referred to as notes in the text.

1 Television Writing and the Screen Idea System

1. In spite of this, as for example, Newcomb has argued, these kinds of publications can sometimes be valuable sources for scholars with an interest in production analysis if dealt with in a careful manner (1991, 99).
2. CPS can be regarded as part of the pragmatic paradigm in creativity research, since the primary focus is to facilitate creative processes, for instance by developing concrete techniques like brainstorming (Sternberg and Lubart 1999, 5). Central to CPS is, thus, the teaching of creativity, but the nuanced breakdown of the different stages also offer a productive understanding of complex production processes if one wants to explore the primary focus, principal participants or main challenges during the making of new products. The CPS models are not the first to attempt to break down these kinds of processes. In *How We Think* from 1910, John Dewey described five stages of reflection in a problem solving process, which are still inspiring to scholars today (e.g. Darsø 2001; Puccio et al. 2005). Graham Wallas described the four steps of preparation, incubation, illumination and verification in *The Art of Thought* (1926). The basic ideas behind CPS were developed by Alex Osborn as part of his attempt to describe how to enhance creativity in groups as well as in individuals (1953). As summarized by Puccio et al. in a historical account of the development of CPS, the thoughts of Osborn are still the basic components in what is now a range of different models (2005).
3. In *Changing the World* (1994), Csikszentmihalyi, Feldman and Gardner present the model as the DIFI Framework ('Domain Individual Field Interaction'). I use the original term from 1988, which Csikszentmihalyi has also used in later studies (e.g. Csikszentmihalyi 1996, 1999; Abuhamdeh and Csikszentmihalyi 2004). As noted by other scholars who have found inspiration in the work of Csikszentmihalyi, the systems model shares similarities with Pierre Bourdieu's theories about the field of cultural production (e.g. Kupferberg 2006; McIntyre 2006, 2008).

4. For more on premises, see Chapter 3.
5. Richard Corliss' attempt to get screenwriting out of the shadows of the auteur theory is still alive in books like David Kipen's *The Schreiber Theory: A Radical Rewrite of American Film History* (2006).

2   Danish Television Drama: A Crash Course

1. http://www.dr.dk/OmDR/Nyt_fra_DR/Nyt_fra_DR/2012/08/223614.htm. Accessed 2 April 2013.
2. In 2012, three Danish feature films sold more than 500,000 tickets in Danish cinemas: *Hvidsten Gruppen/This Life* (764,516 tickets) by Anne-Grethe Bjarup Riis, *Den skaldede frisør/Love is All You Need* (628,477) by Susanne Bier and the Oscar-nominated *En kongelig affære/A Royal Affair* (528,425 tickets) by Nikolaj Arcel. http://www.dfi.dk/FaktaOmFilm/Tal-og-statistik/Billetsalg/Billetsalg-for-danske-film-2012.aspx. Accessed 2 April 2013.
3. http://www.dr.dk/OmDR/Licens/Fakta%20om%20Licens/2009011053652.html. Accessed 9 November 2012.
4. In February 2013, dk4 premiered its first originally produced TV series, the two-episode mini-series *Bødlen*/'The Executioner' (dk4 2013), pointing to the possibility of more broadcasters moving into the production of original scripted series in the years to come.
5. See, for instance, Levine 2008 for a discussion of different discourses on distinguishing features of the television medium and of the changing meanings of television liveness.
6. This latter development is dealt with in more detail in Chapter 3 on formulating dogmas for television drama.
7. For more on the life and work of Leif Panduro, consult the biography by John Christian Jørgensen (1987). For a brief introduction to his television drama work, see Bondebjerg 1991, 155–8.
8. For titles in what Bondebjerg has called the 'Danish line of royalty' in serialized literary classics for television, see Bondebjerg 1991, 158.
9. Satirical DR2 series like *Drengene fra Angora* (2004), *Rytteriet* (2010) or *Normalerweize* (2004–) have found appreciative audiences and created national hit songs, but the viewing figures are in no way similar to the DR drama series. For more on the production of satire in Danish television, see Bruun 2012.
10. According to http://tvtid.tv2.dk/nytomtv/article.php/id-20269086:25-mest-sete-danske-tvprogrammer.html. Accessed 8 November 2012. Other historical series have been the more adventurous attempts to make history come alive as action-filled stories on screen, like *Gøngehøvdingen*/'The Gønge Chieftain' (1992) based on the novel by Carit Etlar (from 1853) about a hero of the Danish-Swedish wars in the 1600s. Another example is the atmospheric and stylized gangster mini-series *Edderkoppen*/'The Spider' (2000), which was inspired by the so-called 'spider case' 1948–1952 dealing with the unravelling of a major criminal web in the post-war underworld of Copenhagen. While the real people and events were used as the basis for creating a more general story of crime and romance, the series seemed more interested in creating cinematic imagery and has been compared to both the spaghetti

westerns of Sergio Leone and classic gangster films like *The Godfather* (1972) (Piil 2008, 651).

11. *Klovn* has been compared to a Danish take on Larry David's *Curb Your Enthusiasm* (2000–present) with comedians Casper Christensen and Frank Hvam as fictionalized versions of themselves. The series was made by Zentropa for the stand up comedy-influenced sister channel TV 2 Zulu and evolved into the feature film *Klovn – The Movie/Clown* (2010), which sold more than 850,000 tickets at the national box office.

12. When the scheme was founded in 2008, it only supported the development and production of scripted drama and documentaries for television. Following discussions of the scheme, the Media Political Agreement for 2011–2014 included programmes for children and young people in all genres as well as radio programmes. The budget for 2011–2014 is DKK 37.5m (EUR 5m) annually.

13. Nordvision is a television and media collaboration between the five Nordic public service broadcasters Danmarks Radio (DR), Norsk Rikskringkastning (NRK), Sveriges Television (SVT), Yleisradio (YLE) and Ríkisútvarpið (RUV) with Sveriges Utbildningsradio (UR), Greenland's Kalaallit Nunata Radioa (KNR) and Kringvarp Føroya (KVP) from the Faroe Islands as associated members.

14. In 2009, The Nordvision Fund allocated DKK 49m (EUR 6.5m) to co-productions between the partners of NV and around DKK 1.8m (EUR 240,000) to research and development (Nordvision.org). As described by Rowold, collaborations on expensive drama productions have been an important part of the Nordic collaborations since the days of the TV Theatre (2009, 42). In 2008, collaborations on drama represented 43 per cent of the co-productions financed by the NV Fund and was the area receiving the most support, but the Nordic drama productions also received the highest numbers of viewers in the neighbouring countries (2009, 42).

3   Dogmas for Television Drama: Changing a Production Culture

1. See Peacock 2009 for a comparison of the original version of *The Kingdom* and the US remake.

2. National series moving from one broadcaster to another is a rare phenomenon in the Danish television landscape with *Lulu & Leon* (2009–2010) premiering on TV 3 and then being bought by DR as one of the only other examples.

3. This will be discussed in more detail in the case study of *Borgen* in Chapter 6.

4. The research project 'Spaces of Television: Production, site and style' is an example of investigating the use of how using, for example, TV studios or locations has conditioned the form and visual style of UK television fiction. For more, see http://www.reading.ac.uk/ftt/research/Spacesoftelevision.aspx. Accessed 3 April 2013.

5. Sven Clausen has given a number of lectures in the industry about the strengths of the Danish set-up over the past five years, for instance at Nordisk

Film & TV Fond's Nordic TV Drama Masterclass 'There is Something Going on' in November 2009 and at the European TV Drama Series Lab in 2012 (Redvall 2012a).

6. The media researchers at DR do traditional audience analysis, but they also conduct qualitative focus group tests once episodes for forthcoming series are finished. Since no pilots are produced, these tests are not to examine whether series should be broadcast or not, but rather to learn more about the audience response to certain aspects, like content and characters, which can then feed back into the further writing and production. Media researchers Lene Heiselberg and Jacob Lyng Wieland kindly allowed me to observe their work and found time for interviews (Heiselberg 2011; Wieland 2011) as did Head of DR Media Research Lars Thunø (Thunø 2012). Their work is the topic of further writings on the DR mode of production, but not described in detail in this book.

7. There are slight differences between the Danish version of the dogmas, which I have received from Ingolf Gabold as an in-house power point presentation, and the English version of the Dogmas, which has recently been published (Hartmann 2012, 55). I have translated the in-house version from Gabold.

8. The term has been translated in different ways to for instance 'double dimension narration' (in Pham 2012).

9. The word 'præmis' (premise) is widely used in the DR framework even though it does not appear in the dogmas. The term grows out of theories of dramaturgy with Lajos Egri's thoughts on premises in *The Art of Dramatic Writing* (1946, 1960) and *The Art of Creative Writing* (1965) as one source of inspiration. Egri has defined a premise as a universal truth for the project at hand containing both character, conflict and resolution (1960, 29), and he has argued that 'a good premise represents the author' (1960, 17).

10. As in other media industries, it is hard to get information on specific salaries, but the writers interviewed for this book have not complained about their pay. According to legal advisor Birna Mohr from the Danish Writers Guild, there is no official agreement on fees between the Guild and DR (similar to the one that exists with the feature film industry), and negotiations on salaries as well as royalties are done on an individual – and confidential – basis (personal communication with Mohr, 3 April 2013). The suggested minimum fees for feature film writing can be accessed from the website of the Writers Guild for an impression of the minimum level of pay in the Danish film industry. The fees are the following as of 1 January 2013: A synopsis: DKK 39,826 (app. EUR 5,300); a treatment: DKK 71,689 (app. EUR 9,560); First draft of script: DKK 127,445 (app. EUR 17,000); Final draft of script: DKK 414,203 (app. EUR 55,230). Accessed 3 April 2013. http://www. dramatiker.dk/spillefilmsoverenskomsten-i-tal.html. It should be noted that all script development fees are paid as percentages (or installments) of the final script fee.

11. Ole Christian Madsen directed episodes 9 and 10 of *Taxa* in 1997, before making his first feature film *Pizza King* (1999). Since then, he has directed the mini-series *Edderkoppen/The Spider* (2000) and four episodes of *Unit One*

(episodes 25 + 26 and the two final more high-profile episodes, 31 and 32).
His feature films are the dogma film *En kærlighedshistorie/Kira's Reason: A Love
Story* (2001), *Nordkraft* (2005), *Prag/Prague* (2006), *Flammen & Citronen/Flame
and Citron* (2008) and *SuperClásico* (2011).

12. Niels Arden Oplev directed several episodes of *Taxa* and was then the conceptualizing director of *Unit One*. He has been moving back and forth between
film and television, directing feature films like *Drømmen/We Shall Overcome*
(2006) and *Män som hatar kvinnor/The Girl with the Dragon Tattoo* (2009)
and episodes of *Forsvar/'Defense'* for TV 2 in 2003 and *The Eagle* in 2005
and 2006. *The Girl With the Dragon Tattoo* was also made in a television
mini-series version (2010).

13. Ole Christian Madsen and Niels Arden Oplev are among the Danish directors
who have gone on to direct episodes for major US series. Madsen as episode
director of *Banshee* (2013) and Oplev of *Unforgettable* (CBS, 2011).

14. The main information in this section is based on the interview with Head of
DR Fiction Nadia Kløvedal Reich (2012).

15. For an introduction to the history of the advent calendar series, see for
instance Monggaard 2012.

4   Training Talent for Television: DR and the 'TV Term'

1. Some scholars have previously analysed the advent of academic film studies as well as courses in practical filmmaking (e.g. Polan 2007; Grieveson and Wasson 2008), while other publications have given the word to
tutors and former students at different schools in order to provide insights
into the differences in the American and European educational structures
(e.g. Boorman et al. 2002). However, Mette Hjort's anthology is the first
comprehensive study on the education of filmmakers on a worldwide
scale.

2. The historical material in the chapter builds on my article 'Teaching Screenwriting in a Time of Storytelling Blindness: The Meeting of the Auteur and
the Screenwriting Tradition in Danish Film-Making'. *Journal of Screenwriting*
1: 57–79.

3. Anders Thomas Jensen is a self-taught screenwriter. He won an Oscar for
his short film *Valgaften/Election Night* (1999) and also gained an international reputation through writing the Dogma films *Mifunes sidste sang/Mifune*
(1999) and *The King is Alive* (2000). Since writing *Elsker dig for evigt/Open
Hearts* (2002) for Susanne Bier, they have had a steady collaboration, leading to an Oscar for best foreign film for *Hævnen/In a Better World* (2010).
Jensen has also directed his own feature film screenplays in *Blinkende
Lygter/Flickering Lights* (2000), *De grønne slagtere/The Green Butchers* (2003) and
Adams æbler/Adam's Apples (2005).

4. Rukov's importance for Danish cinema has been acknowledged by an hon-
orary Bodil award in 2003 and he has also become known abroad. When
the script tutor Dick Ross in 2002 counted NFSD among the leading film
schools in the world he credited Rukov for a lot of the School's success
(2002, 47).

5. TV-Sum refers to 'TV som udtryksmiddel' meaning television as a means of expression.
6. Screenwriter Nikolaj Scherfig (graduated 1990) has described the general impression of classical dramaturgy among the students at this time as 'a bourgeois Hollywood thing that impeded the free, artistic will' (2006, 156).
7. *Dogma 95* and Vinterberg and Rukov's collaborative writing of *Festen/The Celebration* (1998) are among the events that, in the late 1990s, started to make people outside the NFSD aware that something interesting was happening in the Screenwriting Department.
8. Personal email communication with Clausen, 15 September 2012.
9. The budget for the series was to be DKK 45,000 a minute (EUR 6,000) and the suggested time slot was week nights at 8.30 or 9 pm. *Nikolaj and Julie* (2002–2003) and *Rita* (TV 2, 2012–) were mentioned as examples of similar series. The description of the assignment highlighted that the time slot allowed for material with 'an edge' in terms of both content and visuals, but emphasized that students should keep in mind that DR is a public service broadcaster with a broad appeal and an obligation to produce programmes based on stories, 'which tell them something about themselves and make them reflect, on their own and together, on the life they are living' (from the assignment paper of 2012).
10. According to Jakob Ion Wille, the role of the production designers has, however, been a source of some discussions, since the designers have only had ownership of their designs in the contracts made by producers during the term and not any ownership of the concept for the series as such. This changed during the term of 2012, making the designers co-owners of the overall concept. Wille finds that this is an acknowledgement of how production design 'is not only something, which is applied to a text, but that the dramatic and visual universes of a series are connected and developed through collaborations' (Personal email communication with Wille, 23 May 2013).
11. The concept of 'the paramount meeting' is regarded as imported from the US television industry in the 1990s (Gabold 2013; Wille 2013). Paramount meetings are also part of the work processes at DR, where Gabold describes the meeting between the executives of DR Fiction and the creative team as crucial to being on the same page regarding the overall concept for a series. This is not only related to the script, the casting or the arena, but also to issues of the sound and visuals. The often three-hour meeting is normally held two and a half to two months before the first day of production (Gabold 2013).
12. Personal email communication with Clausen, 15 September 2012.
13. NFSD. Accessed 12 February 2013. http://www.filmskolen.dk/english/.

5   Writers, Showrunners and Television Auteurs: Ideas of One Vision

1. Stig Thorsboe and Hanna Lundblad have proposed a new series for TV 2. Peter Thorsboe and Mai Brostrøm have developed a German crime series with Peter Nadermann from ZDF as executive producer.

2. DR made the disclosure into an event by filming the moment of the reading where the actor is revealed as the murderer and posting it on the website of *The Killing* after the airing of the last episode.

6 The Workings of a Writers' Room: *Borgen*

1. Producer Sven Clausen has described how DR considered moving into these genres in the 1990s, but found that there is no large audience for soaps in Denmark. In his view, a main reason for this is that most women are part of the full-time work force, leaving a limited audience for daytime programming (2010), and DR has not tried to develop material in this genre.

2. Access to observing the work in the room in December was granted by the writers based on an inquiry to the producer in September. Following the observation period, interviews about the process and conceptions of best practice were conducted with writers Adam Price, Jeppe Gjervig Gram and Maja Jul Larsen, producer Camilla Hammerich, line producer Pernille Skov Sutherland, researcher Rikke Tørholm Kofoed and Head of DR Fiction Nadia Kløvedal Reich in November and December 2012. Previous interviews related to *Borgen* had been conducted with Price, Hammerich, Gram and former Head of Drama Ingolf Gabold. The case study also draws on documents surrounding the production such as the three 'bibles' for the seasons, written notes and the different drafts of the script. As stated in the acknowledgements, I am thankful to all the *Borgen* practitioners who have allowed me to follow their work and found time for interviews. Special thanks go to Kofoed for her continuous help in numerous ways. When nothing else is noted, statements refer to material from the interviews.

3. A beat can mean (a) a scene or step in the story or (b) a pause in dialogue or action (Douglas 2007, 251). Here it refers to a scene or step in the story.

4. Among the initiatives were scholarly lectures on topics in *Borgen* as part of *Danskernes Akademi* ('The Academy of the Danes'), which was launched in January 2010 as a collaboration between DR, several Danish universities and other educational institutions with the purpose of offering quality lectures, debates and documentaries as both television programming and web content with TED.com and BBC Open University as sources of inspiration. *Borgen* also had an extensive website with teaching material, including two scripts.

5. For more on the politician complaining to DR about episode 25, see e.g. Munksgaard 2013. Several newspapers had articles about the relation between fiction and reality in *Borgen* (e.g. Petersen 2013).

6. Gram and Lindholm also got a special storyline credit with the names of all three writers figuring on the storylining of the first 20 episodes and an agreement that they would write all episodes besides the opening episode by Price. Gram believes the special deal about ownership and responsibility on *Borgen* to be an important reason why the product as well as the process turned out to be successful (2012).

7. An arc refers to the 'progression of a character from one condition to a different dramatic state' (Douglas 2007, 250) as when Nyborg starts as a regular politician in the first season and ends as prime minister.

8. The episode writers are invited to take part in early screenings during the editing. Not only to comment in general but also to discuss the balance of the political and the relational plot. In Larsen's experience directors are often more interested in the closed political case than the episodic personal stories, which might slow down the A-plot and make it less 'clean'. In her opinion, the writers therefore have an important part to play in making sure that the character plotlines get the attention needed and are told in the right way from episode to episode.

9. Birgitte Nyborg discovers that her boyfriend (Alastair Mackenzie) has tried buying sex, much to her dislike; Katrine Fønsmark (Birgitte Hjort Sørensen) finds out that her ex-boyfriend, the spin doctor Kasper Juul (Pilou Asbæk), has affairs with different women, and she ends up sleeping with the new boss at TV1 (Christian Tafdrup). Moreover, to her surprise, Fønsmark learns that her mother had an affair while Fønsmark was a child. In the newsroom, a relationship develops between the Head of News Torben Friis (Søren Spanning) and one of the producers (Lisbeth Wulff). The many doubts about the right way to legislate about prostitution are explicitly brought up in some of the storylines.

10. Written notes on the third draft (dated 10 May) in email correspondence from Kofoed on 22 May 2012.

11. Written notes on the third draft (dated 15 May) in email correspondence from Kofoed on 21 May 2012.

12. The Cultural Director of DR Morten Hesseldahl ended up responding to the larger criticism of DR's public service obligations, insisting that *Borgen* is fiction and that there is no hidden political agenda behind its content (2013a, 2013b). Price was also present in the press, when one politician suddenly proposed similar legislation about prostitution as the one suggested by Nyborg in episode 25. This happened three days before the official airing of the episode, following a preview on the DR website. The politician denied being inspired by the fictional proposal on legislation, but acknowledged using the focus on the topic as a way to get attention (Sæhl 2013). Price commented that he sincerely hoped that no one would rush proposals through based on a fictional story, but that it is 'of course interesting, when a drama series about fictional politics in a fictional Denmark can be part of pushing certain debates' (in Sæhl 2013).

7   Prime-time Public Service Crime: *Forbrydelsen/The Killing*

1. In 'Duchess of Cornwall meets The Killing's Sofie Grabol' bbc.co.uk, 27 March 2013. Accessed 2 April 2013. http://www.bbc.co.uk/news/uk-17529952.

2. *The Killing* premiered on AMC in April 2011. The series was cancelled in 2012 after what *The Hollywood Reporter* called two 'critically adored seasons' (Rose 2013), referring to the 26 episodes (presented as two seasons) about who killed Rosie Larsen. In 2013, the series was somewhat surprisingly revived for a third season based on new material rather than material from the original series, but the third season turned out to be the last.

3. The chapter primarily builds on research interviews with creator Søren Sveistrup (2012), episode writer Michael W. Horsten (2013), former Head of Drama Ingolf Gabold (2010, 2011) and current Head of DR Fiction Nadia Kløvedal Reich (2012) as well as material on the process from *Rushprint* (Berg and Diesen 2012) and *16:9* (2012) and at industry events such as TV Drama Vision 2012 at the Göteborg International Film Festival. When there are no references following summaries, these refer to the interviews by the author.

4. The series was co-produced with German broadcaster ZDF, and until the recent positive response to *Borgen* (2010–2013) abroad, the crime genre has been regarded as the only genre with the potential to attract audiences outside of the Nordic countries. The co-production with Germany has provided money for more production value. According to co-producer Peter Nadermann this was what the Danish series of the 2000s needed to be able to travel (in Redvall 2013, 58), and former DR producer Sven Clausen has described how the German financing for *The Eagle* helped to pay for more location shooting and a more cinematic look, which was important to gain an interest for the series outside of Denmark (Bondebjerg and Redvall 2011, 102).

5. See Nestingen 2012 for an overview of recent Scandinavian crime fiction scholarship.

6. The Millennium Trilogy books by Stieg Larsson (published in Sweden in 2005–2007) were adapted as a combination of feature films and series. Originally, only the adaptation of the first book was intended for a cinema release, but following its enormous success the adaptations of the following books also premiered in cinemas. The material was later shown on television as a six-part mini series. In 2011, David Fincher did a US remake of *The Girl with the Dragon Tattoo* starring Daniel Craig as the investigative journalist Mikael Blomqvist.

7. Accessed 25 March 2013. http://www.zdf-enterprises.de/en/press/press releases/bafta-for-zdf-enterprises-coproduction-the-killing#.UVAoj7Q1ZpQ.

8. Per Daumiller was part of the initial development talks and also wrote four episodes for the first season, but since then the steady writing team has been Hoppe and Horsten.

9. The descriptions of the actual time frame for the process vary quite a bit with, for instance, Bernth presenting that the production starts with four or five weeks of storylining and then two or three weeks to write the first draft at the TV Drama Vision 2012 (2012b), while Sveistrup says that there would normally be two weeks for storylining an episode and then two weeks for a first draft, which quickly turned into ten days because of delays (2012). In an interview on the making of *The Killing*, Bernth presents the beginning of the process as having three weeks for storylining the first draft, a week for the second draft, a week for the third draft and then 'some days' for a final draft (in Berg and Diesen 2012). According to Sveistrup, the storylining of an episode normally begins around one and a half months before shooting the episode (2012).

10. In the UK reception of *The Killing*, there have been several comments on how the series has a different speed than other productions with the words 'slow-moving' appearing repeatedly (e.g. Frost 2011a). This partly refers to the long-running nature of the whodunnit-mystery, partly to the feeling of individual scenes.

11. Other developments in the domain during the making of the seasons led to experts suddenly seeing it in a new light. After its premiere, *Borgen* also used a three-plot structure – about the political scene and the journalists covering it as well as about the private lives of characters. This led to suggestions of the third season of *The Killing* being too much like *Borgen,* and the third season was also discussed in relation to *Bron/The Bridge* (2011–) in its use of a masked killer and kidnapper (Agger 2012).

12. A regular shooting day is 9 hours, including 45 minutes for lunch, but there is a possibility of working 10 hours when on location. In spite of the many scenes taking place at night, there have only been 2 night shoots per episode. Sometimes the dark days of the Scandinavian winter with the light disappearing in the afternoon have been an advantage, since you can then start shooting at 2 pm (according to Bernth in Berg and Diesen 2012).

8   Conclusions and Cliffhangers

1. See Scherfig 2012, for a description of the writing and financing process of *The Bridge*.

2. Tim Kring explains the thoughts behind the augmented reality drama game and 'social benefit storytelling' on the website, http://www.conspiracyforgood.com/about.php. Accessed 3 April 2013.

3. *Conspiracy for Good* and *The Spiral* were case studies at the European TV Drama Series Lab in 2012 when discussing possible transmedia strategies of European drama production (Redvall 2012a).

Bibliography

Abuhamdeh, Sami and Mihaly Csikszentmihalyi. 2004. 'The Artistic Personality: A System's Perspective.' In *Creativity: From Potential to Realization*, edited by Robert J. Sternberg, Elena L. Grigorenko and Jerome L. Singer, 31–42. Washington DC: American Psychological Association.

Agger, Gunhild. 1991. 'Dansk når det er værst og bedst. Om traditioner og gen-reforvaltning i dansk tv-fiktion.' In *Analyser af tv og tv-kultur*, edited by Jens F. Jensen, 173–98. Copenhagen: Medusa.

Agger, Gunhild. 2005a. *Dansk tv-drama: Arvesølv og underholdning*. Frederiksberg: Samfundslitteratur.

Agger, Gunhild. 2005b. 'Folkets teater.' *Information*, 8 April. Accessed 4 April 2013. http://www.information.dk/104020.

Agger, Gunhild. 2006. 'Tv-Drama.' In *Dansk tv's historie*, edited by Stig Hjarvard, 145–78. Frederiksberg: Samfundslitteratur.

Agger, Gunhild. 2010. 'Krimi med social samvittighed. Skandinavisk krimifiktion, medialisering og kulturelt medborgerskab.' In *Den skandinaviske krimi*, edited by Gunhild Agger and Anne Marit Waade, 19–36. Göteborg: Nordicom.

Agger, Gunhild and Anne Marit Waade. 2010a. 'Introduktion. Skandinavisk krimiproduktion og krimiforskning.' In *Den skandinaviske krimi*, edited by Gunhild Agger and Anne Marit Waade, 11–18. Göteborg: Nordicom.

Agger, Gunhild and Anne Marit Waade (eds.) 2010b. *Den skandinaviske krimi*. Göteborg: Nordicom.

Agger, Gunhild. 2011. 'Emotion, Gender and Genre: Investigating *The Killing*.' *Northern Lights* 9: 111–25.

Agger, Gunhild. 2012. 'Er der gået for meget *Borgen* i *Forbrydelsen*?' *Kommunikationsforum*, 7 November. Accessed 14 February 2013. http://www.kommunikationsforum.dk/artikler/anmeldelse-af-forbrydelsen-iii.

Aitken, Ian. 2008. 'European Film Scholarship.' In *The Sage Handbook of Film Studies*, edited by James Donald and Michael Renov, 25–53. London: Sage.

Andersen, Katrine Jo. 2011. 'Branchefolk: DR-drama fortsætter linjen med ny chef.' *Politiken*, 6 October. Accessed 21 March 2013. http://politiken.dk/kultur/tvogradio/ECE1415063/branchefolk-dr-drama-fortsaetter-linjen-med-ny-chef/.

Bach, Steven. 1985. *Final Cut. Dreams and Disaster in the Making of Heaven's Gate*. New York: William Morrow.

Becker, Howard. 1974. 'Art as Collective Action.' *American Sociological Review* 39: 767–76.

Becker, Howard. 1982. *Art Worlds*. Berkeley: University of California Press.

Becker, Howard, Robert Faulkner and Barbara Kirshenblatt-Gimblett (eds.). 2006. *Art from Start to Finish: Jazz, Painting, Writing, and Other Improvisations*. Chicago: University of Chicago Press.

Berg, Ståle S. and Trygve A. Diesen. 2012. 'Berg & Diesen: Kunsten å begå *Forbrytelsen*.' *Rushprint*, 31 October. Accessed 13 March 2013. http://rushprint.no/2012/10/berg-diesen-kunsten-a-bega-forbrytelsen/.

Bernth, Piv. 2012a. 'What Makes Nordic TV Drama Travel?' Session at Nordic TV Drama Vision 2012. Göteborg: Göteborg International Film Festival. http://www.giff.se/start/bransch/nordic-film-market/tv-drama-vision.html

Bernth, Piv. 2012b. 'Works in Progress: The Killing III.' Presentation at Nordic TV Drama Vision 2012. Göteborg: Göteborg International Film Festival. http://www.giff.se/start/bransch/nordic-film-market/tv-drama-vision.html

Bielby, Denise D. and William T. Bielby. 2002. 'Hollywood Dreams, Harsh Realities: Writing for Film and Television.' *Contexts: Journal of the American Sociological Association* 1: 21–7.

Bielby, William T. and Denise D. Bielby. 2001. 'Audience Segmentation and Age Stratification among Television Writers.' *Journal of Broadcast & Electronic Media* 45: 391–412.

Bjørnkjær, Kristen. 2012. 'Forbrydelse og forventninger.' *Information*, 19 September. Accessed 23 March 2013. http://www.information.dk/311392.

Blair, Helen. 2001. ' "You're Only as Good as Your Last Job": The Labour Process and Labour Market in the British Film Industry.' *Work, Employment and Society* 15: 149–69.

Blair, Helen. 2003. 'Winning and Losing in Flexible Labour Markets: The Formation and Operation of Networks of Interdependence in the UK Film Industry.' *Sociology* 37: 677–94.

Bondebjerg, Ib. 1991. 'Dansk tv-fiktion: Indenfor rammen og udenfor.' In *Analyser af tv og tv-kultur*, edited by Jens F. Jensen, 149–71. Copenhagen: Medusa.

Bondebjerg, Ib. 1993. *Elektroniske fiktioner*. Copenhagen: Borgen.

Bondebjerg, Ib. 2005. *Filmen og det moderne*. Copenhagen: Gyldendal.

Bondebjerg, Ib and Eva N. Redvall. 2011. *A Small Region in a Global North: Patterns in Scandinavian Film & TV Culture*. Copenhagen: Think Tank on European Film and Film Policy.

Bondebjerg, Ib and Eva N. Redvall. Forthcoming 2014. 'Breaking Borders: The International Success of Danish TV Drama.' In *Being European: Media, Culture and Everyday Life*, edited by Ib Bondebjerg, Andrew Higson and Caroline Pauwels. Basingstoke: Palgrave Macmillan.

Bondebjerg, Ib, Jesper Andersen and Peter Schepelern (eds.). 1997. *Dansk Film 1972–97*. Copenhagen: Munksgaard/Rosinante.

Boorman, John, Fraser MacDonald and Walter Donohue. (eds.). 2002. *Projections 12: Film-makers on Film Schools*. London: Faber and Faber.

Bordwell, David. 1997. *On the History of Film Style*. Cambridge: Harvard University Press.

Bordwell, David. 2006. *The Way Hollywood Tells It: Story and Style in Modern Movies*. Berkeley and Los Angeles: University of California Press.

Bordwell, David. 2007. 'Risk and Renewal in Danish Cinema.' *FILM* 55: 16–19.

Bordwell, David, Janet Staiger and Kristin Thompson. 1985. *The Classical Hollywood Cinema*. New York: Columbia University Press.

Bordwell, David and Noël Caroll (eds.). 1996. *Post-Theory: Reconstructing Film Studies*. Madison: University of Wisconsin Press.

Born, Georgina. 2005. *Uncertain Vision: Birt, Dyke and the Reinvention of the BBC*. London: Vintage.

Bourdieu, Pierre. 1993. *The Field of Cultural Production*. Cambridge: Polity Press.

Bourdieu, Pierre. 1996. *The Rules of Art*. Cambridge: Polity Press.

Brandstrup, Pil and Eva N. Redvall. 2005. 'Breaking the Borders: Danish Copro-
ductions in the 1990s.' In *Transnational Cinema in Global North*, edited by
Andrew Nestingen and Trevor G. Elkington. Detroit: Wayne State University
Press.

Bro, Arne (ed.). 1991. *Filmskolen: De første 25 år*. Copenhagen: National Film
School of Denmark.

Bruun, Hanne. 2010. 'På vej mod multiplatformkonkurrence: Tv-
produktionsvilkår i forandring i Danmark.' In *Den skandinaviske krimi*,
edited by Gunhild Agger and Anne Marit Waade, 145–55. Göteborg:
Nordicom.

Bruun, Hanne. 2012. 'The Changing Production Culture of Television Satire.'
Northern Lights 10: 41–56.

Buonanno, Milly. 2012. *Italian TV Drama and Beyond*. Bristol: Intellect.

Caldwell, John T. 1995. *Televisuality Style, Crisis, and Authority in American
Television*. New Brunswick: Rutgers University Press.

Caldwell, John T. 2008. *Production Culture: Industrial Reflexivity and Critical Practice
in Film and Television*. Durham: Duke University Press.

Caldwell, John T. 2013. 'Distributed Creativity in Film and Television: Three
Case Studies of Networked Production Labor.' In *The International Encyclopedia of Media Studies. Volume VI: Media Studies Futures*, edited by general
editor Angharad N. Valdivia and volume editor Kelly Gates, 397–9. Boston:
Wiley-Blackwell.

Campbell, James. 1995. *Understanding John Dewey: Nature and Cooperative Intelli-
gence*. Chicago: Open Court Publishing.

Camre, Henning. 2006. 'Hvordan var det nu det var.' In *At lære kunsten*, edited
by Ole John, 21–5. Copenhagen: Aschehoug.

Cantor, Muriel. 1971. *The Hollywood TV Producer: His Work and his Audience*.
New York: Basic Books.

Carringer, Richard L. 1985/1996. *The Making of Citizen Kane*. Berkeley: University
of California Press.

Carringer, Richard L. 2001. 'Collaboration and Authorship.' *PMLA* 116: 370–9.

Caughie, John. 2000. *Television Drama: Realism, Modernism and British Culture*.
Oxford: Oxford University Press.

Caughie, John. 2008. 'Authors and Auteurs. The Uses of Theory.' In *The Sage
Handbook of Film Studies*, edited by James Donald and Michael Renov, 408–23.
London: Sage.

Caves, Richard. 2000. *Creative Industries: Contracts Between Art and Commerce*.
Cambridge: Harvard University Press.

Clarke, M. J. 2013. 'Aggregating Content/Disaggregating Labor in Tentpole TV.'
In *The International Encyclopedia of Media Studies. Volume VI: Media Studies
Futures*, edited by general editor Angharad N. Valdivia and volume editor Kelly
Gates, 399–403. Boston: Wiley-Blackwell.

Collins, Lauren. 2013. 'Letter from Copenhagen: Danish Postmodern.' *The New
Yorker*, 7 January, 22–23.

Collins, Richard. 2004. ' "Isis" and "Oughts": Public Service Broadcasting in
Europe.' In *The Television Studies Reader*, edited by Richard C. Allen and Annette
Hill, 33–51. London: Routledge.

Conor, Bridget. 2010. ' "Everybody's a Writer", Theorizing Screenwriting as
Creative Labour.' *Journal of Screenwriting* 1: 27–43.

Corliss, Richard. 1974. *Talking Pictures: Screenwriters in the American Cinema.* New York: Penguin Books.

Cornea, Christine. 2009. 'Showrunning the *Doctor Who* Franchise: A Response to Denise Mann.' In *Production Studies: Cultural Studies of Media Industries,* edited by Vicki Mayer, Miranda J. Banks and John T. Caldwell, 115–22. New York: Routledge.

Csikszentmihalyi, Mihaly. 1988. 'Society, Culture and Person: A System's View of Creativity.' In *The Nature of Creativity,* edited by Robert J. Sternberg, 325–39. Cambridge: Cambridge University Press.

Csikszentmihalyi, Mihaly. 1996. *Creativity: Flow and the Psychology of Discovery and Invention.* New York: Harper Collins.

Csikszentmihalyi, Mihaly. 1999. 'Implications of a Systems Perspective for the Study of Creativity.' In *Handbook of Creativity,* edited by Robert J. Sternberg, 313–35. Cambridge: Cambridge University Press.

Csikszentmihalyi, Mihaly and Jacob W. Getzels. 1976. *The Creative Vision: A Longitudinal Study of Problem Finding in Art.* New York: John Wiley and Sons.

Cultural Human Resources Council (CHRC). 2009. *Showrunners: Film and Television. A Competency Analysis.* Ottawa: CHRC. Accessed 15 January 2013. http://www.culturalhrc.ca/minisites/Film_and_Broadcasting/e/PDFs/CHRC_Showrunners_Profile_Sample-en.pdf.

Danish Film Institute, The (DFI). 2012. 'Vilkår for støtte til Public Service Puljen.' Copenhagen: The Danish Film Institute. Accessed 9 November 2012. http://www.dfi.dk/Branche_og_stoette/Stoette/Produktion-og-udvikling/Public-Service-Puljen.aspx.

Danske Dramatikere. 2012. *Replikker. Tema: Medlemsundersøgelsen 2011.* Copenhagen: Danske Dramatikere.

Darsø, Lotte. 2001. *Innovation in the Making.* Frederiksberg: Samfundslitteratur.

Davies, Máire Messenger. 2007. 'Quality and Creativity in TV: The Work of Television Storytellers.' In *Quality TV: Contemporary American Television and Beyond,* edited by Janet McCabe and Kim Akass, 171–84. London and New York: L. B. Tauris.

Dawson, Andrew and Sean P. Holmes (eds.). 2012. *Working in the Global Film and Television Industries: Creativity, Systems, Space, Patronage.* London and New York: Bloomsbury Academic.

Del Valle, Robert. 2008. *The One-Hour Drama Series: Producing Episodic Television.* Los Angeles: Silmon-James Press.

Denzin, Norman K. and Yvonne S. Lincoln. (eds.) 2005. *The Sage Handbook of Qualitative Research.* 3rd ed. Thousand Oaks: Sage.

Deuze, Mark. 2007. *Media Work.* London: Polity Press.

Deuze, Mark (ed.). 2010. *Managing Media Work.* London: Sage.

Dewey, John. 1910. *How We Think.* Boston: Heath.

DiMaggio, Paul. 1977.'Market Structure, The Creative Process, and Popular Culture: Toward an Organizational Reinterpretation of Mass Culture Theory.' *Journal of Popular Culture* 11: 436–52.

DiMaggio, Paul and Paul M. Hirsch. 1976. 'Production Organizations in the Arts.' *American Behavioural Scientist* 19: 735–52.

Douglas, Pamela. 2007. *Writing the TV Drama Series.* 2nd ed. Studio City, CA: Michael Wiese Productions.

DR. 2011. *DRs Årsrapport 2011.* Copenhagen: DR.

DR. 2012. 'Hvad er public service?' DR, Accessed 9 November 2012. http://www. dr.dk/OmDR/Fakta%20om%20DR/Public%20Service/20060421140602.html.

DR. 2013. *DR. An Introduction.* Copenhagen: DR.

Dunleavy, Trisha. 2010. 'New Zealand on Air, Public Service Television, and TV Drama.' In *Reinventing Public Service Communication: European Broadcasters and Beyond*, edited by Petros Iosifidis, 298–310. Basingstoke: Palgrave Macmillan.

Dunleavy, Trisha. 2012. 'Maximising Public Value in Costly Areas of Production: TV Drama and the "New Zealand on Air Model".' Paper at the conference Ripe@2012 Conference Value for Public Money – Money for Public Value, Sydney. Accessed 9 November 2012. http://ripeat.org/wp-content/uploads/tdomf/2816/Dunleavy%20Paper%202012.pdf.

Egri, Lajos. 1960/1946. *The Art of Dramatic Writing.* 2nd rev. edition. New York: Simon and Schuster.

Egri, Lajos. 1965. *The Art of Creative Writing.* Seacaucus: Citadel Press.

Ekvall, Göran. 1996. 'Organizational Climate for Creativity and Innovation.' *European Journal of Work and Organizational Psychology* 5: 105–23.

Elefante, Phoebe H. and Mark Deuze. 2012. 'Media Work, Career Management, and Professional Identity: Living Labor Precarity.' *Northern Lights* 10: 9–24.

Elkjær, Jakob. 2011. 'Minister blander sig i DR-satsning.' *Politiken*, 18 February, 2011. Accessed 9 November 2012. http://politiken.dk/kultur/tvogradio/ECE1200423/minister-blander-sig-i-dr-satsning/

Elliott, Philip. 1972. *The Making of a Television Series.* London: Constable.

Ellis, John. 1992. *Visible Fictions.* London: Routledge.

Elsaesser, Thomas, Jan Simons and Lucette Bronk (eds.). 1994. *Writing for the Medium: Television in Transition.* Amsterdam: Amsterdam University Press.

Feldman, David H., Mihaly Csikszentmihalyi and Howard Gardner. 1994. *Changing the World: A Framework for the Study of Creativity.* Santa Barbara: Greenwood Publishing.

Field, Syd. 1979/1994. *Screenplay: The Foundations of Screenwriting.* Expanded ed. New York: Dell Publishing.

Finney, Angus. 1996. *The State of European Cinema.* London: Cassell.

Forshaw, Barry. 2012. *Death in a Cold Climate: A Guide to Scandinavian Crime Fiction.* Basingstoke: Palgrave Macmillan.

Forshaw, Barry. 2013. *Nordic Noir: The Pocket Essential Guide to Scandinavian Crime Fiction, Film & TV.* Harpenden: Oldcastle books.

Frost, Vicky. 2011a. 'The Killing, a Slow-Moving Drama with Subtitles, is a Hit for BBC.' *The Guardian*, 4 March. Accessed 12 March 2013. http://www.guardian.co.uk/tv-and-radio/2011/mar/04/the-killing-bbc-danish-crime-thriller?INTCMP=ILCNETTXT3487.

Frost, Vicky. 2011b. 'The Killing puts Torchlight on Subtitled Drama.' *The Guardian*, 18 November. Accessed 28 February 2013. http://www.guardian.co.uk/tv-and-radio/2011/nov/18/the-killing-torchlight-subtitled-drama.

Gabold, Ingolf. 2006. 'Forord.' In *Den dramaturgiske værktøjskasse*, edited by Per Helmer Hansen, 9–10. Copenhagen: Frydenlund.

Gaut, Berys. 1997. 'Film Authorship and Collaboration.' In *Film Theory and Philosophy*, edited by Richard Allen and Murray Smith, 149–72. Oxford: Clarendon Press.

Gaut, Berys. 2010. *A Philosophy of Cinematic Art.* Cambridge: Cambridge University Press.

Gaut, Berys and Paisley Livingston (eds.). 2003. *The Creation of Art: New Essays in Philosophical Aesthetics.* Cambridge: Cambridge University Press.
Gemzøe, Lynge Agger. 2010. 'Vi har førertrøjen! Interview med producer Sven Clausen i DR om den danske tv-krimi.' In *Den skandinaviske krimi*, edited by Gunhild Agger and Anne Marit Waade, 195–203. Göteborg: Nordicom.
Gilbert, Gerard. 2012. 'How does Danish TV Company DR keep Churning out the Hits?' *The Independent*, 12 May. Accessed 29 March 2013. http://www.independent.co.uk/arts-entertainment/tv/features/how-does-danish-tv-company-dr-keep-churning-out-the-hits-7728833.html
Gitlin, Todd. 1983. *Inside Prime Time*. New York: Pantheon Books.
Goldberg, Lee and William Rabkin. 2003. *Successful Television Writing*. Hoboken: John Wiley & Sons.
Gombrich, Ernst H. 1950/2006. *The Story of Art*. London: Phaidon.
Grainge, Paul. 2007. *Brand Hollywood. Selling Entertainment in a Global Media Age*. London: Routledge.
Gray, Jonathan and Derek Johnson. 2013. *A Companion to Media Authorship*. Oxford: Wiley-Blackwell.
Grieveson, Lee and Haidee Wasson. 2008. *Inventing Film Studies*. Durham: Duke University Press.
Hamilton, Ian. 1990. *Writers in Hollywood 1915–1951*. New York: Harper & Row.
Hammerich, Rumle. 2006. 'Noget vigtigt man husker.' In *At lære kunsten*, edited by Ole John, 91–9. Copenhagen: Aschehoug.
Hammerich, Rumle. 2010. 'Kan filmbranchen levere?' *Rushprint*, 23 November. Accessed 28 November 2012. http://rushprint.no/2010/11/kan-filmbransjen-levere/.
Hammond, Michael and Lucy Mazdon. 2005. *Contemporary Television Series*. Edinburgh: Edinburgh University Press.
Hansen, Klaus. 2009. 'Sæt pris på dansk tv.' *Berlingske Tidende*, 21 December. Accessed via Producentforeningen/The Danish Producers Association, 7 January 2013, http://pro-f.dk/content/sæt-pris-på-dansk-tv.
Hartley, John. 2005. *Creative Industries*. Oxford: Wiley-Blackwell.
Hartmann, Henrik. 2012. 'Borgen, Gabold and Success that Won't Go Away.' In *Nordvision 2011–2012*, edited by Ib Keld Jensen, Mikael Skog, Mikael Horvath and Henrik Hartmann , 49–55. Copenhagen: Nordvision.
Havens, Timothy and Amanda D. Lotz. 2012. *Understanding Media Industries*. New York and Oxford: Oxford University Press.
Henderson, Felicia D. 2011. 'The Culture Behind Closed Doors: Issues of Gender and Race in the Writers' Room.' *Cinema Journal* 50: 145–52.
Hesmondhalgh, David. 2007. *The Cultural Industries*. 2nd ed. London and Thousand Oaks: Sage Publications.
Hesmondhalgh, David and Sarah Baker. 2010. *Creative Labour: Media Work in the Cultural Industries*. New York and Abingdon: Routledge.
Hesseldahl, Morten. 2013a. 'DR: "Borgen" hjernevasker ikke danskerne røde.' *Berlingske Tidende*, 12 February. Accessed 29 March 2013. http://www.b.dk/kommentarer/dr-borgen-hjernevasker-ikke-danskerne-roede.
Hesseldahl, Morten. 2013b. 'Birgitte Nyborg stod ikke bag unges optøjer i Prag.' *Fyens Stiftstidende*, 20 February.

Higson, Andrew. 1995. *Waving the Flag: Constructing a National Cinema in Britain*. Oxford: Clarendon Press.

Hills, Matt. 2013. 'TV Aesthetics in Transition: "Bad" TV Dramas and Discourses of Failure.' Paper in the panel *Beyond the Reruns: Defining the Field of Television Studies*, 7 March. Chicago: Society of Cinema and Media Studies.

Hilmes, Michelle. 2009. 'Nailing Mercury. The Problem of Media Industry Historiography.' In *Media Industries. History, Theory, and Method*, edited by Jennifer Holt and Alisa Perren, 21–33. Malden: Wiley-Blackwell.

Hilmes, Michelle. 2011. *Network Nations: A Transnational History of American and British Broadcasting*. London and New York: Routledge.

Hjarvard, Stig. 2006. 'Tv-mediets halve århundrede.' In *Dansk tvs historie*, edited by Stig Hjarvard, 7–24. Frederiksberg: Samfundslitteratur.

Hjort, Mette. 2005. *Small Nation, Global Cinema: The New Danish Cinema*. Minneapolis: University of Minnesota Press.

Hjort, Mette (ed.). 2007. *On The Five Obstructions*. London: Wallflower Press.

Hjort, Mette. 2013a. *The Education of the Filmmaker in Europe, Australia, and Asia*. Vol. 1. Basingstoke: Palgrave Macmillan.

Hjort, Mette. 2013b. *The Education of the Filmmaker in Africa, the Middle East, and the Americas*. Vol. 2. Basingstoke: Palgrave Macmillan.

Hjort, Mette and Ib Bondebjerg. 2003. *The Danish Directors: Dialogues on a Contemporary National Cinema*. Bristol: Intellect Press.

Hjort, Mette and Scott MacKenzie (eds.). 2003. *Purity and Provocation: Dogme 95*. London: British Film Institute.

Hjort, Mette, Eva Jørholt and Eva N. Redvall (eds.). 2010. *Danish Directors 2: Dialogues on the New Danish Fiction Cinema*. Bristol: Intellect Press.

Holt, Jennifer and Alisa Perren (eds.). 2009. *Media Industries: History, Theory, and Method*. Malden: Wiley-Blackwell.

Isaksen, Scott G. and Donald J. Treffinger. 2004. 'Celebrating 50 Years of Reflective Practice: Versions of Creative Problem Solving.' *The Journal of Creative Behavior* 38: 75–101.

Isaksen, Scott G., K. Brian Dorval and Donald J. Treffinger. 1994. *Creative Approaches to Problem Solving*. Dubuque: Kendall/Hunt.

Iversen, Andreas. 2010. 'Emmyjakt uten en plan.' *Rushprint*, 22 November. Accessed 3 April 2013. http://rushprint.no/2010/11/emmyjakt-uten-en-plan/

Jancovich, Mark. 2003. *Quality Popular Television*. London: British Film Institute.

Jane, Emma. 2012. 'BBC News – The Killing and Borgen: Danish Drama Wins Global Fanbase.' bbc.co.uk, 27 April. Accessed 25 March 2013. http://www.bbc.co.uk/news/magazine-17853928.

Jessen, Catarina Nedertoft. 2013. ' "Borgen" flytter ikke stemmer.' *Information*, 15 February. Accessed 25 February 2013. http://www.information.dk/451260.

Jensen, Klaus Bruhn (ed.). 2002. *A Handbook of Media and Communication Research*. London: Routledge.

Jensen, Lasse. 2013. 'Klummen.' *Information*, 17 April.

John, Ole (ed.). 2006. *At lære kunsten – 40 år med Filmskolen*. Copenhagen: Aschehoug.

John-Steiner, Vera. 2000. *Creative Collaboration*. Oxford: Oxford University Press.

Johnson, Catherine. 2012. *Branding Television*. London: Routledge.

Johnson, David W. and Frank P. Johnson. 2006. *Joining Together: Group Theory and Group Skills*. Upper Saddle River: Pearson Education.

Jørgensen, John Chr. 1987. *Leif Panduro: En biografi*. Copenhagen: Gyldendal.

Kackman, Michael, Marnie Binfield, Matthew T. Payne, Allison Perlman and Bryan Sebok (eds.). 2011. *Flow TV: Television in the Age of Media Convergence*. New York and London: Routledge.

King, Donna and Carrie Lee Smith (eds). 2012. *Men Who Hate Women and Women Who Kick Their Asses: Stieg Larsson's Millenium Trilogy in Feminist Perspective*. Nashville: Vanderbilt University Press.

Kingsley, Patrick. 2012. *How to be Danish. From Lego to Lund: A Short Introduction to the State of Denmark*. London: Short Books.

Kipen, David. 2006. *The Schreiber Theory: A Radical Rewrite of American Film History*. New York: Melville House.

Kragh-Jacobsen, Søren. 2012. 'Filminstruktør på DR Drama.' *Take* 57: 6–9.

Kupferberg, Feiwel. 2006. *Kreative tider. At nytænke den pædagogiske sociologi*. Copenhagen: Hans Reitzel.

Kraszewski, Jon. 2011. 'Hybridity, History, and the Identity of the Television Studies Teacher.' *Cinema Journal* 50: 166–172.

Kåset, Margrete and Jan Strade Ødegårdstuen. 2010. 'NRK Drama – et monster uten hode?' *Rushprint*, 30 November. Accessed 3 April 2013. http://rushprint. no/2010/11/nrk-drama-et-monster-uten-hode/

Lacob, Jace. 2012. ' "Forbrydelsen," "Borgen," "The Bridge": The Rise of Nordic Noir TV.' *The Daily Beast*, 20 June. Accessed 25 March 2013. http://www. thedailybeast.com/articles/2012/06/20/forbrydelsen-borgen-the-bridge-the-rise-of-nordic-noir-tv.html.

Langkjær, Birger. 2012. *Realismen i dansk film*. Frederiksberg: Samfundslitteratur.

Lawson, Mark. 2007. 'Britain's Got Talent – and it's Untouchable.' *The Guardian*, 22 October. Accessed 7 November 2012. http://www.guardian.co.uk/media/ 2007/oct/22/mondaymediasection2.

Levine, Elana. 2001. 'Toward a Paradigm for Media Production Research: Behind the Scenes at General Hospital.' *Critical Studies in Media Communication* 18: 66–82.

Levine, Elana. 2008. 'Distinguishing Television: The Changing Meaning of Television Liveness.' *Media, Culture & Society* 30: 393–409.

Livingston, Paisley. 1997. 'Cinematic Authorship.' In *Film Theory and Philosophy*, edited by Murray Smith and Richard Allen, 132–48. Oxford: Oxford University Press.

Livingston, Paisley. 2007. *Art and Intention: A Philosophical Study*. Oxford: Oxford University Press.

Livingston, Paisley. 2009. *Cinema, Philosophy, Bergman: On Film as Philosophy*. Oxford: Oxford University Press.

Lotz, Amanda D. 2004. 'Textual (im)possibilities in the U.S. Post-Network Era: Negotiating Production and Promotion Processes on Lifetime's *Any Day Now*.' *Critical Studies in Media Communication* 21: 22–43.

Lotz, Amanda D. 2007. *The Television Will be Revolutionized*. New York: New York University Press.

Ludvigsen, Jacob. 2011. 'Skal Public Service Puljen overleve?' *Ekko*, 25 November. Accessed 9 November 2012. http://www.ekkofilm.dk/artikler/skal-public-service-puljen-overleve/.

Lund, Anker Brink, Lars Nord and Johann Roppen. 2009. *Nye udfordringer for gamle medier: Skandinavisk public service i det 21. århundrede*. Göteborg: Nordicom.

Macdonald, Ian W. 2003. 'Finding the Needle. How Readers See Screen Ideas.' *Journal of Media Practice* 4: 27–40.

Macdonald, Ian W. 2004. 'Disentangling the Screen Idea.' *Journal of Media Practice* 5: 89–100.

Macdonald, Ian W. 2010. ' "...So It's Not Surprising I'm Neurotic", The Screenwriter and the Screen Idea Work Group.' *Journal of Screenwriting* 1: 45–58.

Macdonald, Ian W. 2012. 'Behind the Mask of the Screenplay: The Screen Idea.' In *Critical Cinema: Beyond the Theory of Practice*, edited by Clive Myers, 111–40. London: Wallflower Press.

Mann, Denise. 2009. 'It's not TV, It's Brand Management TV: The Collective Author(s) of the Lost Franchise.' In *Production Studies: Cultural Studies of Media Industries*, edited by Vicki Mayer, Miranda J. Banks and John T. Caldwell, 99–114. New York: Routledge.

Maras, Steven. 2009. *Screenwriting: History, Theory and Practice*. London: Wallflower Press.

Maras, Steven. 2011. 'Some Attitudes and Trajectories in Screenwriting Research.' *Journal of Screenwriting* 2: 275–86.

Mayer, Richard E. 1999. 'Fifty Years of Creativity Research.' In *Handbook of Creativity*, edited by Robert J. Sternberg, 449–60. Cambridge: Cambridge UP.

Mayer, Vicki. 2011. *Below the Line: Producers and Production Studies in the New Television Economy*. Durham and London: Duke University Press.

Mayer, Vicki, Miranda J. Banks, and John T. Caldwell (eds.). 2009. *Production Studies: Cultural Studies of Media Industries*. New York: Routledge.

McCabe, Janet. 2012. 'The Girl in the Faroese Jumper: Sarah Lund, Sexual Politics and the Precariousness of Power and Difference.' In *Stieg Larsson's Millennium Trilogy: Interdisciplinary Approaches to Nordic Noir on Page and Screen*, edited by Steven Peacock, 118–30. Basingstoke: Palgrave Macmillan.

McCabe, Janet and Kim Akass. 2007. *Quality TV: Contemporary American Television and Beyond*. London: I B Tauris & Co.

McIntyre, Philip. 2006. 'Paul McCartney and the Creation of "Yesterday": The System's Model in Operation.' *Popular Music* 25: 201–19.

McIntyre, Philip. 2008. 'Creativity and Cultural Production: A Study of Contemporary Western Music Songwriting.' *Creativity Research Journal* 20: 40–52.

McRobbie, Angela. 2002. 'From Holloway to Hollywood: Happiness at Work in the New Cultural Economy?' In *Cultural Economy: Cultural Analysis and Commercial Life*, edited by Paul Du Gay and Michael Pryke, 97–114. London: Sage.

Meskin, Aaron. 2009. 'Authorship.' In *The Routledge Companion to Philosophy and Film*, edited by Paisley Livingston and Carl Platinga, 12–28. London: Routledge.

Meyers, Lawrence (ed.). 2010. *Inside the TV Writer's Woom: Practical Advice for Succeeding in Television*. Syracuse: Syracuse University Press.

Midgley, Neil. 2011. 'BBC Four Buys Second Series of The Killing.' *The Telegraph*, 5 March. Accessed 12 March 2013. http://www.telegraph.co.uk/culture/tvandradio/bbc/8362146/BBC-Four-buys-second-series-of-The-Killing.html.

Miller, Laura. 2010. 'The Strange Case of the Nordic Detectives: The Growing Appeal of Scandinavian Crime Fiction; Existential Malaise and Bad Coffee.' *The*

Wall Street Journal, 15 January. Accessed 12 March 2013. http://online.wsj.com/article/SB10001424052748703657604575004961184066300.html

Ministry of Culture Denmark. 2011. *Bekendtgørelse om lov af radio- og fjernsynsvirksomhed*. Copenhagen: Ministry of Culture Denmark. Accessed 14 November 2012. https://www.retsinformation.dk/Forms/R0710.aspx?id=138757.

Ministry of Culture Denmark. 2013. 'DRs Public Service-Kontrakt for 2011–2014.' Accessed 8 January 2013. http://kum.dk/Documents/Kulturpolitik/medier/DR/public_servicekontrakt.PDF.

Molloy, Tim. 2010. 'AMC and the Triumph of the TV Auteur.' *The Wrap*, 15 December. Accessed 15 January 2013. http://www.thewrap.com/tv/article/amc-and-triumph-tv-auteur-23277.

Monggaard, Christian. 2012. 'Jul i lange baner.' *Information*, 28 November Accessed 7 January 2013. http://www.information.dk/318380.

Mooney, Ross L. 1963. 'A Conceptual Model for Integrating Four Approaches to the Identification of Creative Talent.' In *Scientific Creativity: Its Recognition and Development*, edited by Calvin W. Taylor and Frank Barron, 331–40. New York: Wiley.

Morley, David. 2004. 'Broadcasting and the Construction of the National Family.' In *The Television Studies Reader*, edited by Robert C. Allen and Annette Hill, 418–41. London: Routledge.

Munksgaard, Pia Glud. 2013. 'S-politiker klager til DR over *Borgen*.' *Berlingske Tidende*, 3 February. Accessed 25 February 2013. http://www.b.dk/nationalt/s-politiker-klager-til-dr-over-borgen.

Murphy, J. J. 2007. *Me and You and Memento and Fargo: How Independent Screenplays Work*. New York: Bloomsbury Academic.

Negus, Keith and Mike Pickering. 2004. *Creativity, Communication and Cultural Value*. London: Sage.

Nelmes, Jill (ed.). 2010. *Analysing the Screenplay*. London: Routledge.

Nelson, Robin. 2007. *State of Play: Contemporary 'High-End' TV Drama*. Manchester and New York: Manchester University Press.

Nestingen, Andrew. 2008. *Crime and Fantasy in Scandinavia: Fiction, Film and Social Change*. Seattle/Copenhagen: University of Washington Press/Museum Tusculanum Press.

Nestingen, Andrew. 2012. 'Killer Research: Scandinavian Crime Fiction Scholarship since 2008.' *Journal of Scandinavian Cinema* 2: 153–59.

Nestingen, Andrew and Paula Arvas (eds.). 2011. *Scandinavian Crime Fiction*. Cardiff: University of Wales Press.

Newcomb, Horace and Richard S. Alley. 1983. *The Producer's Medium: Conversations with Creators of American TV*. New York: Oxford University Press.

Newcomb, Horace. 1991. 'The Creation of Television Drama.' In *A Handbook of Qualitative Methodologies for Mass Communication Research*, edited by Klaus Bruhn Jensen and Nicholas W. Jankowski, 93–107. London & New York: Routledge.

Newcomb, Horace (ed.). 2007. *Television: The Critical View*. 7th ed. Oxford: Oxford University Press.

Newcomb, Horace. 2009. 'Toward Synthetic Media Industry Research.' In *Media Industries: History, Theory, and Method*, edited by Jennifer Holt and Alisa Perren, 264–70. Malden: Wiley-Blackwell.

Newcomb, Horace and Amanda D. Lotz. 2002. 'The Production of Media Fiction.' In *A Handbook of Media and Communication Research*, edited by Klaus Bruhn Jensen, 62–77. London: Routledge.

Nielsen, Jakob Isak. 2012a. 'Stort drama på den lille skærm: Interview med Søren Sveistrup.' *16:9*, 10 November. Accessed 28 February 2013. http://www.16-9. dk/2012-11/side05_interview2.htm.

Nielsen, Jakob Isak. 2012b. 'Solen må aldrig skinne, og Sofie må aldrig smile: Interview med Piv Bernth.' *16:9*, 10 November. Accessed 28 February 2013. http://www.16-9.dk/2012-11/side06_interview3.htm.

Nielsen, Jakob Isak. 2012c. 'DR-drama som æstetisk spydspids: Interview med Ingolf Gabold.' *16:9*, 10 November. Accessed 28 February 2013. http://www. 16-9.dk/2012-11/side07_interview4.htm.

Nielsen, Jakob Isak. 2012d. 'Den kreative fabrik. Interview med Nadia Kløvedal Reich.' *16:9*, 10 November. Accessed 28 February 2013.

Nordisk Film & TV Fond. 2011. 'News: Bornedal Wins Battle Over 100DKK Million DR Historical Series.' 13 May. Accessed 9 November 2012. http://www. nordiskfilmogtvfond.com/news_story.php?cid=2783&sid=11&ptid=4.

Nordstrøm, Pernille. 2004. *Fra Riget til Bella*. Copenhagen: DR Multimedie.

Nordvision. 2010. *Annual Report for 2009*. Copenhagen: Nordvision.

Osborn, Alex F. 1953. *Applied Imagination: Principles and Procedures of Creative Thinking*. New York: Charles Scribner's Sons.

Parker, Philip. 1998. *The Art & Science of Screenwriting*. Bristol: Intellect Press.

Paulus, Paul B. and Bernhard A. Nijstad. 2003. *Group Creativity: Innovation Through Collaboration*. Oxford: Oxford University Press.

Peacock, Steven. 2009. 'Two Kingdoms, Two Kings.' *Critical Studies in Television* 4: 24–36.

Peacock, Steven (ed.). 2012. *Stieg Larsson's Millennium Trilogy: Interdisciplinary Approaches to Nordic Noir on Page and Screen*. Basingstoke: Palgrave Macmillan.

Perkins, Victor F. 1972. *Film as Film: Understanding and Judging Movies*. Baltimore: Penguin Books.

Perren, Alisa. 2011. 'In Conversation: Creativity in the Contemporary Cable Industry.' *Cinema Journal* 50: 132–8.

Perren, Alisa. 2013. 'From Producer's Medium to Producer's Media: The Showrunner's Shifting Authority in the Convergent Era.' Paper presented at the research symposium *Generation(s) of Television Studies*, 12 April. The University of Georgia.

Petersen, Trine Munk. 2013. 'DR-fiktionschef: "Borgen" skal ikke give et billede af virkeligheden.' *Berlingske Tidende*, 4 February. Accessed 25 February 2013. http://www.b.dk/kultur/dr-fiktionschef-borgen-skal-ikke-give-et-billede-af-virkeligheden-0.

Peterson, Richard A. and N. Anand. 2004. 'The Production of Culture Perspective.' *Annual Review of Sociology* 30: 311–34.

Petrie, Duncan. 2010. 'Theory, Practice and the Significance of Film Schools.' *Scandia* 76: 31–46.

Petrie, Duncan. 2011. 'Theory/Practice and the British Film Conservatoire.' *Journal of Media Practice* 12: 125–38.

Petrie, Duncan. 2012. 'Creative Industries and Skills: Film Education and Training in the Era of New Labour.' *Journal of British Cinema and Television* 9: 357–76.

Phalen, Patricia and Julia Osellame. 2012. *Writing Hollywood: Rooms With a Point of View. Journal of Broadcasting & Electronic Media* 56: 3–20.

Pham, Annika. 2012. 'DR's Queens of Drama Give the Ingredients to Their Winning Recipe.' News from Nordisk Film & TV Fond, 11 May. Accessed 7 November 2012. http://www.nordiskfilmogtvfond.com/news_story.php?cid=3356&sid=10&ptid=4.

Pham, Annika. 2013. 'Stefan Baron Details SVT Drama's New Projects and Leadership.' Nordisk Film & TV Fond Newsletter, 18 January. Accessed 18 January 2013. http://www.nordiskfilmogtvfond.com/news_story.php?cid=3725&sid=10&ptid=4.

Philipsen, Heidi. 2005. *Dansk films nye bølge: Afsæt og aftryk fra Den Danske Filmskole*. PhD thesis. Odense: University of Southern Denmark.

Piil, Morten (ed.). 2008. *Gyldendals danske filmguide*. Copenhagen: Gyldendal.

Polan, Dana. 2007. *Scenes of Instruction: The Beginnings of the U.S. Study of Film*. Berkeley: University of California Press.

Powdermaker, Hortense. 1950. *Hollywood: The Dream Factory: An Anthropologist Looks at the Movie-Makers*. Boston: Little, Brown.

Price, Steven. 2010. *The Screenplay: Authorship, Theory and Criticism*. Basingstoke: Palgrave Macmillan.

Puccio, Gerard J., Mary C. Murdock and Marie Mance. 2005. 'Current Developments in Creative Problem Solving for Organizations: A Focus on Thinking Skills and Style.' *The Korean Journal of Thinking & Problem Solving* 15: 43–76.

Pye, Michael and Lynda Myles. 1979. *The Movie Brats: How the Film Generation Took Over Hollywood*. New York: Henry Holt.

Rasmussen, Anita Brask. 2007. 'Succesens farlige nabo.' *Information*, 26 July Accessed 29 March 2013. http://www.information.dk/118399

Redvall, Eva N. 2005. 'DR skaber legeplads.' *Information*, 18 April. Accessed 13 February 2013. www.information.dk/104332.

Redvall, Eva N. 2009. 'Scriptwriting as a Creative, Collaborative Learning Process of Problem Finding and Problem Solving.' *MedieKultur* 46: 34–55.

Redvall, Eva N. 2010a. *Manuskriptskrivning som kreativ process: De kreative samarbejder bag manuskriptskrivning i dansk spillefilm*. PhD Thesis. University of Copenhagen: Department of Media, Cognition and Communication.

Redvall, Eva N. 2010b. 'Teaching Screenwriting in a Time of Storytelling Blindness: The Meeting of the Auteur and the Screenwriting Tradition in Danish Film-Making.' *Journal of Screenwriting* 1: 57–79.

Redvall, Eva N. 2010c. 'Gabolds vision.' *Ekkofilm*, 24 August. Accessed 8 January 2013. http://www.ekkofilm.dk/artikler/gabolds-vision/.

Redvall, Eva N. 2010d. 'Kampen om sofavælgerne.' *EKKO* 50: 64–66.

Redvall, Eva N. 2011. 'Dogmer for tv-drama. Om brugen af *one vision*, den dobbelte historie og *crossover* i DR's søndagsdramatik.' *Kosmorama* 248: 180–98.

Redvall, Eva N. 2012a. *European TV Drama Series Lab. Summary of Module 1*. Berlin: Erich Pommer Institut.

Redvall, Eva N. 2012b. 'A Systems View of Filmmaking as a Creative Practice.' *Northern Lights* 10: 57–73.

Redvall, Eva N. 2012c. 'Encouraging Artistic Risk Taking through Film Policy: The Case of New Danish Screen.' In *Film and Risk*, edited by Mette Hjort, 209–26. Detroit: Wayne State University Press.

Redvall, Eva N. 2012d. 'Fra folkeligt fællesfjernsyn til kvalitetskræs med kant.' *Kulturo* 18: 69–75.

Redvall, Eva N. 2013. *European TV Drama Series Lab. Summary of Module 2*. Berlin: Erich Pommer Institut.

Redvall, Eva N. and Michael Gubbins. 2011. *Scandinavian Think Tank: On Films, Markets, Audiences and Film Policy*. Copenhagen: Think Tank on European Film and Film Policy.

Reich, Nadia Kløvedal. 2013. 'Producentforeningen i et farligt ærinde.' *Jyllands-Posten*, 29 January. Accessed 20 March 2013. http://m.jyllands-posten.dk/jp/opinion/breve/ECE5121244/producentforeningen-i-et-farligt-aerinde/

Rhodes, Mel 1961. 'An Analysis of Creativity.' *Phi Delta Kappan* 42: 305–10.

Rollinson, David. 2011. 'Small Screens and Big Voices: Televisual Social Realism and the Popular.' In *British Social Realism in the Arts since 1940*, edited by David Tucker, 172–217. Basingstoke: Palgrave Macmillan.

Romano, Andrew. 2012. 'Borgen: The Best TV Show You've Never Seen.' *Newsweek*, 30 July. Accessed 25 February 2013. http://www.thedailybeast.com/newsweek/2012/07/29/borgen-the-best-tv-show-you-ve-never-seen.html.

Rose, Lacey. 2013. 'It's Official: "The Killing" Being Revived at AMC.' *Hollywood Reporter*, 15 January. Accessed 25 March 2013. http://www.hollywoodreporter.com/live-feed/killing-being-revived-at-amc-412703.

Rosenlund, Peter. 2012. 'Forfatteren i sentrum.' *Rushprint*, 5 November Accessed 29 March 2013. http://rushprint.no/2012/11/forfatteren-i-sentrum/.

Ross, Dick. 2002. 'Dick Ross. Tutor.' In *Projections 12*, edited by John Boorman, Fraser MacDonald and Walter Donohue, 39–53. London: Faber and Faber.

Rosten, Leo. 1941. *Hollywood: The Movie Colony, the Movie Makers*. New York: Harcourt Brace.

Rowold, Finn. 2009. *Nordvision gennem 50 år. Tilbageblik på et enestående nordisk tv-samarbejde*. Copenhagen: Danmarks Radio.

Rukov, Mogens. 1991. 'Om at lave skole.' In *Filmskolen: De første 25 år*, edited by Arne Bro, 38–41. Copenhagen: National Film School of Denmark.

Runco, Mark A. 2007. *Creativity: Theories and Themes: Research, Development, and Practice*. Burlington: Elsevier Academic Press.

Ryhammar, Lars and Catarina Brolin. 1999. 'Creativity Research: Historical Considerations and Main Lines of Development.' *Scandinavian Journal of Educational Research* 43: 259–73.

Sandeen, Cathy A. and Ronald J. Compesi. 1990. 'Television Production as Collective Action.' In *Making Television: Authorship and the Production Process*, edited by Robert J. Thompson and Gary Burns, 161–74 New York: Praeger Publishers.

Sandler, Ellen. 2007. *The TV Writer's Workbook*. New York: Delta Trade Paperbacks.

Sarris, Andrew. 1962. 'Notes on the Auteur Theory in 1962.' *Film Culture* 27: 1–8.

Sarris, Andrew. 1968. *The American Cinema: Directors and Directions 1929–68*. New York: Dutton.

Sawyer, Keith. 2008. *Group Genius: The Creative Power of Collaboration*. New York: Basic Books.

Schatz, Thomas. 1996. *The Genius of the System: Hollywood Filmmaking in the Studio Era*. New York: Henry Holt.

Schatz, Thomas. 2009. 'Film Industry Studies and Hollywood History.' In *Media Industries: History, Theory, and Method*, edited by Jennifer Holt and Alisa Perren, 45–56. Malden: Wiley-Blackwell.

Schepelern, Peter. 1986. 'Det uendeligt små: En vis tendens i moderne dansk tv-dramatik.' In *Sekvens 1986: Dansk TV*, edited by Lene Nordin, 53–66. Copenhagen: University of Copenhagen.

Schepelern, Peter. 1995. 'Mellem lyst og pligt: Filmkultur og filmkritik i Danmark.' *Medie Kultur* 23: 5–25.

Schepelern, Peter. 2000. *Lars von Triers film: Tvang og Befrielse*. Copenhagen: Rosinante.

Schepelern, Peter. 2005. 'The Making of an Auteur: Notes on the Auteur Theory and Lars von Trier.' In *Visual Authorship: Creativity and Intentionality in Media*, edited by Torben Grodal, Bente Larsen and Iben T. Laursen, 103–37. Copenhagen: Museum Tusculanum.

Scherfig, Nikolaj. 2006. 'Erindringer om skandaløse taler og andre anekdoter fra senfirserne.' In *At lære kunsten*, edited by Ole John. Copenhagen: Aschehoug.

Scherfig, Nikolaj. 2012. 'Broen til suksess.' *Rushprint*, 6 December. Accessed 20 March 2013. http://rushprint.no/2012/12/broen-til-suksess/

Sellors, Paul C. 2007. 'Collective Authorship in Film.' *Journal of Aesthetics and Art Criticism* 65: 263–71.

Smethurst, William. 2009. *How to Write for Television*. 6th ed. Oxford: How To Books.

Staiger, Janet. 1979. 'Dividing Labor for Production Control: Thomas Ince and the Rise of the Studio System.' *Cinema Journal* 18: 16–25.

Staiger, Janet. 2012. 'Considering the Screenplay as Blueprint.' *Northern Lights* 10: 75–90.

Stake, Robert E. 2000. 'The Case Study Method in Social Inquiry.' In *Case Study Method* Roger Gomm, Martyn Hammersley and Peter Foster, 19–27. London: Sage.

Stake, Robert E. 2005. 'Qualitative Case Studies.' In *The Sage Handbook of Qualitative Research*, 3rd ed, edited by in Norman K. Denzin and Yvonne S. Lincoln, 443–66. Thousand Oaks: Sage.

Stanley, Alessandra. 2012. 'She Seems To Have it All, A Whole Nation in Fact', *The New York Times*, 11 October. Accessed 25 February 2013. http://www.nytimes.com/2012/10/12/arts/television/borgen-a-danish-political-drama-series-on-link-tv.html.

Steffensen, Mads D. 2009. 'Tv-stationer kæmper om at levere efterårets dramaserie.' *Information*, 25 September 2009.

Stempel, Tom. 1996. *Storytellers to the Nation: A History of American Television Writing*. New York: Continuum.

Sternberg, Robert J. 1999. *Handbook of Creativity*. Cambridge: Cambridge University Press.

Sternberg, Robert J. and Todd I. Lubart. 1999. 'The Concept of Creativity: Prospects and Paradigms.' In *Handbook of Creativity*, edited by Robert J. Sternberg, 3–31. Cambridge: Cambridge University Press.

Sæhl, Marie. 2013. 'Adam Price: Jeg tror da ikke, at K laver politik ud fra "Borgen" ' *Politiken*, 1 February. Accessed 26 February 2013. http://politiken.dk/kultur/tvogradio/ECE1885797/adam-price-jeg-tror-da-ikke-at-k-laver-politik-ud-fra-borgen/.

Søndergaard, Henrik. 2006. 'Tv som institution.' In *Dansk tvs historie*, edited by Stig Hjarvard, 25–64. Frederiksberg: Samfundslitteratur.

Taylor, Thom. 1999. *The Big Deal: Hollywood's Million-Dollar Spec Script Market*. New York: William Morrow.

Thompson, Kristin. 1999. *Storytelling in the New Hollywood*. Cambridge: Harvard University Press.

Thompson, Kristin. 2003. *Storytelling in Film and Television*. Cambridge: Harvard University Press.

Thompson, Robert J. and Gary Burns (eds.) 1990. *Making Television: Authorship and the Production Process*. New York: Praeger Publishers.

Thorsboe, Peter. 2006. 'Om at lære et håndværk.' In *At lære kunsten*, edited by Ole John, 142–7. Copenhagen: Aschehoug.

Thorsen, Lotte. 2013. 'Amerikansk kabelkanal bag de fede serier flirter med DR.' *Politiken*, 15 January. Accessed 2 April 2013. http://politiken.dk/kultur/tvogradio/ECE1867954/amerikansk-kabelkanal-bag-de-fede-serier-flirter-med-dr/

Thorsen, Nils. 2013. 'Danmark som science fiction.' *Politiken*, 6 January.

Tybjerg, Casper. 2005. 'The Makers of Movies: Authors, Subjects, Personalities, Agents?' In *Visual Authorship: Creativity and Intentionality in Media*, edited by Torben Grodal, Bente Larsen and Iben T. Laursen, 37–65. Copenhagen: Museum Tusculanum.

Vinterberg, Thomas and Ole John. 2006. 'Samtale.' In *At lære kunsten*, edited by Ole John, 177–87. Copenhagen: Aschehoug.

Waade, Anne Marit. 2010. 'Små steder – store forbrydelser. Stedspecifik realisme, provinsmiljø og rurale landskaber i skandinaviske krimiserier.' In *Den skandinaviske krimi*, edited by Gunhild Agger and Anne Marit Waade, 63–78. Göteborg: Nordicom.

Wallas, Graham. 1926. *The Art of Thought*. New York: Harcourt, Brace and Company.

Wasko, Janet. 2003. *How Hollywood Works*. London: Sage.

Weisberg, Robert W. 1993. *Creativity. Beyond the Myth of Genius*. New York: W. H. Freeman.

Weissmann, Elke. 2012. *Transnational Television Drama: Special Relations and Mutual Influence Between the US and UK*. Basingstoke: Palgrave Macmillan.

Wind-Friis, Lea. 2013. 'Adam Price arbejder på ny BBC-serie med markant skrivemakker.; *Politiken*, 7 April. Accessed 10 April 2013. http://politiken.dk/kultur/ECE1939173/adam-price-arbejder-paa-ny-bbc-serie-med-markant-skrivemakker/

Wivel, Anne and Arne Bro. 1991. 'Interview med Henning Camre.' in *Filmskolen: De første 25 år*, edited by Arne Bro, 6–15. Copenhagen: Den Danske Filmskole.

Wyatt, Justin. 1994. *High Concept: Movies and Marketing in Hollywood*. Austin: University of Texas Press.

List of interviews

Brostrøm, Mai. 2012. Interview by the author. 18 December.

Clausen, Sven. 2010. Interview by the author. 23 August.

Detlefsen, Lars. 2012. Interview by the author. 11 December.
Gabold, Ingolf. 2010. Interview by the author. 21 July.
Gabold, Ingolf. 2011. Interview by the author. 17 March.
Gabold, Ingolf. 2013. Telephone interview by the author. 17 May.
Gram, Jeppe Gjervig. 2011. Interview by the author. 16 September.
Gram, Jeppe Gjervig. 2012. Interview by the author. 9 November.
Hammerich, Camilla. 2011. Interview by the author. 16 September.
Hammerich, Camilla. 2012. Interview by the author. 9 November.
Hammerich, Rumle. 2012. Interview by the author. 7 June.
Heiselberg, Lene. 2011. Interview by the author. 1 April.
Horsten, Michael W. 2013. Interview by the author. 29 January.
Ilsøe, Maya. 2012. Interview by the author. 13 November.
Kofoed, Rikke Tørholm. 2012. Interview by the author. 9 November.
Larsen, Maja Jul. 2012. Interview by the author. 8 November.
Lundblad, Hanna. 2012. Interview by the author. 3 September.
Price, Adam. 2010. Interview by the author. 17 July.
Price, Adam. 2012. Interview by the author. 20 December.
Rank, Christian. 2012. Interview by the author. 22 November.
Reich, Nadia Kløvedal. 2012. Interview by the author. 6 November.
Sutherland, Pernille Skov. 2012. Interview by the author. 9 November.
Sveistrup, Søren. 2012. Interview by the author. 6 November.
Thorsboe, Peter. 2012. Interview by the author. 18 December.
Thorsboe, Stig. 2012. Interview by the author. 3 September.
Thunø, Lars. 2012. Conversation with the author. 16 November.
Wieland, Jacob Lyng. 2011. Interview by the author. 1 April.
Wille, Jakob Ion. 2013. Interview by the author. 28 January.

List of films

Adams æbler/Adam's Apples. 2005. Wr: Anders Thomas Jensen, Dir: Anders Thomas Jensen, Denmark, 97 mins.
Blinkende Lygter/Flickering Lights. 2000. Wr: Anders Thomas Jensen, Dir: Anders Thomas Jensen, Denmark, 109 mins.
Citizen Kane. 1941. Wr: Herman J. Makiewicz and Orson Welles, Dir: Orson Welles, USA, 119 mins.
Dagbog fra midten/'Diary from the Middle'. 2009. Documentary, Dir: Christoffer Guldbrandsen; Denmark, DR, 74 mins.
De fem benspænd/The Five Obstructions. 2003. Wr: Jørgen Leth, Lars von Trier and Asger Leth, Dir: Lars von Trier, Denmark, 92 mins.
De grønne slagtere/The Green Butchers. 2003. Wr: Anders Thomas Jensen, Dir: Anders Thomas Jensen, Denmark, 99 mins.
De Unge År/The Early Years – Erik Nietzsche Part 1. 2007. Wr: Lars von Trier, Dir: Jacob Thuesen, Denmark, 92 mins.
Den skaldede frisør/Love is All You Need. 2012. Wr: Anders Thomas Jensen. Dir: Susanne Bier, Denmark, 112 mins.
Drømmen/We Shall Overcome. 2006. Wr: Steen Bille and Niels Arden Oplev, Dir: Niels Arden Oplev, Denmark, 105 mins.

Elsker dig for evigt/Open Hearts. 2002. Wr: Anders Thomas Jensen, Dir: Susanne Bier, Denmark, 114 mins.

En kærlighedshistorie/Kira's Reason: A Love Story. 2001. Wr: Ole Christian Madsen and Mogens Rukov, Dir: Ole Christian Madsen, Denmark, 93 mins.

En kongelig affære/A Royal Affair. 2012. Wr: Nikolaj Arcel and Rasmus Heisterberg, Dir: Nikolaj Arcel, Denmark, 128 mins.

Epidemic. 1987. Wr: Niels Vørsel and Lars von Trier, Dir: Lars von Trier, Denmark, 106 mins.

Europa. 1991. Wr: Lars von Trier and Niels Vørsel, Dir: Lars von Trier, Denmark, 113 mins.

Festen/The Celebration. 1998. Wr: Thomas Vinterberg and Mogens Rukov, Dir: Thomas Vinterberg, Denmark, 106 mins.

Flammen & Citronen/Flame and Citron. 2008. Wr: Ole Christian Madsen and Lars K. Andersen, Dir: Ole Christian Madsen, Denmark, 130 mins.

Forbrydelsens element/The Element of Crime. 1984. Wr: Niels Vørsel and Lars von Trier, Dir: Lars von Trier, Denmark, 103 mins.

Hævnen/In a Better World. 2010. Wr: Anders Thomas Jensen, Dir: Susanne Bier, Denmark, 119 mins.

Heaven's Gate. 1980. Wr: Michael Cimino, Dir: Michael Cimino, USA, 219 mins.

Hvidsten Gruppen/This Life. 2012. Wr: Ib Kastrup, Jørgen Kastrup and Regner Grasten (as Thorvald Lervad), Dir: Anne-Grethe Bjarup Riis, Denmark, 110 mins.

Idioterne/The Idiots. 1998. Wr: Lars von Trier, Dir: Lars von Trier, Denmark, 117 mins.

Klovn – The Movie/Clown. 2010. Wr: Casper Christensen and Frank Hvam, Dir: Mikkel Nørgaard, Denmark, 94 mins.

Män som hatar kvinnor/The Girl with the Dragon Tattoo. 2009. Wr: Nikolaj Arcel and Rasmus Heisterberg based on novel by Stieg Larsson, Dir: Niels Arden Oplev, Sweden/Denmark/Germany/Norway, 152 mins.

Mifunes sidste sang/Mifune. 1999. Wr: Anders Thomas Jensen and Søren Kragh-Jacobsen, Dir: Søren Kragh-Jacobsen, Denmark, 102 mins.

Nattevagten/Nightwatch. 1994. Wr: Ole Bornedal, Dir: Ole Bornedal, Denmark, 107 mins.

Nightwatch. 1997. Wr: Ole Bornedal and Steven Soderbergh, Dir: Ole Bornedal, USA, 101 mins.

Nordkraft/Angels in Fast Motion. 2005. Wr: Ole Christian Madsen, Dir: Ole Christian Madsen, Denmark, 120 mins.

Pizza King. 1999. Wr: Ole Christian Madsen, Janus Nabil Bakrawi and Lars K. Andersen, Dir: Ole Christian Madsen, Denmark, 103 mins.

Prag/Prague. 2006 Wr: Ole Christian Madsen and Kim Fupz Aakeson, Dir: Ole Christian Madsen, Denmark, 96 mins.

SuperClásico. 2011. Wr: Ole Christian Madsen and Anders Frithiof August, Dir: Ole Christian Madsen, Denmark, 99 mins.

The Godfather. 1972. Wr: Mario Puzo and Francis Ford Coppola, Dir: Francis Ford Coppola, USA, 175 mins.

The King is Alive. 2000. Wr: Kristian Levring and Anders Thomas Jensen, Dir: Kristian Levring, Denmark/USA, 110 mins.

Valgaften/Election Night. 1999. Wr: Anders Thomas Jensen, Dir: Anders Thomas Jensen, Denmark, 12 mins.

List of TV series

1864. forthcoming 2014. Cr: Ole Bornedal; Denmark, Miso Film for DR, 8 eps.
2 Broke Girls. 2011–. Cr: Michael Patrick King and Whitney Cummings; USA, CBS, 22 mins eps.
24. 2001–2010. Cr: Joel Surnow and Robert Cochran; USA, Fox, 42 mins × 192 eps.
2900 Happiness. 2007–2009. Wr: Thomas Glud and Iben Gylling; Denmark, TV3, 30 mins × 142 eps.
Absalons hemmelighed/'Absalon's Secret'. 2006. Cr: Maya Ilsøe; Denmark, DR, 30 mins × 24 eps.
Absolutely Fabulous. 1992–2012. Cr: Jennifer Saunders and Dawn French; UK, BBC One, 30–60 mins × 39 eps.
Album. 2008. Wr: Bo Hr. Hansen, Dir: Hella Joof; Denmark, Fine & Mellow for DR, 58 mins × 5 eps.
Anna Pihl. 2006–2008. Wr: Adam Price and others; Denmark, TV 2, 50 mins × 30 eps.
Anthonsen. 1984–1985. Wr: Peter Thorsboe and Stig Thorsboe, Dir: Erik Balling; Denmark, Nordisk Film *for* DR, 54 mins × 5 eps.
Arvingerne/The Legacy. forthcoming 2014. Cr: Maya Ilsøe; Denmark, DR, 58 mins eps.
Banshee. 2013–. Cr: David Schickler and Jonathan Tropper; USA, Cinemax, 50 mins eps.
Blekingegade/The Left Wing Gang. 2009–2010. Wr: Lars Kjeldgaard, Dir: Jacob Thuesen; Denmark, TV2, 45 mins × 5 eps.
Boardwalk Empire. 2010–. Cr: Terence Winter; USA, HBO, 60 mins eps.
Bødlen/'The Executioner'. 2013. Wr: Nikolaj Scherfig, Dir: Frode Højer Pedersen; Denmark, dk4, 60 mins × 2 eps.
Bored to Death. 2009–2011. Cr: Jonathan Ames; USA, HBO, 30 mins × 24 eps.
Borgen. 2010–2013. Cr: Adam Price; Denmark, DR, 58 mins × 30 eps.
Borgia. 2011–. Cr: Tom Fontana; USA, Canal+, 52 mins eps.
Boss. 2011–2012. Cr: Farhad Safinia; USA, Starz, 54–60 mins × 18 eps.
Breaking Bad. 2008–2013. Cr: Vince Gilligan; USA, AMC, 47 mins × 62 eps.
Bron/The Bridge. 2011–. Cr: Hans Rosenfeldt; Sweden/Denmark, Filmlance and Nimbus Film *for* SVT and DR, 60 mins eps.
Bryggeren/'The Brewer'. 1996–1997, Cr: Kaspar Rostrup; Denmark, DR, 55 mins × 12 eps.
Californication. 2007–. Cr: Tom Kapinos; USA, Showtime, 28 mins eps.
Charlot & Charlotte. 1996. Cr: Ole Bornedal; Denmark, DR, 52 mins × 4 eps.
Coronation Street. 1960–. Cr: Tony Warren; UK, ITV, 22 mins eps.
Criminal Minds. 2005–. Cr: Jeff Davis; USA, CBS, 42 mins eps.
Crusoe. 2008–2009. Cr: Justin Bodle, Stephen Gallagher; USA, NBC, 60 mins × 12 eps.
Curb Your Enthusiasm. 2000–. Cr: Larry David; USA, HBO, 30 mins eps.
Dallas. 1978–1991. Cr: David Jacobs; USA, CBS, 50 mins × 357 eps.

Den som dræber/Those Who Kill. 2011. Wr: Elsebeth Egholm and Stefan Jaworski; Denmark, TV2, 55 mins × 10 eps.

De udvalgte/'The Chosen Ones'. 2001. Cr: Jens Dahl and Nicolas Winding Refn. Denmark, DR1, 40 mins × 13 eps. Later shown on DR2 in a re-edited version as 12 eps.

Dexter. 2006–2013. Cr: James Manos, Jr; USA, Showtime, 45–60 mins × 96 eps.

Dicte. 2013–. Wr: Elsebeth Egholm, Dorthe Warnøe Høgh and Ida Maria Rydén; Denmark, TV2, 45 mins eps.

Doctor Who. 2005–. Cr: Russell T. Davies; UK, BBC One, 45 mins eps.

Drengene fra Angora/'The Boys from Angora'. 2004. Cr: Simon Kvamm, Esben Pretzmann and Rune Tolsgaard; Denmark, DR2, 30 mins × 24 eps.

Dynasty. 1981–1989. Cr: Esther Shapiro and Richard Alan Shapiro; USA, ABC, 46 mins × 220 eps.

Edderkoppen/'The Spider'. 2000. Wr: Lars Kjeldgaard and others, Dir: Ole Christian Madsen; Denmark, DR, 58 mins × 6 eps.

Een gang strømer . . ./ 'Once a Cop . . .'. 1987. Wr: Anders Refn and Flemming Quist Møller, Dir: Anders Refn; Denmark, Nordisk Film for DR, 60 mins × 6 eps.

Eleventh Hour. 2006. Cr: Stephen Gallagher; UK, ITV, 90 mins × 4 eps.

Eleventh Hour. 2008–2009. Cr: Stephen Gallagher; USA, CBS, 44 mins × 18 eps.

En by i provinsen/'A Town in the Provinces'. 1977–1980. Wr: Leif Panduro; Dir: Bent Christensen; Denmark, DR, 17 eps.

Engrenages/Spiral. 2005–. Cr: Alexandra Clert and Guy-Patrick Sainderichin; France, Canal+, 52 mins eps.

Fabian of the Yard. 1954–56. Wr: Robert Fabian et al.; UK, BBC, 30 mins × 36 eps.

Follow the Money. Forthcoming 2015. Cr: Jeppe Gjervig Gram; Denmark, DR.

Forbrydelsen/The Killing. 2007–2012. Wr: Søren Sveistrup; Denmark, DR, 55 mins × 40 eps.

Forestillinger/'Performances'. 2007. Wr: Lars Kjeldgaard, Per Fly and Kim Leona, Dir: Per Fly; Denmark, Zentropa for DR, 58 mins × 6 eps.

Forsvar/'Defense'. 2003–2004. Wr: Lars Kjeldgaard and others; Denmark, TV2, 44 mins × 29 eps.

Game of Thrones. 2011–. Cr: David Benioff and D. B. Weiss; USA, HBO, 60 mins eps.

Gøngehøvdingen/'The Gønge Chieftain'. 1992. Wr: Bjarne O. Henriksen and Gert Henriksen, Dir: Peter Eszterhás; Denmark, DR, 30 mins × 13 eps.

Heroes. 2006–2010. Cr: Tim Kring; USA, NBC, 42 mins × 77 eps.

Hill Street Blues. 1981–1987. Cr: Steven Bochco and Michael Kozoll; USA, NBC, 49 mins × 146 eps.

Homicide: Life on the Street. 1993–1999. Cr: Paul Attanasio; USA, NBC, 49 mins × 122 eps.

Hotellet/At the Faber. 2000–2002. Wr: Morten Arnfred, Peter Nyrén, Søren Sveistrup and others; Denmark, TV2, 60 eps.

House. 2004–2012. Cr: David Shore; USA, Fox, 42 mins × 177 eps.

House of Cards. 1990. Wr: Andrew Davies and Michael Dobbs; UK, BBC, 55 mins × 4 eps.

House of Cards. 2013–. Wr: Beau Willimon and others; USA, Netflix, 55 mins eps.

Hunted. 2012. Cr: Frank Spotnitz; UK, BBC, 60 mins × 8 eps.

Huset på Christianshavn/'The House in Christianshavn'. 1970–1977. Wr: Henning Bahs, Paul Hammerich, Leif Panduro and others, Dir: Erik Balling, Tom Hedegaard and Ebbe Langberg; Denmark, DR, 25 mins × 84 eps.

Hvide løgne/White Lies. 1998–2001. Wr: Winnie Haarløv and others; Denmark, TV3, 25 mins × 447 eps.

In Treatment. 2008–. Cr: Rodrigo Garcia; USA, HBO, 30 mins eps.

Julestjerner/'Christmas Stars'. 2012. Wr: Michael Wikke, Steen Rasmussen; Denmark, DR, 25 mins × 25 eps.

Ka' de li Østers?/Do you like Oysters? 1967. Wr: Leif Panduro and Bent Christensen, Dir: Ebbe Langberg; Denmark, DR, 28–40 mins × 6 eps.

Kingdom Hospital. 2004. Cr: Stephen King based on the series by Lars von Trier; USA, ABC, 40 mins × 13 eps.

Klovn/Clown. 2005–2009. Cr: Casper Christensen and Frank Hvam; Denmark, TV 2 Zulu, 25 mins × 60 eps.

Krøniken/Better Times. 2004–2007. Wr: Hanna Lundblad and Stig Thorsboe; Denmark, DR, 58 mins × 22 eps.

Lærkevej/Park Road. 2009–2010. Wr: Mette Heeno and others; Denmark, TV2, 43 mins × 22 eps.

Landsbyen/'The Village'. 1991–96. Cr: Stig Thorsboe and Peter Thorsboe; Denmark, Nordisk Film for DR, 25 mins × 44 eps.

Langt fra Las Vegas/'Far from Las Vegas'. 2001–2003. Cr: Casper Christensen, Frank Hvam; Denmark, TV2 Zulu, 30 mins × 53 eps.

Lilyhammer. 2012–. Cr: Anne Bjørnstad and Eilif Skodvin; Norway, NRK/Netflix, 46 mins eps.

Limbo. 2012. Cr: Karina Dam and Poul Berg; Denmark, DR, 28 mins × 10 eps.

Livvagterne/The Protectors. 2008–2010. Cr: Mai Brostrøm and Peter Thorsboe; Denmark, DR, 58 mins × 20 eps.

Lost. 2004–2010. Cr: J. J. Abrams, Damon Lindelof and Jeffrey Lieber; USA, ABC, 42 mins × 121 eps.

Lulu & Leon. 2009–2010. Cr: Jens Dahl and Lolita Belstar; Denmark, TV3, 43 mins × 24 eps.

Lykke/Happy Life. 2011–2012. Cr: Hanna Lundblad and Stig Thorsboe; Denmark, DR, 58 mins × 18 eps.

Mad Men 2007–. Cr: Matthew Weiner; USA, AMC, 47 mins eps.

Matador. 1978–81. Cr: Lise Nørgaard and Erik Balling; Denmark, DR, 50 mins × 24 eps.

McCloud. 1970–1977. Cr: Herman Miller; USA, NBC, various lengths, 46 eps.

Medea. 1988. TV film, Wr: Preben Thomsen and Lars von Trier, Dir: Lars von Trier, Denmark, DR, 76 mins.

Mille. 2009. Cr: Karina Dam and Poul Berg; Denmark, DR, 28 mins × 10 eps.

Morten Korch – Ved Stillebækken. 1999–2000. Wr: Ole Meldgaard, John Stefan Olsen, Peter Thorsboe and Lone Scherfig; Denmark, TV 2, 30 mins × 26 eps.

Murder One. 1995–1997. Cr: Steven Bochco, Charles H. Eglee and Channing Gibson; USA, ABC, 60 mins × 41 eps.

Nikolaj og Julie/Nikolaj and Julie. 2002–2003. Wr: Søren Sveistrup; Denmark, DR, 43 mins × 22 eps.

Normalerweize. 2004–. Cr: Lærke Winther Andersen and Anna Neye Poulsen; Denmark, DR2, 28 mins eps.

Nynne. 2006. Wr: Iben Gylling, Camilla Hübbe; Denmark, TV3, 45 mins × 13 eps.

NYPD Blue. 1993–2005. Cr: Steven Bochco, David Milch; USA, ABC, 44 mins × 261 eps.

Ørnen/The Eagle. 2004–2006. Cr: Mai Brostrøm and Peter Thorsboe; Denmark, DR, 58 mins × 24 eps.

Pagten/'The Pact'. 2009. Cr: Maya Ilsøe; Denmark, DR, 25 mins × 24 eps.

Regnvejr og ingen penge/'Rainy Weather and no Money'. 1965. Wr: Henning Ipsen, Dir: Gabriel Axel; Denmark, DR, 50 mins × 4 eps.

Rejseholdet/Unit One. 2000–2004. Cr: Peter Thorsboe; Denmark, DR, 60 mins × 30 eps, 90 mins × 2 eps.

Riget/The Kingdom. 1994 and 1997. Cr: Lars von Trier; Denmark, DR, 72 mins 8 eps.

Rita. 2012–. Cr: Christian Torpe; Denmark, TV2, 40 mins eps.

Rytteriet/'The Cavalry'. 2010. Cr: Martin Buch and Rasmus Botofte; Denmark, DR2, 25 mins × 10 eps.

Sommer/Summer. 2008. Cr: Jesper W. Nielsen, Karina Dam; Denmark, DR, 60 mins × 20 eps.

Station 13/'Precinct 13'. 1988–89. Wr: Peter Thorsboe and Stig Thorsboe, Dir: Edward Fleming; Denmark, Nordisk Film for DR, 30 mins × 8 eps.

Store drømme/Big Dreams. 2009. Wr: Iben Gylling, Christian Torpe and Kari Vidø; Denmark, TV2, 30 mins × 10 eps.

Strisser på Samsø/Island Cop. 1997–1998, Wr: Eddie Thomas Petersen and others, Dir: Eddie Thomas Petersen; Denmark, TV 2, 58 mins × 12 eps.

Taxa/Taxi 1997–1999. Wr: Stig Thorsboe and others; Denmark, DR, 45 mins × 56 eps.

The Dick van Dyke Show. 1961–1966. Cr: Carl Reiner; USA, NBC, 24 mins × 159 eps.

The Killing. 2011–2013. Cr: Veena Sud based on Søren Sveistrup's *Forbrydelsen/The Killing*; USA, AMC, 45 mins × 38 eps.

The Sopranos. 1999–2007. Cr: David Chase; USA, HBO, 58 mins × 86 eps.

The Spiral. 2012. Cr: Hans Herbots; Belgium/Netherlands and others, Caviar for several European broadcasters, 60 mins × 5 eps.

The West Wing. 1999–2006. Cr: Aaron Sorkin; USA, NBC, 42 mins × 156 eps.

The Wire 2002–2008. Cr: David Simon; USA, HBO, 60 mins × 60 eps.

True Blood. 2008–. Cr: Alan Ball; USA, HBO, 50 mins × 60 eps.

Twin Peaks. 1990–1991. Cr: David Lynch and Mark Frost; USA, ABC, 47 mins × 30 eps.

Ugeavisen/'The Weekly Newspaper'. 1990–1991. Wr: Various; Denmark, DR, 47 mins × 52 eps.

Unforgettable. 2011–. Cr: John Bellucci and Ed Redlich; USA, CBS, 45 mins eps.

Unge Andersen/Young Andersen. 2005. Wr: Rumle Hammerich and Ulf Stark, Dir: Rumle Hammerich; Denmark, Nordisk Film for DR, 55 mins × 2 eps.

Wallander. 2005–2006 and 2009–2010. Wr: Henning Mankell and others; Sweden, TV4, 89 mins × 26 eps.

Wallander. 2008–. Wr: Henning Mankell and others; UK/Sweden, BBC, 89 mins eps.

Z Cars. 1962–1978. Wr: Troy Kennedy Martin and Allan Prior; UK, BBC, 25/45 mins × 799 eps.

Index

The manufacturer's authorised representative in the EU is Springer
Nature Customer Service Centre GmbH, Europaplatz 3, 69115 Heidelberg,
Germany. If you have any concerns regarding our products, please
contact ProductSafety@springernature.com

Printed and bound by CPI Group (UK) Ltd, Croydon, CR0 4YY
23/04/2026
02095595-0011